THE
PAGE'S DRIFT

THE PAGE'S DRIFT

R.S. THOMAS at EIGHTY

Edited by
M. Wynn Thomas

Seren

SEREN BOOKS is the book imprint of
Poetry Wales Press Ltd
Andmar House, Tondu Road, Bridgend, Mid Glamorgan

Selections and Introduction © M. Wynn Thomas, 1993
The essays © the essayists, 1993
'The One' © R.S. Thomas, 1993
'The Poet' © Gillian Clarke, 1993

A British Library Cataloguing in Publication Data record is
available from the CIP office.

ISBN 1-85411-093-4
ISBN 1-85411-100-0 pbk

*The publisher acknowledges the financial support of the
Welsh Arts Council*

Printed in Palatino by WBC Print Ltd, Bridgend

Contents

vi   Acknowledgements

vii   **R.S. Thomas**, 'The One'

viii   Abbreviations

9   Introduction

22   **Sandra Anstey**, 'Some Uncollected Poems and Variant Readings from the Early Work of R.S. Thomas'

36   **Anne Stevenson**, 'The Uses of Prytherch'

57   **Helen Vendler**, 'R.S. Thomas and Painting'

82   **Rowan Williams**, '"Adult geometry": Dangerous Thoughts in R.S. Thomas'

99   **William V. Davis**, '"The Verbal Hunger": the Use and Significance of "Gaps" in the Poetry of R.S. Thomas'

119   **Marie-Thérèse Castay**, 'The Self and the Other: the Autobiographical Element in the Poetry of R.S. Thomas'

148   **Tony Brown**, '"Over Seventy Thousand Fathoms": the Sea and Self-definition in the poetry of R.S. Thomas'

171   **Walford Davies**, 'Bright Fields, Loud Hills and the Glimpsed Good Place: R.S. Thomas and Dylan Thomas'

211   **Ned Thomas**, 'R.S. Thomas and Wales'

221   **Gillian Clarke**, 'The Poet'

222   Bibliography

226   Notes on Contributors

229   Index

Acknowledgements

The publishers thank R.S. Thomas for permission to include 'The One' at the beginning of this book, and to quote from his work.

Acknowledgement is also due to Gillian Clarke for the inclusion of 'The Poet'. The Estate of René Magritte and ADAGP, Paris and DACS, London granted permission for the use of 'The Red Model' by René Magritte. The paintings by Monet, Degas and Pissarro are reproduced by kind permission of the Louvre, Paris.

The One

I gird myself for the agon;
and there at the centre
is the word. What does it mean
and who initiated it?
Behind the word is the name
not to be known for fear
we should gain power over it.
It is buried under the page's
drift, and not all our tears,
not all our air-conditioning
can bring on the thaw. Our sentences
are but as footprints, arrested
indefinitely on its threshold.

Perhaps our letters for it
are too many. Nearer the sound,
neither animal nor human,
drawn out through the wrenched
mouth of the oracle at Delphi.
Nearer the cipher the Christ
wrote on the ground, with no one
without sin to peer at it
over his shoulder.
                Male
as I am, my place, perhaps,
is to sit down in a mysterious
presence, leaving the vocabularies
to toil, the machine to evacuate
its resources, learning we are here
not necessarily to read on,
but to explore with blind
fingers the word in the cold,
until snow turn to feathers
and somewhere far down we come
upon warmth and a heart beating.

R.S. Thomas

Abbreviations

SF	*The stones of the field*
AL	*An acre of land*
SYT	*Song at the year's turning*
PS	*Poetry for supper*
T	*Tares*
BT	*The bread of truth*
P	*Pietà*
NBF	*Not that he brought flowers*
H'm	*H'm*
SP	*Selected poems, 1946-1968*
WW	*What is a Welshman?*
LS	*Laboratories of the spirit*
WI	*The way of it*
F	*Frequencies*
BHN	*Between here and now*
LP	*Later poems, 1972-1982*
IT	*Ingrowing thoughts*
Neb	*Neb*
EA	*Experimenting with an amen*
WA	*Welsh airs*
ERS	*The echoes return slow*
C	*Counterpoint*
MHT	*Mass for hard times*
Prose	*Selected prose*, ed., Sandra Anstey
PMI	*Pe medrwn yr iaith*, goln., Tony Brown a Bedwyr Lewis Jones

Introduction

On 17 May, 1983 the Welsh Arts Council celebrated R.S. Thomas's seventieth birthday with tributes and readings. The poet himself stalked on stage at the Sherman Theatre, unslung his hiker's rucksack, unceremoniously fished out his poems, and proceeded to read. True to his reputation, he kept his accompanying remarks to an austerely bare minimum. He did, however, wryly mention that his regret at having not played rugby for Wales was tempered by a satisfaction at being included in the first fifteen of Welsh poets — even if he was condemned to languish way out on the wing. Ten years on, his place in that first fifteen seems if anything even more assured, but his standing as a poet outside Wales remains uncertain.

Of course such reservations as younger writers and critics have are these days mostly muffled by courtesy. There is a decent, though grudging, impulse to pay lip service to an elder poet of imperious spirit, even if it is suspected he no longer has any clothes. Occasionally, though, repressed feelings surface with a predictable vengeance, as in Peter Reading's dismissive review of *Ingrowing Thoughts* which concludes: "The work is nicely, and probably expensively, produced by Poetry Wales Press with the financial support of the Welsh Arts Council — a measure of parochial wealth and chauvinism."[1] Most of the stereotypes that dog assessment (both positive and negative) of R.S. Thomas's work are here on flagrant display. R.S. Thomas = 'Welsh' = parochial = a cleric = boring/quaint/...: the adjectival conclusion may vary, but the equation remains much the same. It is a tried and tested formula for critical condescension.

The Iago Prytherch poems have not helped — although the fault lies much less in them than in the blind and disproportionate attention that has been paid to them. As Kingsley Amis in a way foresaw in 1956, the garlands of adjectives draped for years around Thomas's neck by Prytherch's admirers have turned into millstones.[2] It is scarcely possible any longer to discuss these poems— probably the major achievement, as Anne Stevenson

9

here claims, of Thomas's first twenty years as a poet — without lapsing into Iago-speak, a kind of critical discourse involving the mantra-like repetition of certain key terms such as 'bleak', 'muck', 'spittle', etc. This is automatic writing dictated by cultural cliché — a view of Wales as a mean and peasant land, immemorially sunk in bible-black gloom. When BBC2 televised a Bookmark programme about R.S. Thomas, the highlight for many English reviewers was a rural churchwarden's claim that upon becoming vicar Mr Thomas had insisted all the pews in the church should be repainted black.[3]

With Welsh life thus neatly edited down to conform to (stereo)-type, there is no incentive for outsiders to search for the cultural materials out of which Prytherch's character was fashioned, yet before his gaunt figure can be properly understood it has to be seen as rooted in cultural history quite as much as in 'the soil'. The ancestry of Prytherch can be traced back at least as far as 1847 when English government inspectors produced a notorious report condemning Welsh rural life as backward, pig-ignorant and highly licentious. Partly by way of reaction, Welsh-speaking Non-conformists proceeded to construct a counter-image, an idyll of a pious, musical, cultured 'volk' which was in its turn savagely challenged by Caradoc Evans in *My People* (1915). This fiercely original collection of iconoclastic stories established the terms in which a whole thirties generation of anglicised, urbanised, Anglo-Welsh writers, including the young Dylan Thomas, tended to represent life in the Welsh countryside. When R.S. Thomas, with his refined bourgeois and Romantic attitudes towards the country, was shocked into bewildered poetry by his first direct experiences of life in his rural parish, his work therefore became implicated in this longstanding struggle in Wales between two bitterly opposed styles of representation. Behind Thomas's end-lessly conflicting personal impulses to praise Prytherch and to blame him (in a style which originally owed something to Patrick Kavanagh) lies a very complex and intimate cultural dialectic.

There must be times when R.S. Thomas wishes he could write R.I.P. over his I.P. Prytherch so continues to monopolise such attention as critics pay to Thomas's earlier poetry that few notice 'unrepresentative' passages like the following from *Pietà*:

Introduction

> There are no signposts
> There but bones of the dead
> Conger, no light but the pale
> Phosphorous, where the slow corpses
> Swag. (*P*, 12)

This comes from one of those poems of unflinching self-assessment at which Thomas, Rembrandt-like, excels. They form part of a gallery of portraits — of self, of wife, of son, of parents, of others (Rhodri, Evans, Marged, farm wife, tramp, Mrs Li, schoonermen, commuters, expatriots, etc.) — that critics seldom visit, though some of his best work is to be found there. (The essays by Tony Brown and Marie-Thérèse Castay in the present collection show how versions of autobiography permeate his poetry.[4]) As for his devoted readers, they seem mostly to prefer to keep their R.S. simple. While his grand obsessions — with Iago Prytherch or the absent God — are felt to be intensely compelling, little notice is taken of the care with which he arranges the poems within his individual volumes in order to produce rich resonances of meaning. This is of course an advertised feature of such recent collections as *Counterpoint* or *The Echoes Return Slow*, but few have been instructed by them to return, say, to *Between Here and Now* to examine anew the relation between the religious poetry and the picture poems; or to ask (as Helen Vendler does here) why in that volume pictures invariably precede the related text whereas in *Ingrowing Thoughts* the relationship of painting to 'commentary' is constantly being reversed; or to wonder, as William V. Davis does in the case of *Frequencies*, at the play of meaning in a volume's title; or to note that poems such as 'Rose Cottage' and 'Hafod Lom' are carefully paired in *Pietà*; or to notice how the Spanish countryside becomes a witty surrogate for the Welsh landscape in *Not that he brought flowers*; or to register the fact that *The Bread of Truth* is delicately suspended in spirit between the optimism of the opening poem 'A Line from St David's' and the pessimism of the concluding 'Looking at Sheep'.

Considered separately these examples matter much less than they do together, when they signify that little attempt has as yet been made to take the full measure of R.S. Thomas. The fault, if such there be, is partly his own, for as Sandra Anstey mentions, not only has no complete collection of his poetry so far appeared, but a significant number of his widely scattered poems have never been gathered into any of his published books. A truly complete collection — one which included even his juvenilia — would at least bring home the fact that he has been publishing poetry for well over fifty years, having started out as that strange anachronism, a Georgian poet of the late thirties. He therefore began, we now might say, as he meant to continue, namely as a writer who had been born too late. He is like Miniver Cheevy, however, far less than like Cheevy's creator Edwin Arlington Robinson. In both poets a consciously cultivated air of belatedness was the bedrock on which their originality was founded, proof against successive shockwaves of fashion. Moreover throughout his long writing life Thomas has self-protectively used a reputation for provincialism and insularity to decoy critics away from the wide intellectual interests that have secretly and steadily been feeding his writing. Art, music, modern theology and philosophy (from Kierkegaard to Wittgenstein and Heidegger), and of course poetry, occupied much of the time left over from parish work when he was a priest. Furthermore, any description of him as a moors-wandering, bird-watching, Nature-loving poet (i.e. as a worthy relic of sub-Wordsworthian Romanticism) should at least be accompanied by a footnote mentioning that scarcely a day has passed in thirty years without his reading a poem by Wallace Stevens.[5] Geoffrey Hill has for some considerable time been at least as important to him as the George Herbert with whom he is routinely compared, and Rowan Williams's essay helps us understand why.

"Art," Edward Thomas shrewdly remarked, "knows no must, only an infinite may." One would have thought that critics would have learned, by now, from the innumerable gaffes of the past, not to attempt to legislate for the artists of the present. However, every age seems compelled to produce its self-righteous musts — the supposed ratifiers of contemporary practice — and the current critical favourites include self-reflexive writing, language poetry and streetwise thinking. R.S. Thomas can scarcely expect to be approved by these critical standards. He would hardly wish, let alone hope, to be accepted as a fully paid-up postmodernist. His practice as a poet remains fairly tenaciously rooted in the old Romantic-Modernist belief in the cognitive power of metaphor, although his thinking has branched out in opposite directions. In fact, his best poetry during the last twenty years has proceeded by calling some of its own fundamental practices into question. His religious poetry, for instance, broods on the conceit of faith — taking that word 'conceit' in its multiple senses. The truth of a poem is made to hang on a vulnerably exposed trope, sometimes pushed to a breaking point of exaggeration; the very possibility of faith is implicitly queried from the sceptical viewpoint of the enlightened humanist and the worldy-wisdom of the relativist; and at the same time the presumptions of human faith are questioned by a quizzical, almost perversely elusive deity. In all these senses, then, the practice of religious faith in modern times seems for R.S. Thomas to involve the artistic and spiritual daring of a necessary conceit.

Such a faith requires that he take risks in order to find for it adequate forms of expression, and his experiments have by no means met with general approval. John Wain, for instance, has mourned the disappearance of the earlier writer of "graceful, lyrical poems"; and Donald Davie, in a short but sympathetic essay, has noted how the later Thomas has "[gone] to great lengths to offend and disappoint the reader's ear."[6] His "ruthless enjambements" have in particular been felt to be insensitive, disconcerting, even arbitrary. I would myself argue that more often than not they have the music that is consonant with their function — a Schoenbergian music of dissonance as authoritativeness is janglingly harmonised with misgiving. However, the point I prefer to stress here is that Thomas is, in his scrupulously undemonstrative and conscientiously functional way, an experimental writer. Nor are his innovations confined to his religious poetry. His poems about painting involve fascinating attempts to dramatise the process of imputing moral meaning to a picture. And in a volume such as *The Echoes Return Slow*, Thomas investigates ways in which we retrospectively construct for ourselves a life out of our remembered experiences. By juxtaposing prose passages with what we call 'poetry' he even raises questions about the respective status of these two forms of discourse as modes of autobiography.

The publication of his complete poems might just possibly dispel the general lazy impression that in spite of his considerable output he is a poet of limited formal range and of regrettably few themes. On the other hand, judging by the reactions of those recent reviewers inclined to regard the post-Prytherch poet as insignificant,[7] the sight of all Thomas's religious poems gathered together in one place might provoke some critics to bury the bulk of the collection. That, in my opinion, would be a serious error of literary judgement, but there's no denying that his later poetry can sometimes prominently exhibit those weaknesses that are related to its strengths, and occasionally (as in the case of *Experimenting with an Amen*) a whole volume seems to be very much fuller of the former than of the latter. Even the way Thomas's mind keeps revolving around the same old spiritual dilemmas and paradoxes undoubtedly irritates some, but for me he thus movingly demonstrates the provisionality of all spiritual utterance: "I write it down in visible ink", says the American poet Charles Wright, "Black words that disappear when held up to the light —/I write it down/not to remember but to forget,/ Words like thousands of pieces of shot film/exposed to the sun."[8] As Rowan Williams emphasises, Thomas's spiritual poetry is essentially a "language poetry", i.e. a poetry that keeps calling into question the very nature of the language it nevertheless persists in putting to the most serious of uses. The absoluteness of Thomas's flat statements, the pithiness of his images, the epigrammatic quality of his formulations — all are destabilised by intrusive line-breaks and strange enjambements. Whereas Herbert could envisage the ideal preacher as a stained glass window through whom the light of God's life shone in a strong mingling of colour and light, Thomas can offer us only the coarse pebble-glass of an inevitably compromised mortal utterance.

An almost Stevensian awareness of the inescapable fictiveness of the terms in which we image our spiritual concerns is already very evident in *H'm*, the first of his volumes entirely devoted to spiritual exploration. In a rabbinical way Thomas there toys with story — fantasticating by devising new parables of the God-man relationship. Sometimes these are sportively satirical versions of the old stories of orthodoxy, at other times they are the extravagant conceits of a modern faith, but always Thomas seems aware that to explore the realm of the spirit is to be almost irremediably lost in a wilderness of stories each of which is capable of alternating between truth and illusion as rapidly as the flashings of a

14

fluorescent light. A similar preoccupation is evident in his recent collection, *Counterpoint* (1990), accompanied in places by a scepticism about the very grammar of the language of our human being. So God is described as "repudiating.../...a syntactical /compulsion to incorporate /him in the second person" (*C*, 15). Elsewhere in that volume, however, it is in the predominance of the first person singular in our everyday discourse that Thomas finds the surest grammatical sign of original sin:

> I want...Help me. Listen...I —
> no time. What is life but
> deciduous? That I in my day, no
> other...I, I, I, before the world,
> in the present tense; so, now,
> here, stating my condition —
> whose else? Not my fault; I
> at the centre, everything else
> echoes, reflections. (*C*, 18)

These stammering phrases plainly show how the power of Thomas the poet is rooted in precisely those equivocations of language which Thomas the spiritual searcher regrets. In the same way the pursuit of an absent God brings him repeatedly into creative contact with the limiting conditions of mankind's existence. In short the greatness that I, at least, would want to claim for some of Thomas's religious poems derives from the abiding humanness of the world of uncertainties in which he there reluctantly dwells.[9]

As for Thomas's Welshness, that is a subject much more often knowingly mentioned in passing than knowledgeably discussed, and as Ned Thomas shows there is always the danger of supposing Wales to be present in the poetry only when specifically mentioned. A mistake to which outsiders are particularly prone is to suppose that, Wales being a small country, any writer named Thomas, whether Dylan or R.S., must come from much the same background. In fact these two Thomases came from opposite ends of Wales, one from the reticent far north, the other from the garrulous deep south, and they therefore naturally came at Welsh life from two very different directions — indeed a fixed dislike for the industrial, anglicised culture of south Wales has (for better and for worse) been one of the significant determinants of R.S. Thomas's whole style and stance as a writer. As Walford Davies shows, the relationship between Dylan and R.S. Thomas, both as poets and as Welshmen, is ultimately a subtle and complex matter, but one single dominating figure decisively marks the great divide between them on cultural and political affairs. That figure is Saunders Lewis, arguably the greatest writer and intellectual produced by Wales this century. A founder-member of Plaid Cymru (the Welsh nationalist party), the controversial Lewis was also an outstanding Welsh-language dramatist, poet, critic and cultural ideologue in the mould and on the scale of T.S. Eliot. Although he denied that such a beast as a genuine Anglo-Welsh literature could exist in nature, Lewis was an important influence on several of the English-language writers in Wales who came to prominence immediately after World War II.[10] These (R.S. Thomas among them) constituted the second flowering of Anglo-Welsh writers, the first having occurred with those writers of the thirties of whom Dylan Thomas had been one.

Nor is it to Saunders Lewis alone one should look in order to appreciate the exact colour of Welshness in R.S. Thomas's saying. Several of the main aspects and concerns of Welsh-language literature during this century are translated into powerful English in Thomas's poetry. Indeed, his whole concept of poetry has been strongly marked by the tradition of politically-engaged writing that has been a feature of twentieth-century literature in Welsh. Whereas outsiders tend to regard Thomas simply as a loner, there is a very important sense in which he belongs to a whole body of writers in Wales whose talents have been committed to the preservation of an increasingly threatened culture. Since the war several of these writers have written in English, like Thomas himself, but their models have almost invariably been Welsh-language writers of an earlier period, such as the poet Gwenallt about whom R.S. has written a revealing poem under the ironically bland title 'A Lecturer':

> A little man,
> Sallow,
> Keeping close to the wall
> Of life; his quick smile
> Of recognition a cure

For loneliness; he'll take you
Any time on a tour
Of the Welsh language, its flowering
While yours was clay soil.

It seeds in him.
Fitfully,
As the mood blows, poetry
In this small plot
Of manhood opens
Its rich petals; the smell
Is familiar. Watch hlm,
As with short steps he goes.
Not dangerous?
He has been in gaol. (*WA*, 23)

That warning, at the end, of the political activism that underlies
and underwrites Gwenallt's poetry, is one that should be particu-
larly heeded by R.S. Thomas's readers, since the direction taken
by his own work over the years has been strongly, even when
silently, influenced by the turn of political events in Wales. The
drowning of a Welsh rural valley to provide Liverpool with water,
Saunders Lewis's dire warnings in a radio lecture of the imminent
death of the language, the subsequent formation of the militant
action group called The Welsh Language Society, the Investiture
of Prince Charles as Prince of Wales — these are simply a few of
the most obvious episodes to which his imagination has reacted,
not always in predictable or directly political ways.[11] One won-
ders, for example, how far his turn away from the matter of Wales
and to religious poetry during the early seventies was due not only
— as he has himself repeatedly explained — to his tolerably
contented homecoming to the heartland of Welsh-speaking cul-
ture on the distant peninsula of Llŷn, but also to his disillusion-
ment with the compromising terms (as he no doubt saw it) on
which Plaid Cymru (the nationalist party) was by then making
headway with voters. To put it simply, these were not the terms
in which his own nationalist poems of the sixties, with their
emphasis on the centrality of the language issue, had been writ-
ten.[12]

Thomas's obsessive fingering of his Welshness has seemed,
even to some of his warmest admirers, to be embarrassing and

distasteful. They are often secretly inclined to turn his scathing description of his own nation back on himself, dismissing him as typical, at least in this one unfortunate respect, of a small people "sick with inbreeding."[13] Behind such dismissals lies not infrequently an attitude towards Wales that is as blithely ignorant as it is patronising.[14] However, since the arguments of a Welsh-speaking Welshman such as myself — and a Thomas at that — will always be open, in this connection, to the charge of cultural nepotism and special pleading, let me requisition the words of two impeccably disinterested commentators. The first is Donald Davie, noting in an essay on Anglo-Welsh poets that "it is R.S. Thomas who has articulated and suffered through the predicament of the modern Welshman [and woman]". He associates Thomas with Heaney, seeing them both as choosing to act out in their lives and writings the painful plight of their respective peoples:

> This is presumptuous, and in both cases the presumption has been fastened on, and derided, by the poet's compatriots[15].... But the presumption is allowable, and indeed necessary, in the case of those who aspire to be national poets. The national poet holds up a glass in which his nation shall see itself as it is, not as it figures in the beguiling image available alike for internal and external consumption; and so one has heard Welsh people complain that whereas R.S. Thomas's portrait of the Welsh was faithful, he should have registered it only in Welsh, not in a language that outsiders could read... But it is the presumptuousness of Thomas and Heaney that seems to keep the faith with great national poets of the past — or for that matter of the present, as in the case of many subjugated nations in Eastern Europe.[16]

Davie's last insight is an especially important one. It is not when we avert our embarrassed eyes from his cultural nationalism that R.S. Thomas assumes the stature of an 'international poet'; rather, it is precisely in and through his anguished, troubling relationship to Wales (a relationship darkly shadowing all his poetry) that he relates to a wider world, beyond the shores of an intervening England.[17]

Appropriately enough, it is the Heaney with whom Davie felicitously chose to compare him who can, I feel, best enable us to understand the way in which R.S.Thomas's poetry — of Wales, of

Iago Prytherch, of spiritual search, and of painful self-examination
— is profoundly all of a piece. It is a single, unified body of work
because it stems from a single source; from an indomitable con-
science that refuses to acknowledge the *de facto* authority of the
established order of things. And by virtue of this conscience,
Thomas belongs in the spiritual company of those writers for
whom (as Heaney has written) "literature provides a court of
appeal in which the imagination can seek redress against the
affronts of the prevailing conditions. 'Obedience to the force of
gravity is the greatest sin,' said Simone Weil. This redress of poetry
comes from its being a revelation of potential that is denied or
constantly threatened by circumstance". Then however, Heaney
adds, the poet "comes under the strain of bearing witness in his
or her own life to the plane of consciousness established in the
poem."[18] Not the least of the reasons for respecting and saluting
R.S. Thomas at the age of eighty is that he has for so long borne
lonely stubborn witness in his life to the values that have so
fiercely animated his writing.

Notes

1. 'Doubting Thomas?', a review of *Experimenting with an Amen* and
Ingrowing Thoughts, TLS (Oct. 3, 1986), 118.
2. 'A True Poet', *The Spectator* (Jan. 13, 1956), reprinted in Sandra Anstey,
ed., *Critical Writings on R.S.Thomas* (Bridgend: Poetry Wales Press, 1982),
29-30.
3. *TLS* (Feb. 28, 1986), 220. Peter Kemp there uses the usual agricultural
lexicon with particular relish: "Hearing him speak — as the camera
tracked a cow-man slopping through the slurry — of his initial shocked
revulsion from the muck and manure of farming life reminded you how,
in stanzas spattered with spittle, phlegm and filth, his Christian pastor-
ship often reels under his recoil from people he sees as near-brutish
creatures, reeking of stale sweat and animal contact."
4. See also M. Wynn Thomas, 'Songs of "ignorance and praise": R.S.
Thomas's poems about the four people in his life', in *Internal difference: the
literature of Wales in the twentieth century* (Cardiff: University of Wales
press, 1992), 130-155.
5. Information obtained in a private conversation with the poet.
6. Donald Davie, 'R.S. Thomas', in *Under Briggflatts: a history of poetry in
Britain, 1960-1988* (Manchester: Carcanet, 1989), 147-150. John Wain's
comments are quoted, 146-147.

7. David Bromwich, *TLS* (Feb. 27, 1976), 215; William Scammell, 'Acid rain on a burning bush', *TLS* (March 1, 1991), 18.

8. Charles Wright, *Zone Journals* (New York: Farrar/Strauss/ Giroux, 1988), 32.

9. The religious poetry is particularly thoughtfully discussed by Grevel Lindop in the *TLS* (Dec. 16, 1983), 1411, and by Stephen Medcalf, 'Divine presentiments', *TLS* (April 17, 1987), 418.

10. See M. Wynn Thomas, 'Keeping his pen clean: R.S. Thomas and Wales', in William V. Davis, ed., *Miraculous simplicity: essays on R.S. Thomas* (Fayetteville: U. of Arkansas Press, 1993); J.P. Ward, 'R.S. Thomas's poems of Wales', *Poetry Wales* vol.23, no.2/3, 20-25; John Barnie, 'Never forget your Welsh', *The King of Ashes* (Llandysul: Gomer Press, 1989), 14-19.

11. Still the best introduction to the politico-cultural ferment in Wales during the sixties is Ned Thomas, *The Welsh Extremist: a culture in crisis* (London: Gollancz, 1971).

12. An important document in this connection is the essay by Dafydd Elis Thomas (later to become a Plaid Cymru M.P.), 'The image of Wales in R.S. Thomas's poetry', *Poetry Wales*, R.S. Thomas special number (Spring, 1972), 59-66.

13. For example: "The feeling is that he will, at whatever risk of monotony, go on enumerating the smells of his dead nation. He does it very well." (*TLS* [Dec. 12, 1968], 1407.)

14. For example, the following facetious remark about the wholesale purchase of cottages in Welsh-speaking west Wales at highly advantageous prices: "One may wonder whether this discovery of Wales by the hard-up English intelligentsia is such a tragedy." (*TLS* [Feb. 27, 1964], 158.)

15. An outstanding study of Thomas in relation to his Welsh audience is Tony Bianchi, 'R.S. Thomas and his readers', in Tony Curtis, ed., *Wales: the imagined nation: essays in cultural and national identity* (Bridgend: Poetry Wales Press, 1986), 69-95.

16. *Under Briggflatts*, 163. Exceptionally sensitive understanding of the Welsh situation is shown by P.J. Kavanagh in his review of a collection of Thomas's prose writings, *TLS* (March 2, 1984), 226.

17. Although, of course, he can also be seen as related to those English, Scottish and Irish poets for whom, as Alan Robinson has put it, "nationalism, class- and gender- consciousness converge in opposition to the Establishment's marginalisation of 'the Other'" (*Instabilities in contemporary British poetry* [London: Macmillan, 1988], ix). For further discussion of such writing see Jeremy Hooker, *The Presence of the Past: essays on modern British and American poetry* (Bridgend: Poetry Wales Press, 1987). A key text for understanding the decentralisation of culture in the British Isles is Seamus Heaney, 'Englands of the mind', in *Preoccupations* (London:

Faber and Faber, 1980), 150-169.

18. Seamus Heaney, 'The redress of poetry', an abridged version of his inaugural lecture as Professor of Poetry at Oxford, *TLS* (Dec. 22-28, 1989), 1412 & 1418.

Sandra Anstey

Some Uncollected Poems and Variant Readings from the Early Work of R. S. Thomas

Many of R.S. Thomas's poems and occasional pieces of prose remain uncollected. Those interested in tracing the prose writings can turn to *Selected Prose* and *Pe Medrwn yr Iaith* which contain listings of material in English and Welsh, but details of the uncollected poems are not as yet available in such a convenient published form.

During my research at the University of Wales I found in literary periodicals some poems by R.S. Thomas that I could not trace in published collections of his poetry. Discussion with R.S. Thomas revealed that he had no record of poems that he had sent to journals, so I began compiling an index of my findings. The index grew, and has continued to grow over the years, to reveal a network of references to first and subsequent appearances of poems, plus details of variant readings; some of the variants appear to be printing errors, but others are too marked to be explained in that way.

In 1990 Gwydion Thomas, R.S. Thomas's son, asked me to send him my findings so that he could read through the material in preparation for a publication of R. S. Thomas's poems to celebrate his eightieth birthday. Assembling material that might be useful to Gwydion and his father provided an opportunity to reconsider the wealth of poems by R.S. Thomas that remain uncollected. In this essay I will draw together details of these uncollected poems that appeared up to and including 1955 and will comment on variant readings covering the same period. Such material will, therefore, focus on the early stages of R.S. Thomas's poetic career leading up to the publication of *Song at the Year's Turning* (1955), his first London-based collection.

R.S. Thomas's poems began appearing in literary periodicals in 1939, seven years before the publication of *The Stones of the Field*, his first book of verse. Other earlier compositions include his contributions while still a student to *Omnibus*, a college magazine based in Bangor, under the pseudonym of Curtis Langdon and then Figaro,[1] plus some pieces in the possession of the National Library of Wales.[2] The latter holograph poems, purchased by the National Library of Wales in 1968, are undated but their style and presentation suggest that they belong to the same period as the poems published in 1939. One of these poems, 'The Bridge', bears the signature of R.S. Thomas, the other five are without titles and signatures. The first lines are "A blue snake in the valley ran", "Once through the friendless dark so close I came", "How many men have loved", "The waters strive to wash away" and "Like slender waterweeds to my mind".

When R.S. Thomas read in a newspaper that the National Library of Wales claimed to have bought holograph poems by him, he wrote a short letter in Welsh to the librarian in Aberystwyth in which he expressed his incredulity and indignation; he made it clear that he always refused to sell manuscripts, copies and such like and therefore failed to understand how some of his poems could have been purchased by the library. After receiving details of the poems R.S. Thomas wrote to the librarian again acknowledging that the poems were his, that they had most likely been kept by some editor from the early days and then sold. These six holograph poems, examples of a pronouncedly Georgian style of writing, provide the reader with an interesting perspective from which to view the poet's later work. R.S. Thomas has commented himself on the way in which the style of the Georgian poets became a feature of his own early poetry:

> In the late twenties, at a time when I should have been in touch with what Eliot, Joyce and Pound were doing, I was receiving my ideas of poetry via Palgrave's *Golden Treasury*, and through such Georgian verse as was compulsory reading for my examinations in English. I was also a confirmed open-air nature lover so that such verses as I then achieved myself were almost bound to be about trees and fields and skies and seas. No bad thing if I had been familiar with the poets who knew how to deal maturely with such material, Wordsworth and Hardy for instance. But my efforts were based on the weaker poems of Shelley and the more sugary ones of the Georgians.[3]

The holograph poems reveal a careful attention to rhyming

schemes which is coupled with a pedantic adherence to syllabic balance: the latter gives rise on occasion to such banal line-fillers as "Lest this, perchance, may be".[4] Such material is the work of a writer who had yet to find his own voice as a poet.

In 1939, the year in which poems by R.S. Thomas began to appear in literary journals, the poet was in his third year as curate of Chirk, having prepared for the ministry at St Michael's College, Llandaff. His first poem, published in *The New English Weekly* under the title 'Fragment', appears in full below:

> Deep in the blue of April skies
>   I have seen the cruel pair
> Hawk and kestrel pierce the air
>   With needle eyes,
> Stitching to the ground with unseen thread
> The tender shrew-mouse as it sped.[5]

The presentation of a simple yet memorable central image is a technique that R.S. Thomas has returned to frequently throughout his poetic career. In 'Fragment' the focus is on observation of nature, a choice of subject that R.S. Thomas commented on in the opening of a broadcast that he made in 1961:

> I was not born in the country, but I was brought up in it, and most of my later life has been spent in it or in contact with it. It was natural, therefore, that when I began to write, I should take my first subjects for poems from the countryside, as many of the Romantic poets did.[6]

R.S. Thomas's two contributions to *The Dublin Magazine* in 1939, 'The Bat' and 'Cyclamen', look to nature once again for their subjects. These pieces offer an interesting contrast. The series of observations in 'The Bat' is arranged in two four-line stanzas:

> The day is done, the swallow moon
>   Skims the pale waters of the sky,
> And under the blossom of sunset cloud
>   Is hidden from the eye.
>
> And now when every spectral owl
>   Is mindful of the ancient wars,
> A withered leaf comes fluttering forth
>   To hunt the insect stars.[7]

This poem remains uncollected whereas 'Cyclamen', which appeared on the same page of the 1939 issue of *The Dublin Magazine*, later reappeared in *The Stones of the Field* in 1946. 'Cyclamen' moves away from the formal stanzaic pattern of 'The Bat'; its content depends on the extension of a single metaphor following the pattern established in 'Fragment'. Here a cyclamen is described as a white moth that is restrained from flying by its awareness of its own image in the water below:

> They are white moths
> With wings
> Lifted
> Over a dark water
> In act to fly,
> Yet stayed
> By their frail images
> In its mahogany depth. (*SF*, 11)

This poem was not included in the selection of poems from *The Stones of the Field* that later reappeared in *Song at the Year's Turning*.

In 1940 *The Dublin Magazine* printed three more poems by R.S. Thomas, all of which remain uncollected: one is entitled 'Birches', the other two are known by their first lines only, "I know no clouds" and "Look, look at the sky".[8] 'Birches' and "I know no clouds" are both arranged in four-line stanzas with rhyming second and fourth lines. This pattern is broken by "Look, look at the sky" in a manner that recalls the opening of Gerard Manley Hopkins's 'The Starlit Night', "Look at the stars! look, look up at the skies!" In their respective poems both Thomas and Hopkins are expressing an ecstatic joy, having been excited by a visual phenomenon. The religious overtones of the closing lines of Hopkins's poem is suggested in Thomas's use of "virgin" as an adjective to describe the blue of the sky:

> Look, look at the sky
> Above you,
> Where the keen winds
> Since dawn were busy
> Quarrying the dark clouds to find
> This virgin blue.[9]

Richard Burnham in an article entitled 'The Dublin Magazine's

Welsh Poets' has contrasted the economy of R.S. Thomas's 'Cyclamen' with stanzas of the untitled poem which opens " I know no clouds". He notes in relation to "I know no clouds" "a sing-song rhyme that lacked subtlety"[10] and attributes these features to the influence of Seamus O'Sullivan (as editor and poet) on the contributor to his magazine. From these early beginnings R.S. Thomas went on to contribute over the years a total of twenty-two poems[11] and one review to *The Dublin Magazine*.

The next poems by R.S. Thomas that are as yet uncollected appeared in 1943 in *Wales*, a literary magazine edited by Keidrych Rhys.[12] *Wales*, like many other publications at that time, had been affected by war-time paper-rationing. Its appearance from 1937 was suspended in 1940 (one broadsheet was printed in 1941) to be resumed in 1943. It was in this magazine that ten of R.S. Thomas's poems appeared in the three years from 1943 to 1945: three remain uncollected while seven were brought together in 1946 to reappear in *The Stones of the Field*. The three uncollected poems are a curious group. In 'Confessions of an Anglo-Welshman',[13] R.S. Thomas dwells on the problems of being an English-speaking Welshman. It is interesting to note that here the poet is ready to use the label 'Anglo-Welsh' in the title of a composition which relates so directly to his own position whereas, just three years later, in his reply to the *Wales* questionnaire, he was determined to deny the title.[14] The position of a poet who is brought up in Wales without knowledge of the Welsh language is portrayed in dramatic imagery within the poem:

> Even at my christening it was she decreed
> Uprooted I should bleed.[15]

The "she" referred to in these lines is the Anglo-Welsh poet's own country, Wales. But the poem closes on a different note as the poet explains that despite his strong feeling of patriotism, he is linked to the tradition of English literature, through the writing of Blake, Shelley, Shakespeare and Keats.

'A Farmer'[16] and 'Gideon Pugh',[17] the other uncollected pieces that made their first appearance in *Wales* during this period, take descriptions of country characters as their subjects, and in both compositions the admiration of poet for subject is evident. 'A

Farmer' presents

> A man so small in the green surge of grass
> Lapping his limbs...[18]

Yet this same man is a

> stranger to despair,
> Sure of his mastery in the age-old war
> Of fibre and sinew, blood and bone
> With the crude earth and the indifferent stone.[19]

The poem ends with an essentially romanticised view of the life of a man who works in the country:

> Ah, could we appropriate for the subtler strife
> Of mind and spirit with a seven-fold death
> Tithe of his courage, tithe of his faith,
> How firm the gesture of each puny life![20]

In 'Gideon Pugh' a rural character (a Welshman by name) is chosen for study.[21] Here the length of the piece and the choice of one particular figure allow for a more detailed examination of subject within the composition. Loneliness and monotony are underlined as prominent features of Gideon Pugh's life. The picture is a depressing one but, in the last of the three stanzas, the poet suggests that Gideon Pugh, a man who is battling against nature, has the capacity to transport himself, in his mind, beyond the immediate physical struggle:

> Leave him, then, leave him alone with his secret dream,
> The dream of a stone in the grass, the hunger of a tree
> For the soft touch of the sky, of the land for the sea.[22]

In both 'A Farmer' and 'Gideon Pugh' the adjective "indifferent" is used to describe aspects of nature against which these men are struggling. The men continue with their tasks despite the land's indifference; the poet underlines this endurance as a quality to be admired.

Such poems are evidence of R.S. Thomas's awakening to the richness of his surroundings in Manafon as subject-matter for his writing. This marks the beginning of the poet's movement away from a nature poetry written in the style of the Georgian poets to a different kind of writing, a change which has been commented on by R.S. Thomas himself:

> My awakening to the possibility of a more robust poetry came with my removal to my first incumbency in the Montgomeryshire foot-hills in 1942... I came in contact for the first time with the rough farm folk of the upland valleys. These were pre-tractor days. Their life was a hard slog in wind and mire on hill slopes with the occasional brief idyllic interludes. Their life and their attitudes, administered an inward shock to my Georgian sensibility. I responded with the first of my poems about Iago Prytherch, a sort of prototype of this kind of farmer. It was called 'A Peasant'.[23]

'A Peasant', first published in *Life and Letters Today* in 1943,[24] certainly is written in a style which is very different from R.S. Thomas's early nature poems outlined above. This poem, with its well-known opening lines — "Iago Prytherch his name, though, be it allowed,/Just an ordinary man of the bald Welsh hills" (*SF*,14) — is by now well anthologised; in 1944 it appeared in *Modern Welsh Poetry* and *Poetry London*, 1946 in *The Stones of the Field*, then in *Song at the Year's Turning* (1955) and again in 1973 in *Selected Poems*. Indeed, 'A Peasant' is one of twenty poems that had appeared in print before their publication in *The Stones of the Field*, and of those all but three underwent some slight alterations in punctuation, wording or format for their appearance in the 1946 collection. For the most part the revisions are minor — the insertion or disappearance of a comma perhaps — but there are a few instances in which some interesting word changes take place. 'A Priest to his People' provides an example. In that poem's first appearance in *Counterpoint* in 1945,[25] line 21, in which a priest addresses his parishioners, reads "And why should you come like sparrows for comfort"; in the 1946 publication, this line has become "And why should you come like sparrows for prayer crumbs" (*SF*, 29), a change which emphasises the religious aspect of the priest's role within the community.

Variant readings extend to titles of poems as well as content. Examples of such changes are found in a close examination of the poems in *An Acre of Land* (1952). Fourteen of the poems in that collection had appeared previously in literary magazines, and, of those fourteen, ten were reprinted with revisions to the text including four that were making their second appearance under new titles. The expansive implications of changing 'The Hill Country, Montgomeryshire'[26] to 'The Welsh Hill Country' (*AL*, 7) are reversed in the effect achieved by reprinting 'The Farmer Speaks'[27] as 'The Hill Farmer Speaks' (*AL*, 17) for the 1952 collection. 'Welsh History' (*AL*, 23) had originally appeared as 'Welsh Nation' in 1950[28] (this was also the title of the publication in which it appeared), and 'The Lonely Furrow' (*AL*, 36) had been titled 'Song' on the occasion of its first appearance in *The Dublin Magazine*.[29]

I have found eight uncollected poems by R.S. Thomas in literary periodicals between 1946 and 1952,[30] the dates of publication of his first two books of verse. It is only too easy to speculate on the poet's reasons for leaving these compositions aside — repetition of ideas that had already been included in collected pieces would present itself as one of the obvious considerations. The subjects of these eight poems are indeed familiar: a reference to Iago Prytherch in 'Welsh Shepherd', the comments of a man who works in the hills in 'Hill Farmer', words delivered by a figure from the Welsh past in 'Lines from Taliesin', and a comparison of the attributes of England and Wales (presented allegorically) in 'The Two Sisters'. In four of the eight uncollected pieces R.S. Thomas employs a three-stanza, quatrain form which allows the ideas of each poem to be developed within a concise and controlled framework.

A particularly interesting uncollected poem from this period is 'Y Gwladwr'. This poem, written in sonnet form, appeared in *Y Fflam* in 1950. It is one of only two poems in the Welsh language that R.S. Thomas has published to date.[31] The content of the composition, a restatement of the poet's belief in the worth of the Welsh hill farmer, is linked closely to poems like 'A Peasant' and 'Affinity'. R.S. Thomas had been learning the Welsh language for only a short time prior to the appearance of 'Y Gwladwr', and in an article based on an interview with Dyfed Evans[32] — one of the few occasions on which the poet has acknowledged the existence of 'Y Gwladwr' — he is reported to have indicated his dissatisfaction with this Welsh poem.

1952, as well as being the year of publication of *An Acre of Land*, was also the year in which R.S. Thomas completed a script he had been commissioned to write by the BBC. The result, entitled *The Minister*, was broadcast by the Welsh Home Service in that same year as one in a series of poems under the title of 'Radio Odes'.[33] The text of this broadcast was published by the Montgomery Printing Company in 1953, and it was reprinted in 1955 in *Song at the Year's Turning*.

A comparison of the 1953 and 1955 texts of *The Minister* reveals an important revision within the closing section. In the 1955 version the narrator's final contribution includes the following comment on Morgan the Minister:

> He never listened to the hills'
> Music calling to the hushed
> Music within... (*SYT*, 92)

The same lines of the 1953 edition are very different:

> He never listened to the moor's
> Silence speaking to the slow
> Silence within...[34]

This revision reveals a marked change in content; in the original text it is the quality of silence that is shared by moors and man, in the later version it is the music which provides the common factor between, not moors and man, but now the hills and man. Silence as a characteristic of the moors is underlined within the text of *The Minister*. For example, in the description of Morgan's reaction to the tricks played on him by the Sunday School children:

> Say nothing, say nothing. Morgan was learning
> To hold his tongue, the wisdom of the moor. (*SYT*, 87)

The original version of the revision under discussion says that Morgan "never listened to the moor's/Silence", but such an idea is contradicted by the lines quoted above. The revised version "hill's/Music", however, avoids this awkward contradiction. The setting for the chapel is "the hill country at the moor's edge"(*SYT*, 77): during his time in the area Morgan learns to adopt the silence of the moor, but he never becomes aware of the music of the hills.The reference to the "hill's /Music" in the 1955 text evokes a reference to something celestial and fulfilling, echoing the lines of R.S. Thomas's earlier poem 'Maes-yr-Onnen':

> You cannot hear as I, incredulous, heard
> Up in the rafters, where the bell should ring,
> The wild, sweet singing of Rhiannon's birds. (*AL*,10)

But for Morgan there is only silence.

Song at the Year's Turning, which appeared in October 1955, was the first collection of R.S. Thomas's poems to be published outside Wales. It is divided into four sections: three are devoted to a selection from earlier publications, and the fourth consists of nineteen 'Later Poems'. In selecting from his early publications for the 1955 collection, R.S. Thomas omitted eighteen poems from *The Stones of the Field*, and six from *An Acre of Land*. *The Minister* reappears in its complete form.

There are some changes in punctuation and vocabulary in a few of the poems from *The Stones of the Field* and *An Acre of Land* that are reprinted in the 1955 collection. Two of the more significant examples include a change of title and a substantial textual revision. The change of title involves the poem which is printed as 'The Lonely Furrow' on page 36 of *An Acre of Land*; it reappears in *Song at the Year's Turning* as 'The One Furrow', altering the centre of focus within the poem. The replacement of "lonely" by "one" shifts the centre of attention from a condition that is dominated by a sense of loneliness to an emphasis on concentration. The new title echoes a phrase in the penultimate line of the poem; it suggests singularity of purpose and, perhaps, narrowness of vision as the features to be linked with the fate of the speaker in the poem.

A textual revision also appears in the final lines of 'Welsh History'. In the 1952 text these lines read:

> we will arise
> And greet each other in a new dawn. (*AL*,23)

In the 1955 print these lines have become:

> we will arise ,
> Armed, but not in the old way. (*SYT*, 61)

This revision leaves behind the magical awakening suggested in the earlier text. The emphasis of the new final line falls on the opening word "Armed": the conclusion to that line — "but not in the old way" — serves to qualify the meaning of the stressed word and leaves the reader to unravel possible interpretations.

In *Song at the Year's Turning* material from R.S. Thomas's earlier publications is followed by a final section of nineteen 'Later Poems'. Of these nineteen poems only two were appearing in print for the first time: the others had already appeared in periodicals between 1952 and 1955 inclusive.

Besides the material that was published in *Song at the Year's Turning,* I have traced twelve other poems by R.S. Thomas in literary periodicals between 1953 and 1955 which were not subsequently collected together into a volume of the poet's work.[35] Of these pieces 'Proportions', 'Auguries', 'Original Sin' and 'No Answer' dwell on a reassessment of the figure whose life is spent working on the land; a more personal note is revealed in the lines of 'Growing Up' and 'Commission'. This latter poem is printed with the epigraph "for Raymond Garlick", a dedication to a man whom the poet recognised as sharing his own passionate commitment to Wales. 'Commission' ends with an appeal to Raymond Garlick urging him to "Open their eyes, show them the heart that's breaking". This line echoes the Welsh epigraph that appeared at the beginning of *The Minister,* "Sŵn y galon fach yn torri",[36] in which the heart that is breaking belongs to the Reverend Elias Morgan. However, the heart referred to in 'Commission' is not a human one, but that of Wales.

When R.S. Thomas was asked his reasons for not including 'Original Sin' in one of his volumes of poetry, his answer put emphasis on the rhythm of the composition:

> ...it's the rhythm, I suppose. I don't like that jaunty sort of jog-trot rhythm, and that's probably why so... I've gone right away from any sort of jingle in the poem. I used to fall into it in my earlier days, much to my annoyance. So that's probably why it didn't get into a collection.[37]

So it appears that 'Original Sin' was one of the poems that R.S. Thomas put aside on the grounds of metrical insufficiency. This same aversion to "jingle" in poetry is also alluded to in John Betjeman's introduction to *Song at the Year's Turning* which states that R.S. Thomas "does not read nineteenth-century poems because he thinks that their obvious and jingly rhythms might upset his own sense of metre" (*SYT*, 14). This is obviously an overstatement of the situation but, nevertheless, it underlines neatly the importance that this poet attaches to his innate sense of metre.

This essay has included details of some of R.S. Thomas's uncollected poems plus variant readings up to and including 1955. As the years have passed so the number of poems has grown. By the beginning of the nineteen eighties I had traced over one hundred such pieces and the number has been increasing steadily since that date. These uncollected poems have appeared in such established journals as *The Times Literary Supplement*, *The Listener*, *Critical Quarterly*, *Agenda*, *Transatlantic Review*, *Encounter* and *Poetry Wales*, as well as locations that are not so obvious, such as *Forethought* (a publication from Eton College, in aid of famine relief), the Australian journals *Helix* and *Overland*, *The New York Times*, *Night Ride and Sunrise* (an anthology prepared on behalf of the British Migraine Association) and *Ishmael* (a quarterly review which in 1970 operated from an editorial address in Paris). Many of these uncollected poems fall into the linguistic and thematic areas that were characteristic of the collected compositions published during the same period, others provide an interesting counterpoint. All, plus details of variant readings, contribute to an understanding of R.S. Thomas's development as a poet.

Notes

1. R.S. Thomas comments on these early poems in 'Probings: An Interview with R.S. Thomas', *Planet* 80 (1990), 30.
2. NLW MS 20006 C.
3. From a tape of R.S. Thomas reading and discussing his own poems, 'Norwich Tapes Ltd: The Critical Forum', 1978.
4. "How many men have loved", NLW MS 20006 C.
5. 'Fragment', *The New English Weekly*, 13 July 1939, 204.
6. 'The Living Poet: R.S. Thomas', Third Programme, 27 August 1961, unpublished.
7. 'The Bat', *The Dublin Magazine* X1V:3 (1939), 8.
8. These three poems appear on a single page: *The Dublin Magazine* XV:3 (1940), 6.
9. "Look, look at the sky", loc. cit.

10. Richard Burnham, 'The Dublin Magazine's Welsh Poets', *The Anglo-Welsh Review* XXVII:60 (1978), 52.

11. Not 21 as stated by Richard Burnham.

12. Keidrych Rhys was also responsible for organizing the publication of *The Stones of the Field* at his Druid Press, Carmarthen.

13. 'Confessions of an Anglo-Welshman', *Wales* 2 (1943), 49.

14. 'Replies to *Wales* Questionnaire', *Wales* VI:3 (1946), 22-23. Here in answer to the question "Do you consider yourself an Anglo-Welsh writer?" R.S. Thomas wrote "No! A Welsh writer...".

15. 'Confessions of an Anglo-Welshman', loc. cit.

16. 'A Farmer', *Wales* 2 (1943), 48.

17. 'Gideon Pugh', *Wales* IV:6 (1944), 47.

18. 'A Farmer', loc. cit.

19. 'A Farmer', loc. cit.

20. 'A Farmer', loc. cit.

21. The poet's name is given as S.R. Thomas at the foot of this poem.

22. 'Gideon Pugh', loc. cit.

23. 'Norwich Tapes Ltd: The Critical Forum', 1978.

24. *Life and Letters Today* XXXVI: 67 (1943), 154.

25. *Counterpoint* 1 (1945), n.p.

26. *The Welsh Nationalist* XVI:1 (1947), 4.

27. *The Dublin Magazine* XXVI:4 (1951), 5.

28. *The Welsh Nation* XIX:11 (1950), 1.

29. *The Dublin Magazine* XXIV:2 (1949), 4-5.

30. 'Hill Farmer', *Wales* VIII:29 (1948), 511; 'Llandewi Brefi', *Wales* VIII:29 (1948), 521; 'Song', *The Dublin Magazine* XXIII:1 (1948), 3-4; 'Lines for Taliesin', *The Welsh Nation* XVIII:3 (1949), 5; 'Three Countries', *The Dublin Magazine* XXIV:2 (1949), 5; 'Welsh Shepherd', *The Dublin Magazine* XXIV:4 (1949), 5; 'Y Gwladwr', *Y Fflam* 9 (1950), 42; 'The Two Sisters', *The Welsh Nation* XIX:3 (1950), 1.

31. The other Welsh-language poem is 'Mae Ganddo Bleidlais', inspired by the 1984 General Election campaign, which appeared in *Barn* 256 (1984), 151.

32. 'Bachgen oeddwn i yng Nghaergybi — nid Cymro', *Y Cymro* 30 November 1967, 2.

33. Broadcast 18 September 1952, 8.00-8.30 p.m. The producer, Aneurin Talfan Davies, also commissioned John Ormond, Lynette Roberts and Glyn Jones to contribute to this series.

34. *The Minister* (Newtown: Montgomeryshire Printing Co., 1953), 23-24.

35. 'Auguries', *The Listener* 15 October 1953, 632; 'Darlington', *Rann* 19 (1953), 17-18; 'No Answer', *The Dublin Magazine* XXIX:2 (1953), 10-11; 'Peasant Girl Weeping', *The Listener* 9 July 1953, 67; 'Original Sin', *The Dublin Magazine* XXX:2 (1954), 9; 'Proportions', *The Dublin Magazine* XXX:2

(1954), 9; 'Somersby Brook', *TLS* 13 August 1954, 518; 'A Welsh Ballad Singer', *Encounter* III:6 (1954), 64; 'Commission: for Raymond Garlick', *Dock Leaves* VI:7 (1955),17; 'Farm Wives', *The Dublin Magazine* XXX:4 (1955), 1-2; 'Growing Up', *The New Statesman* 12 March 1955, 361; 'Midnight on the Farm', *The Dublin Magazine* XXXI:2 (1955), 4-5.

36. "The sound of the little heart breaking". The Welsh words appear as the last line of one of the traditional folk verses (hen benillion) which can be found together with an English translation in Gwyn Williams, *The Rent That's Due To Love* (London: Editions Poetry London, 1950), 86-87.

37. From an unpublished transcript of the author's interview with R.S. Thomas, 21 March 1978.

Anne Stevenson

The Uses of Prytherch

Once upon a time, on a gusty, wet afternoon in November, a young American mother parked her pram and sleeping baby in the lobby of the Hammersmith Public Library and guiltily ducked inside. She was looking for a book of poems. At her American university, before marrying in England, she had studied with passion the poetry of Herbert and Donne, Frost, Yeats and Eliot. Now England (not, alas, Bloomsbury) and marriage (not out of Jane Austen) had pretty well driven poetry out of her life. Foundering, bewildered, cold, not very happy, she was seeking the poems of a famous Welshman, not long dead, called Dylan Thomas. I can still see her forefinger travelling along the celluloid-covered titles on the poetry shelf: Auden, Bridges, Eliot, Hopkins, Muir — ah, Thomas. But the book she pulled out (a stone wall depicted on the binding) was not by the anticipated Dylan; it was the work of a poet she had never heard of: *Song at the Year's Turning*, by R.S. Thomas.

On the point of returning the volume to the shelf, she leafed through it. An introduction by a 'name', John Betjeman, warmly recommended the work of a country parson whose appeal went "beyond the Welsh border". R.S. Thomas was evidently another Welsh poet who wrote in English. It was impressive, though, that he had learned the Welsh language to help him understand "the remote hill people" among whom he lived. He was a nature poet, too, without the stigma of being Georgian or neo-Georgian. His feeling for Wales and Welsh dissent had enabled him to identify with the Minister of his narrative poem...and so on. All this sounded strange enough to that young American. (She has since come to realise how little Betjeman comprehended — despite the generosity of his recommendation — of R.S. Thomas's complicated conscience; or of the Wales in which is rooted his prolonged quarrel with himself.)

Nevertheless, opening the book at random, she read to the end a poem called 'Affinity'.

The Uses of Prytherch

Consider this man in the field beneath,
Gaitered with mud, lost in his own breath,
Without joy, without sorrow,
Without children, without wife,
Stumbling insensitively from furrow to furrow,
A vague somnambulist; but hold your tears,
For his name also is written in the Book of Life. (*SYT*,25)

Simple lines, but masterly. The rhymes and half-rhymes, enviably smooth, guided the sense through the stanza with none of the exhibitionist bravura of that other Thomas by now so familiar to Americans like my apprentice self — for why pretend any longer that bewildered young mother was anyone else? Especially striking was the way the line-beat varied, from two stresses in the generally anapestic "Without joy, without sorrow,/Without children, without wife" to five stresses in the last: "For his name also is written in the book of life."

English prosody has yet to evolve a notation that can represent the subtleties of phrase and rhythm in poetry like this. Anyone with an ear will unconsciously register the pattern of stresses, light syllables and pauses that in each line combine to achieve unostentatious wholeness. What the poem says is inseparable from what it is. A tone of moral injunction secures itself in the diction, yet every time a line veers towards rhetoric, the taut verse intervenes and pulls it back into the immediacy of the poem's occasion. If, for example, the rhymed couplet in the middle of the second stanza verges on preachiness, the sequel carries the verse into the realm of vision:

From the standpoint of education or caste or creed
Is there anything to show that your essential need
Is less than his, who has the world for church,
And stands bare-headed in the woods' wide porch
Morning and evening to hear God's choir
Scatter their praises?...

Again, if "God's choir" edges towards bathos, the effect is soon dissipated by the right-thereness of

Don't be taken in
By stinking garments or an aimless grin...

37

The Page's Drift: R.S. Thomas at Eighty

So it was that on a dark English day thirty-five years ago, this poem — not one Thomas chose to reprint in later collections — revealed itself to me instantly as the real thing: clear, closely-knit, spare and forceful by reason of its appropriate form. How much of this I understood at the time I don't know. After I had read 'Affinity' and the lovely translation from the Welsh, 'Night and Morning', on the facing page, I checked out Thomas's book and, with my crying baby and bulky shopping, returned home to read it when I needed it.

In part, my reason for attempting an essay on work which R.S. Thomas may by now reject or regret having published is to thank this poet whose fastidious ear and assured command of English verse brought poetry back to me — or me to poetry — in a bleak time of my youth. *Song at the Year's Turning* has remained a touchstone through the years. It seems important to emphasise that it was (and is) Thomas's *poetry* that impressed me; not only his fine technique, but the passion that seemed to well up from within it. That the passion was Welsh and its expression English can be seen today as the source of harrowing tension. But that was not so conspicuous then.

Speaking of 'The Making of a Poem' in 1969, Thomas himself declared "One of my objections to...reviewers and columnists is that they...nearly always go over what [my] poems are about... the hill country of Wales; the Welsh political and social existence; the natural world; the struggle between time and eternity; the struggle between reason and the emotions." While Thomas readily admits, in this talk to librarians, that he himself may be responsible for such reviews because he "pushes" his ideas at people, still, he says, this "is not what a poet should do at all." He goes on to explain that poetry, for him, as for all poets deserving of the name, "is a matter of technique" (*Prose*, 109).

> If a poet realises that it has been his privilege to have a certain gift in the manipulation of language...then he is obviously committed from the very beginning to a life-time of self discipline, struggle, disappointment, failure, with just possibly that odd success which is greater in his eyes than it probably is in the eyes of anybody else. (*Prose*, 111)

Later on in the same passage, Thomas adds in a characteristic tone of self-questioning, "...there must be some kind of music which one is after, and indeed isn't this what makes poetry memorable? Isn't it just the way of saying things which really is part of our appreciation of poetry, and the thing that makes poetry last through the centuries?"

It is pertinent to keep those remarks on technique and music in mind while considering the overall direction and development of Thomas's poems over twenty-five years; roughly, from 1942, when he became Rector of Manafon in the border county of Montgomeryshire, to 1967, when he left Eglwys-fach, south of the Dyfi estuary, and moved further west and north to Aberdaron on Welsh-speaking Llŷn. His geographical migration parallels the thematic configuration of his poetry; and both manifest a conscious and deliberate withdrawal from England (including the forms of English verse) and a correspondingly self-monitored identification with Wales and Welsh culture. In Aberdaron, after the publication of *Not that He Brought Flowers* in 1968, he severely winnowed his earlier work, dropping from the six (really nine) collections represented in his *Selected Poems, 1946-1968* many poems that his readers knew well and must have expected to find. Why? Why, in the early 1970s, did he discard from this retrospective volume good poems that recorded step by step the process of a spiritual and mental dialectic that for twenty-five years had empowered his verse? Can a shape or paradigm be found in the early books that will shed light on the direction of the later ones?

II

Thomas's 'early' poems — Thomas was forty-two when *Song at the Year's Turning* was published (1955); two years older than George Herbert when he died — are sometimes known as the 'Prytherch poems', after Iago Prytherch, a name the poet "jestingly" invented for a hill-farmer he once saw docking mangles while "visiting a 1,000 feet up farm in Manafon".[1] The name Iago Prytherch, strange to English ears, is common enough in Welsh. Iago simply means James, pronounced with a short a, as in 'baggage' or 'map'; it bears no relation, probably, to the long-aed villain of *Othello*. Prytherch, or Prydderch in Welsh, would be a contraction of ap Rhydderch, or son of Rhytherch. It is not likely that 'Prytherch' has significance as a name, apart from its being a Welsh surname given to an English-speaking hill-farmer, rooting him in Wales and its hereditary Celtic 'tree'.[2] When he first appears in 'A Peasant', Iago Prytherch more or less merges with other, often unnamed men of the soil and mixen: "Just an ordinary man of the bald Welsh hills,/who pens a few sheep in a gap of cloud." Like Davies who died "with his face to the wall...in his stone croft" (*SYT*, 59), like Twm of 'The Airy Tomb', Prytherch represents an amalgam of labourers and poor farmers in *The Stones of the Field* and *An Acre of Land* who "compelled" the poet's gaze.

It has long been apparent, though, that Iago Prytherch, perhaps 'real' to begin with, through the years came to represent a good deal more than a rural type. Writing on the Prytherch Poems in 1971, H.J. Savill confirmed what is surely plain to anyone who reads them in sequence: that Prytherch evolved to become a conscience or *alter ego* for Thomas; as Savill puts it "a control, a sounding board for the poet's personal sense of conflict...".[3]

Thomas himself has recorded, in Welsh prose, how, upon arriving in Manafon, his parish of materialistic border-Welsh hill-farmers at first shocked and repelled him. "Manafon was an eye-opener to me," he wrote in the radio talk *Y Llwybrau Gynt* in 1972:

> Here I became aware of the clash between dream and reality. I was a proper little bourgeois, brought up delicately, with the mark of the church and the library on me. I had seen this part of the country from the train in the evening through a romantic haze. I now found myself among hard, materialistic, industrious people, who measured each other in acres and pounds; Welshmen who turned their backs on their inheritance...farmers of the cold, bare hillsides, who dreamed of saving enough money to move to a more fertile farm on the plains. (*Prose*, 138)

The conflicts that resulted in the Manafon poems were born, surely, of that first confrontation with the 'real world'. The "clash between dream and reality" — the same that beset Yeats in Ireland — would seem to set the younger Thomas, too, in the mainstream of the late romantic tradition. His self-doubt ("a proper little bourgeois") bespeaks disdain for his own intellectual status ("the mark of the church and the library"). At the same time, the poet was disturbed by the crudeness and materialism of the hill farmers, in whom he had hoped to find a "magical and mysterious" Welshness he had not found in a previous parish on the plains of Flintshire (*Prose*, 138).[4]

How Thomas responded and dealt with romantic disillusion is hinted at in his prose, although one has to read poems such as 'Memories' (*SYT*, 45) to realise how, when romantic fantasy gave way to a sense of 'reality', he tried on alternative romantic ideas, conspicuously those developed in the early nineteenth century by Coleridge and Wordsworth. In Manafon, Thomas's imagination abandoned the "magical and mysterious" and instead looked hard at the place where he was. He remained, however reluctantly (or so it seems to me), a precarious and increasingly self-conscious, self-critical Romantic. Ned Thomas, in an essay introducing the *Selected Prose*, writes convincingly of what he calls R.S. Thomas's "clash of Romanticisms", for example "The late Romanticism of the far horizon that was so often projected onto the Celtic West is rejected but in its place appears a new and fresh romanticism, grounded in this place and welling up in the heart in the manner of the great early Romantics" (*Prose*, 9). The essay goes on to associate Thomas's evolving outlook not only with the German and English movement of the nineteenth century but, to a limited extent, with a Welsh-language tradition nearer at hand in the work of his contemporary, Waldo Williams (*Prose*, 11).

Whatever Thomas may believe about romanticism, his writing repeatedly insists that the feelings "welling up in his heart" in Manafon radically affected the tenor of his ideas and the dilemmas those ideas brought to his poetry.[5] The passage from *Y Llwybrau Gynt* quoted above continues,

> [Manafon] was in some ways an old-fashioned district. When I went there in 1942, there was not a single tractor in the area. The men worked with their hands, hoeing, sheep-shearing, collecting hay, and cutting hedges. The horse was still in use. There was a smithy there; I can hear the sound of the anvil still, and see the sparks flying. I can remember the lonely figures in the fields, hoeing or docking mangles, hour after hour. What was going on in their heads, I wonder? The question remains unanswered to this day. (*Prose*, 138-9)

Such recollections, exact, moving, tinged slightly with nostalgia, provide no evidence that Thomas came to know or understand his hill-farmers. On the contrary, as he repeatedly lamented in poetry and prose, their existence seemed inconceivably distant from his own. It was, surely, the gnawing bafflement and pity he felt when faced with people like Prytherch that set him writing. When the dream was lost, responsibilities to other ideals began to emerge. If the Wales he loved, with its birds and trees and mountains, was also a nation of "old fashioned ways" and inarticulate farmers, then the poet would have to forge links with them, as with their "cold, bare hillsides" and the Welsh language they had forgotten. Confronting what he saw as insensibility in his rural parishioners, he contemplated them — the conundrum of their minds and the harsh realities of their lives — with a view not so much of teaching them as of learning from them how to approach himself. If he could not show them how to value what they, as Welshmen, so preciously possessed, could he himself believe in that idyll — so dear to him — of a shared inheritance: cultural, natural, Christian and national? In the context of his ideal, "What was going on in their heads, I wonder?" became absolutely pivotal to the pro-longed self-interrogation that sustains the dramatic tension in Thomas's first five or six books.[6]

As Thomas set it up for himself, the dispute with the farmers of Montgomeryshire (i.e., with his own ideas) that pervades *Song at the Year's Turning* and continues to break out in *Poetry for Supper*, *Tares* and *The Bread of Truth* was bound to result in the poet's seeming defeat. (If it had been a real defeat, Thomas would not have gone on writing.) "All in vain. I will cease now/My long absorption with the plough," Thomas declares in 'No Through Road', the last poem in *Song at the Year's Turning* (*SYT*, 115).

> I have failed after many seasons
> To bring truth to birth,
> And nature's simple equations
> In the mind's precincts do not apply.

This acknowledgement of failure, though, is tantamount to a statement of purpose: the poet has tried, he says, first to lay bare the truth in art, and secondly to reconcile nature's rules or "simple equations" with the complex mind that creates poetry. In confess-ing that such connections can't be made, he shows, in the following stanza, that they must. "But where to turn?" He answers himself immediately by returning to 'nature', even as he despairs of representing it in language.

> Earth endures
> After the passing, necessary shame
> Of winter, and the old lie
> Of green places beckons me still
> From the new world, ugly and evil,
> That men pry for in truth's name.

More forbidding than anything in nature is the "new world" that science and technology are bringing about in the name of truth: notice that men now "pry" for it; i.e. no longer 'pray'. The "old lie" for Thomas, is preferable to the new 'truth'. One sees here that the argument has veered away from the puzzle of Prytherch and other men of the soil. It seems now to take place in the pained consciousness of a man who, having got rid of his romantic, idealised illusions, faces with horror the intolerable condition of the world without them.

The apparent finality of 'No Through Road' is really, then, a point of new departure: the poet, now allied with Prytherch, stands in opposition to the "evil" mechanizing treads of contemporary culture. This poem's place, moreover, at the end of Thomas's first selection seems to inform us that a chapter of the poet's mental travelling is over.

It is helpful, I think, to regard each of Thomas's books as a lap in a personal journey — a quest that seems bound to fail because it seeks a truth that, on one hand, cannot be logical or proved by reason, but on the other, has to be 'proved' against the romantic lie. A map can be imagined that would chart the contradictions and temptations this poet forced himself to overcome as he persevered on his barefoot way. His books, of course, overlap; and the line (or maze) that connects them is continuous. Nevertheless, there are halting places, pits of despair, a few dazzling peaks of arrival, interspersed with shifts or changes in the overall topography. These latter tend to occur after a subject has worn itself out, working through every possible cranny of the poet's consciousness.

Such a subject was Prytherch and his brothers of the Montgomeryshire hills. *Song at the Year's Turning* did not, in fact, exhaust Thomas's "long absorption with the plough", although at least thirty of its sixty-three lyrics dwell on the enigma of unthinking labouring man. When Prytherch returns in subsequent collections, it is to a somewhat less solidly earthed, more metaphysical and defensive context. Up to 1955 or so, the figure of Prytherch invited, over and over, the same amazed gaze of revulsion and fascination, followed usually by self-castigation and a humbled acknowledgement of his status as a man. The struggle was never one, however, in which the labourer participated; it occurred within the mind of the poet even when, as in 'Invasion on the Farm', Prytherch himself was given an anxious, protesting monologue.

> I am Prytherch. Forgive me. I don't know
> What you are talking about; your thoughts flow
> Too swiftly for me... (SYT, 102)

The farm workers described in the more typical 'A Peasant' and 'Affinity' are spoken about, but have nothing to say for themselves. "Blind? Yes, and deaf and dumb, and the last irks most," cries the speaker in 'Enigma' (*SYT*, 68). Repeatedly the peasant is seen to be rooted in the land, more plant than man, "enduring like a tree under the curious stars" ('A Peasant', *SYT*, 21); or as one who pulls "the reluctant swedes" until "his back comes straight/ Like an old tree lightened of the snow's weight" ('A Labourer', *SYT*, 18). In *An Acre of Land*, the same labourer, or one identical to him, is seen as "A wild tree still, whose seasons are not yours..." ('The Labourer', *SYT*, 70).

As Ned Thomas demonstrates (*Prose*, 11-12), the tree is an image or emblem that weaves through all Thomas's work. Converging with the image of the fountain,[7] it knits up the apparent contradictions, again and again appearing as a symbol of endurance, of hope, of nature, of poetry "that is eternity wearing/the green leaves of time" ('Prayer', *LP*, 214). It is in terms of a tree, finally, that Prytherch gains his victory over the world and the poet alike:

> Power, farmer? It was always yours.
> Not the new physics' terrible threat
> To the world's axle, nor the mind's subtler

Manipulation of our debt

To nature; but an old gift
For weathering the slow recoil
Of empires with a tree's patience,
Rooted in the dark soil.
('Iago Prytherch', *PS*, 37)

Open, almost anywhere, any of Thomas' books published before
1961 to find Prytherch or Prytherch's double, described as a crea-
ture more of nature than of humanity, rooted in the land, some-
times sensitive to his surroundings, "your soul made strong/ By
the earth's incense" ('Absolution', *PS*, 44), sometimes "Wasting
his frame under the ripped coat,/...Contributing grimly to the
accepted pattern,/The embryo music dead in his throat" ('The
Welsh Hill Country', *SYT*, 46). Yet a penetrating reading shows us
such figures, not only as trees, rooted in the soil, but as potential
inheritors of the one "great tree" that is Wales: "Its roots were
nourished with their blood" ('The Tree: Owain Glyn Dŵr Speaks',
SYT, 56-58). This heraldic tree of Welsh legend, together with the
Christian tree that is the cross, are invoked often enough in the
early poems to offset the bitterness of their realism with a lyrical,
even mystical, iconography.

He kneeled long,
And saw love in a dark crown
Of thorns blazing, and a winter tree
Golden with fruit of a man's body.
('In a Country Church', *SYT*, 114)

As early as 1946, after the publication of *The Stones of the Field*,
Thomas was being attacked by fellow Welshmen for the grimness
of his rural portraits. Dr. Pennar Davies, in a broadcast on 21
November of that year, commented, "R.S. Thomas sees far more
uncouthness in the men of the Welsh hills than I have ever been
able to detect."[8] Such criticism is understandable. With the spread
of nonconformity through Wales "a yawning gulf", in the words
of the historian Kenneth O. Morgan, "opened up between the
anglicized gentry and the...Welsh-speaking majority": Welsh cul-
ture "emerged from below, from the tenant farmers and labourers
on their smallholdings".[9] The extension of the franchise and the

reform of local government in the late nineteenth century, with the great transfer of landownership before and after the First World War, made these farmers masters of their own land. The Welsh tradition they inherited, founded on the nonconformism which had saved their language and culture, was one in which education, poetry and music were cherished. In his (Welsh) poem 'Ffermwr Rhyddfrydol' ('Liberal Farmer') Bobi Jones — a younger contemporary of R.S.Thomas — brings one such farmer vividly to life: "He was so stout: but when he spoke his pure harsh consonants/I felt like an exile on a distant continent/Hearing through bars the forgotten echo/Of the language of his boots...".[10] Even before the advent of tractors and electricity, Bobi Jones's "stout farmer" would scarcely have recognised himself in Iago Prytherch. But, of course, Prytherch, almost from the beginning, was a projection of an idea; a partner in a purely internal dialogue.

Moreover, as H.J. Savill points out, Thomas's farmers and labourers did not belong to Welsh-speaking Wales. They were, in Thomas's eyes, impoverished English-speaking border-people, indifferent to the Welshness that he desired to restore to them. Importantly for Thomas, too, they were a people left out by advancing civilization, and therefore, through their very backwardness and ignorance, salvageable as representatives of an 'old world' everywhere threatened by the 'evil' new one.

It is not surprising, either, that Thomas, who was born and educated outside the Welsh cultural tradition, looked at Prytherch and his kind, and saw there a curious affinity; both he and they were anomalies in Wales. His disgust with himself and his background could be transferred to them, and shared. That the Anglican priest was articulate and the hill-farmers mute meant that, in reaching out to them, he could try to speak for them. And yet, paradoxically, this poet's romantic vision gave him to understand that education and articulation (especially in English) was itself a form of corruption. So it was that Thomas found himself torn between revulsion at the passive insensitivity of his hill-farmers, and admiration (eventually reverence) for the the strength of their innocence. The tension bore fruit in all the poetry of the Prytherch period.

Part of the paradox of Thomas's position in Manafon was that he represented the recently disestablished Anglican Church of

Wales. Welsh-speaking farmers would have attended a non-conformist Baptist, Presbyterian or Methodist chapel. In 'The Minister' Thomas lambasts the Calvinism preached by Elias Morgan:

> Protestantism — the adroit castrator
> Of art; the bitter negation
> Of song and dance and the heart's innocent joy —
> You have botched our flesh and left us only the soul's
> Terrible impotence in a warm world. (*SYT*, 92)

In 'Dau Gapel' (1948), however, Thomas wrote of nonconformism with enthusiasm: "Speaking of denominations, I must admit that Nonconformity wins hands down... The Church in Wales isn't any longer Welsh enough in Spirit" (*Prose*, 46-47). Here was another source of contradiction for the Anglican priest and artist struggling to come to terms with the 'truth', with the farmers who were his parishioners and with the Wales he associated with spiritual wholeness.

A poem that seems central to the tangle of conflicts that runs right through *Song at the Year's Turning* is one called 'A Priest to his People' (*SYT*, 29). It is not as dramatically affecting as 'The Minister', but it is typical of Thomas's struggle at the time. The huge swing of its dialectic, from harangue to celebration, with its uneasy resolution in baffled submission is like a blueprint of this period's (productive) continuing battle. The poem begins brutally.

> Men of the hills, wantoners, men of Wales
> With your sheep and your pigs and your ponies, your sweaty
>   females,
> How I have hated you for your irreverence, your scorn even
> Of the refinements of art and the mysteries of the Church...

"Hated" is a strong word; "sweaty females" is shocking. But notice how Thomas puts the priest in a false position he is bound to forfeit. Hatred, disgust, arrogance — such powerfully unChristian feelings are spat out in an invective of self-defence. Protecting the "refinements" of his tastes, the speaker is ignoring the earth of his origin. The "men of bone" he addresses, "who have not yet shaken the moss from [their] savage skulls", detect his falseness: the priest's "true heart" is "wandering in a wood of lies." And what are these lies? The forms of the Church, "the pale words in the black Book" offered so unprofitably to people "whose hands can dabble in the world's blood." Equally suspect are the forms of art:

> I have taxed your ignorance of rhyme and sonnet,
> Your want of deference to the painter's skill,
> But I know, as I listen, that your speech has in it
> The source of all poetry, clear as a rill
> Bubbling from your lips...

Today Thomas would almost certainly reject such lines — cleverly rhymed, rhythmical, conventionally romantic in sentiment. Implied is a criticism of all that culture stands for, couched in 'poetic' English that he now bitterly stands against. In the 1940s, when *Stones of the Field* was being written, Thomas was still attracted by the pastoral ideal. Nonetheless, the priest soon sees how "indifferent they are to all I can offer,/Caring not whether I blame or praise." This is where Thomas, of course, departs from the traditional model. Pastoral encomiums will not satisfy the 'truth'. In the end, priest and people remain irremediably separated, the priest locked within his Church of "refinements" and "mysteries", the people unaware that 'higher' sentiments exist.

> With your pigs and your sheep and your sons and holly-
>   cheeked daughters
> You will still continue to unwind your days
> In a crude tapestry under the jealous heavens
> To affront, bewilder, yet compel my gaze.

A theme common to the poems of *Song at the Year's Turning* can be identified as intense romantic longing, frustrated by the poet's faithfulness to the truth he perceives. His defeat at the hands of reality is paradoxically a victory for the 'failure' he unearths, after he has cast away his false illusions. The question arises, how much of his residual, hard-won insight is true, how much still false? Determined to be scrupulously honest, conditioning himself by renouncing the lyrical pulse that thrust him into poetry in the first place, Thomas set out, it appears, in pursuit of a metaphysic that would supersede his endemic intellectuality by giving him access to some holy unity of body and spirit, earth and mind, that he glimpsed only at moments. Such a longed-for state of exalted reality became for Thomas the uncertain promise that sanctified his quest — Wordsworth's "central peace subsisting at the heart/ of endless agitation", Eliot's "still point of the turning world."

Keeping such an elusive, essential possibility alive — while the dialogue with Prytherch rumbled on — meant that a number of intermediate poems, written along the way, as it were, had to be pruned once they had served their purpose. Of the eighteen published poems in which Prytherch appears,[11] Thomas preserved only three for his *Selected Poems*: 'A Peasant', which first introduced him (it also introduces the selection and is its point of departure); 'Invasion on the Farm' which reverses the roles of poet and persona, allowing Prytherch to voice his misgivings under threat from the poet's challenge; and finally, some late consolations of philosophy offered by the poet to the labourer in a curt 'Aside' (*SP*, 100).

> Take heart, Prytherch.
> Over you the planets stand,
> And have seen more ills than yours.
> This canker was in the bone
> Before man bent to his image
> In the pool's glass. Violence has been
> And will be again. Between better
> And worse is no bad place
>
> For a labourer, whose lot is to seem
> Stationary in traffic so fast.
> Turn aside, I said; do not turn back.
> There is no forward and no back
> In the fields, only the year's two
> Solstices, and patience between.

'Aside' partakes of the self-searchings and assertions of *Pietà*, in which it appeared in 1966. At once didactic and resigned, it signals an end to the long question and answer of the Prytherch debate, and may have seemed to Thomas the most satisfying of his attempts finally to reconcile the outlooks of priest and peasant. Between 'A Peasant' and 'Aside', some of the best of Prytherch has been lost ('The Gap in the Hedge' [*SYT*, 53] for instance, with its haunting ambiguity) along with weaker chapters in the story: the nostalgic, somewhat patronising 'Memories' (*SYT*, 45), the almost melodramatic 'Temptation of a Poet' (*PS*, 14), the embittered 'Too Late' (*T*, 25). None of the shifts in attitude explored in *Poetry for Supper* appear in the *Selected Poems*, although the former book, with *Tares*, traces Prytherch's metamorphoses from a mute toiler in the fields to a "scholar of the soil" who is seen to have been "right the whole time" ('Absolution', *PS*, 44), and is now chiefly threatened, not by the poet who loves him, but by modern methods of farming "That will destroy you and your race" ('Too Late', *T*, 25).

By the time *Tares* appeared in 1961, Prytherch was clearly a type Thomas honoured and wished to preserve in Wales, but his symbolic presence was not so urgently relied on. The nonconformist farmer Walter Llywarch (*SP*, 63), describing his isolated life in a Welsh valley, delivers a cool monologue of defeat that has little to do with the poet's metaphysical conflict. Likewise 'On the Farm' (*SP*, 89) departs from the Prytherch pattern, presenting the "no good" Puw family objectively, in grim ironical stanzas that, at the end, plunge into dark hints of corruption:

> And lastly there was the girl:
> Beauty under some spell of the beast.
> Her pale face was the lantern
> By which they read in life's dark book
> The shrill sentence: God is love.

Poems like this — detached, pared to the bone and technically stunning — rightly, in my opinion, filtered out a good deal of self-questioning and ideological gesturing from the *Selected Poems*. Prytherch is interesting to those who have followed the tos and fros of Thomas's mental strife, but in the later poems he is better placed behind the scenes. Thomas, it would seem, having sputtered at his critics and openly explained his relationship to Prytherch in 'Iago Prytherch' (*PS*, 36) while beseeching him for forgiveness (see also 'Absolution', *PS*, 44) at last felt ready to release him. 'Servant', from *The Bread of Truth* says as much, providing the title of that collection in its last line.

> You served me well, Prytherch.
> From all my questioning and doubts;
> From brief acceptance of the times'
> Deities; from ache of the mind
> Or body's tyranny, I turned...

To where you read in the slow book
Of the farm, turning the fields' pages...
...proving in your bone and in your blood
Its accuracy....

Prytherch had not, of course, given "the whole answer". The poem goes on to balance the equation:

Is truth so bare,
So dark, so dumb, as on your hearth
And in your company I found it?
Is not the evolving print of the sky
To be read, too; the mineral
Of the mind worked?.....

The poet, given his eye for beauty and capacity for working "the mineral of the mind" can choose his 'higher' truth "With a clear eye and free hand,/From life's bounty". Prytherch has no such advantage:

Not choice for you,
But seed sown upon the thin
Soil of a heart, not rich, nor fertile,
Yet capable of the one crop,
Which is the bread of truth that I break. (BT, 41)

As R.S. Thomas increasingly abandoned the prosodic models of English verse and secured his poetry in a voice that drew strength from conceptual imagery ("evolving print of the sky"; "mineral of the mind"), certain ideas he found himself promoting — such as 'higher' truth for the educated and plain "bread of truth" for Prytherch — may well have distressed him. Poems like 'Servant' made the conflict between beauty and truth seem more, rather than less insoluble. Even to call Prytherch a "servant" seems to relegate the values he represents to a lesser status: and this was not, I believe, what Thomas intended to do. The dialectic of assertion, withdrawal and pained reconsideration that characterises the Prytherch poems seeks, surely, to represent Prytherch and priest as equals. The chasm they are asked to bridge lies between nature's truth and the ideas educated people formulate in language in order to comprehend and communicate 'truth'. Yet language, to Thomas (as to Wittgenstein and subsequent linguistic philosophers) is not, in the end, capable of bridging the gap between reality and itself. This state of affairs is plainly set forth in 'Epitaph' (*PS*, 48):

> The poem in the rock and
> The poem in the mind
> Are not one.
> It was in dying
> I tried to make them so.

How is a reader to take such a poem's despairing assertion? As resignation? As a threat? Or as the stripped bedrock on which to found new attempts to build truth out of language? It appears that at a stage in his progress, Thomas was willing to 'die', or in the words of his essay, to "commit suicide" as a poet,[12] in order to marry the irreconcilable concepts of intellect and instinct, body and mind, language and reality. As he must have seen, when he attempted synthesis by argument or plain assertion, he failed to convince himself. He seems to have 'said' things in his poems in order to prove himself wrong. It was by airing his arguments that he discovered where he was mistaken. The poem he called 'Green Categories' (*PS*, 19) in which he confronts Prytherch with Kant, is a case in point.[13] However, it appears that Thomas often did succeed in satisfying himself when, exhausted by mental strife, he dropped naturally into images. "Don't think, look," Wittgenstein advised, after anguished years of fighting the antinomies Kant categorically had forced into partnership.

As a poet, though, Thomas had the advantage over the philosophers. For where philosophy, of its very nature, has to expound abstract ideas, poetry is like painting; it talks with images. Like music, too, it is a 'language' of sound. To be art, of course, images and sound have to communicate through a logic of their own. Yet the vital ambiguity and multiple resonances of imagistic expression give the poet a chance.

In 'Absolution' (*PS*, 44), Thomas grants to Prytherch a patient wisdom denied to the poet, but he still reserves to himself the intelligence that finds this out. The very acknowledgement, "It was you who were right", opens a loophole through which the poet can escape into a field of 'things', i.e. *away* from his ideas. He cannot become a Prytherch, docking mangels in the dusk, but he knows now where he fell into error: "I have worn my soul bare/ On the world's roads, seeking what lay/Too close *for the mind's lenses to see*..." (my italics). Seeing, then, offers the poet salvation, and it is, after all, Prytherch who has shown him how to look.

When, in the first poem of *Tares*, Thomas sets forth his compassionate reasons for making Prytherch central to his story, he ignores the infinitely valuable lesson he has been taught in return. 'The Dark Well' (*T*, 9) is a poem of conscience; it tells us why Prytherch deserves compassion.

> There are two hungers, hunger for bread
> And hunger of the uncouth soul
> For the light's grace. I have seen both,
> And chosen for an indulgent world's
> Ear the story of one whose hands
> Have bruised themselves on the locked doors
> Of life; whose heart, fuller than mine
> Of gulped tears, is the dark well
> From which to draw, drop after drop,
> The terrible poetry of his kind.

To say that, as a poem, 'The Dark Well' is overstated (though heart-felt) probably does Thomas an injustice. But as so often, Thomas here asserts, in lines of verse, feelings that he asks his readers to accept as statements. The sentiments are strongly felt, and yes, they are couched in metaphor. Nevertheless, the figurative language is illustrative, and not really intrinsic to the poem. A quality of exegesis, of sermonising explanation, 'pushes' them (Thomas's own word, see *Prose*, 109) at the reader, and the words speak darkly from the priest's conscience, not from the poet's freedom. For that *élan* we sometimes call revelation — that outward push from the traps of 'truth' and guilt — one has to turn to something like 'The Place', with which Thomas chose to end his *Selected Poems*.

> Summer is here.
> Once more the house has its
> Spray of martins, Proust's fountain
> Of small birds, whose light shadows
> Come and go in the sunshine
> Of the lawn as thoughts do
> In the mind.

The Page's Drift: R.S. Thomas at Eighty

Poetry happens when image and thought are fired simultaneously by language, compounding idea and vision in an indivisible whole. Towards the end of 'The Place', Thomas lets the fountain of martins "build in" himself, and their "bitter migrations" represent his; but the analogy is so delicately drawn that the birds remain in the ascendant — images of renewal and certainty that may well have suprised the poet, as he came joyfully to see them.

> ... my method is so
> To have them about myself
> Through the hours of this brief
> Season and to fill with their
> Movement, that it is I they build
> In and bring up their young
> To return to after the bitter
> Migrations, knowing the site
> Inviolate through its outward changes.

Notes

1. H.J. Savill, 'The Iago Prytherch Poems of R.S. Thomas', *The Anglo-Welsh Review*, XX:45 (1971), 143. Reprinted in Sandra Anstey, ed., *Critical Writings on R.S. Thomas* (Bridgend: Poetry Wales Press, 1982), 51. Page references are to *Critical Writings*.
2. The author is grateful to the Welsh poet Dewi Stephen Jones for his comments and translations from the Welsh.
3. Savill, *Critical Writings*, 53.
4. Writing of himself in the third person in his autobigraphy, *Neb (Nobody)* Thomas vividly describes the Manafon he found in 1942: "Manafon scarcely existed. There was no village, only a church, a tavern, a school and a shop. The farms were spread across the hills as small-holdings mostly, but with the occasional larger farm. The people were anglicised Welsh, with Welsh names and Shropshire accents. They became the subject of his poetry. To him the country and its surroundings were beautiful. He wished to continue to sing poems of praise about them. But how could one reconcile the lives and attitudes of these farmers to this? On a cold, dark day in November, on his way to visit a family living in a farm a thousand feet above sea-level, he noticed the farmer's brother out in the field docking mangels. This made a deep impression on him and when he returned home after the visit he began writing 'A Peasant', his first poem to face the reality of the scenes before him." (*Neb* [Caernarfon: Gwasg Gwynedd, 1985], 42, translation, Dewi Stephen Jones.)

5. A further passage from *Neb*: "Was it because of the hardness of the people and their work, or because of some nicey-nice quality in himself that the tension arose which was to be a part of his spiritual and literary problems for some years to come?...After long hours of hard work in all kinds of weather, what was there to do each night after a meal but nod by the fire before they went to bed under the slates?...Earth from earth were they; their only interests were the farm, the animals, prices and the personal lives of their neighbours. The horizons of some of them did not extend beyond the far side of the valley where they lived." (42-43)

6. R.S. Thomas, 'Abercuawg' (1976), *Prose*, 159: "When I began writing I devised a character called Iago Prytherch — an amalgam of some farmers I used to see at work on the Montgomeryshire hillsides. In the opinion of some, he developed into a symbol of something greater. And yet I had to ask myself whether he was real at all. And there was something else that would worry me as I saw him sweating or shivering hour after hour in the fields: 'What is he thinking about? What's going on inside his skull? And of course there was always the awful possibility that the answer was — 'Nothing'. Nothing. What is nothing?"

7. In 1956 Waldo Williams published his visionary Welsh poem 'Mewn Dau Gae' ('In Two Fields') which contains these lines, seemingly important to R.S.Thomas:

> Great was the leaping of hearts, after their ice-age.
> The fountains burst up toward heaven, till,
> Falling back, their tears were like leaves of a tree.

Translation, Anthony Conran [See also *Prose*, 12].

8. Quoted by Savill in Anstey, *Critical Writings*, 54.

9. Kenneth O. Morgan, *Rebirth of a Nation: Wales 1880-1980*, (Oxford: Oxford University Press, 1982), 13-27.

10. John Emyr, *Bobi Jones* (Cardiff: University of Wales Press, 1991), 29-30.

11. H.J. Savill puts the total number of Prytherch poems at eighteen, to include an earlier romantic, "almost euphoric" 'Iago Prytherch' that R.S. Thomas suppressed after the publication of *Stones of the Field* in 1946 (*Critical Writings*, 58).

12. R.S. Thomas, 'The Creative Writer's Suicide' (1978), *Prose*, 167-174. See also the introduction by Ned Thomas: "The pressures of the modern world which turned R.S. Thomas' Wales into something with a status close to that of pure idea also have an internalized dimension in language itself" (*Prose*, 13). It seems that Thomas was prepared to sacrifice his English lyricism in order to forge a distinctive Anglo-Welsh voice, but he was *not* prepared to give up the English language in poetry, because Welsh was not his mother tongue".

13. 'Green Categories' ends with a reference to the last lines of Kant's *Critique of Pure Reason*: "der besternte Himmel über mir, und das moralische Gesetz in mir." In the final stanza of 'Green Categories' Thomas writes: "[Kant's] logic would have failed; your mind, too,/Exposed suddenly to the cold wind/Of genius, faltered. Yet at night together/In your small garden, fenced from the wild moor's/Constant aggression, you could have been at one,/Sharing your faith over a star's blue fire."

Helen Vendler

R.S. Thomas and Painting

Between Here and Now (1981) and *Ingrowing Thoughts* (1985) are sufficiently unusual among R.S. Thomas's books to be considered as a unit. The first in part, and the second as a whole, contain poems reflecting on paintings; in the first (according to Thomas's notes), the thirty-three paintings are drawn from Germain Bazin's *Impressionist Paintings in the Louvre*; in the second, the twenty-one paintings are drawn from Herbert Read's two books, *Surrealism* and *Art Now*.[1] Opposite his poem-commentaries, Thomas reproduces the paintings in black-and-white small-format, and it is fair to say that the poems would on the whole be unintelligible without the paintings. On the other hand, many aspects of the paintings go unmentioned in the poetry; the poems do not refer to genre, dimension, colour, brushwork, or art-historical allusion in the painting. The subject-matter of the paintings is clearly important to Thomas, as, from time to time, is the structure. Thomas's reader is expected to possess some minimal cultural information (Gauguin's madness, the events at Guernica).

Of the two volumes of painting-poems, I prefer, and will concentrate on, *Between Here and Now*, but I shall also refer to *Ingrowing Thoughts* as occasion offers. (All poems quoted are from *Between Here and Now* unless otherwise noted.)

Thomas's volumes take up in fresh ways the historic and uneasy relation between poesis and the picture, a theme necessarily recalling the most memorable lyrics theorising the relation, Keats's odes to the nightingale and on the urn. In the first title, Keats emphasises the living nature of (musical and poetic) temporal art, as something that can be addressed, something to sing *to*. In the second title, Keats represents himself as a commentator, speculating on the nature of non-temporal visual art, as something to think *about*. Thomas's first title, invoking both space (*Here*) and time (*Now*), suggests that he will complicate Keats's division. For Thomas, art is neither spatial nor temporal, but occupies a space outside of our categories, "between here and now":

The Page's Drift: R.S. Thomas at Eighty

> Creatures of time and space as we all are, we are yet haunted by
> dreams of eternity and we have a conception of ourselves as arrest-
> ing the flow of time. When we love somebody, or we see something
> very beautiful, or when we are experiencing something very won-
> derful or very strange which has a dreamlike quality about it, there
> is on that occasion something within us which wants to arrest this
> and keep it forever, and we know that in so far as we are creatures
> of time and space this does not seem to be possible. Almost before
> we have really had our attention drawn to it either we have passed
> on or it has gone in the slip-stream and is no more. Most of us would
> feel that if only we had the gift of language, or if only we had the
> hand of the painter, or if only we were musicians, we should try to
> formalise and crystallise or trap this evanescent experience, and
> arrest it and take it out of the time-flow. And this is surely what the
> better poets are able to do. (*Prose*, 112)

To "arrest it and take it out of the time-flow" is perhaps harder to
do in poetry than in visual art. In Thomas's new technique in these
volumes, the art-transaction of his poems occurs in the space
between the reproduced (spatial) painting and the opposite (tem-
poral) commentary, and is located in the invisible intersection
(first in the poet's mind, then in the reader's) where the two
art-works illuminate each other. Although Thomas gives onto-
logical priority to the painting (first he contemplates it, next he
comments on it — a relation that cannot be reversed), still, since
we have not truly 'seen' the painting until we have read his poem,
the painting eventually becomes a *post-hoc* commentary on the
verse, which then becomes (as the prescriptive guide to interpre-
tation of the painting) ontologically prior in its turn.

Each of Thomas's poems is small enough to fit on the page
opposite its painting, so that a single glance can take in both
art-works. In *Between Here and Now*, the painting is always on the
left, the poem on the right, so that the eye sees first the painting,
then the reflection on/of it; but in the later book the paintings
alternate from the left side of the double page to the right side, all
through the volume, thereby suggesting that sometimes the paint-
ing 'comments'on the poem, rather than the converse. However,
logical priority remains with the painting (in that the poem, to
become intelligible, must be referred to the painting in every case).
The alternating positions of the paintings in *Ingrowing Thoughts* do
not seem to me integral to Thomas's work, except in so far as they

force us to ask why that arrangement has replaced the earlier one — I believe to call our attention to the alternating ontological priority of the two art-forms.

Though many poets have written about paintings, they rarely themselves reproduce the artworks on which they comment. They must describe in the poem whatever aspects of the painting they wish the reader to know about (or to remember). Thomas's enigmatic and epigrammatic reflections mimic, instead, the instant responses of the mind (which does not need to describe to itself what its eyes are resting on) and are pointedly designed to draw the reader into an identity with the writer as he stands before the work. There is no air of leisured reflection or connoisseurship in Thomas's poems (and most of the things a connoisseur might mention are in fact omitted). Thomas confronts his artworks rather as Rilke confronted the archaic torso of Apollo, as a topical and ethical challenge. In fact, Thomas takes a grim amusement in being so resolutely the subject-centred amateur before the artwork. The amateur always takes his thematic and ethical responses as primary, and is generally oblivious to the technical difficulties (and triumphs) of the artist. Thomas — though he knows from his own work about the trials of technique — deliberately mentions technique only to dismiss it when he looks at Degas's 'Portrait of a Young Woman':

> I imagine he intended
> other things: tonal
> values, the light and shade
> of her cheek.
>   To me innocence
> is its meaning. If the lips
> opened a little, blessings
> would come forth. Those eyes
> have looked upon evil
> and not seen it. Her young being
> waits....

The immediate 'humanising' and 'moralising' of the portrait suggests a defense against technical intention (which is nonetheless freely ascribed to Degas). Thomas implies that it is 'wrong'— or at least no part of his wish — to look at an artwork as a *tour de force* of tonal values, of chiaroscuro. He will take from it what he

Degas: Portrait of a Young Woman

needs of human reassurance, and ignore its aesthetic experimentation. On the other hand, his own stylization-technique can scarcely be missed: each line of his description of the young woman stops on a noun — "innocence", "lips", "blessings", "eyes", "being" — which hesitates on a brink before tipping over into its verb. The syntactic momentum thus maintained makes innocence only temporary; the "reluctant feet" of this Tennysonian maiden will have to advance into experience. And yet the poem finds a way to let the final tip-over verb belong not to her (as the earlier ones do) but to someone else, the eventual husband whose hands will undress her:

> Her young being
> waits to be startled
> by the sweetness in roughness
> of hands that
> with permitted boldness
> will remove her bark
> to show under how smooth a
> tree temptation can shelter.

The "permitted" deflowering (de-barking) of this Eve by her Adam, since it takes place in a postlapsarian world, will still bring "temptation" to her "innocence"; and the poet, as he slides, in gazing at the portrait, from "innocence is its meaning" to his voyeuristic identification with the "permitted" sexuality that nonetheless shelters "temptation", reveals the unsatisfactoriness of remaining humanly "innocent" if this means remaining pre-sexual.

Throughout the painting-poems Thomas shows himself to be as susceptible to women as Hardy was, and women and sexuality are among the thematic constants of these collections, sometimes with the moral overtones of the poem just quoted, sometimes not. Even while seeming to write only thematically, repudiating direct remarks on technique, Thomas usually describes a painting in such a way that we perceive its symbolic value to its painter (and to Thomas), its structural choices, and even aspects of its technical decisions. At the same time, Thomas is deploying a number of technical strategies himself, which guarantee, by a species of sympathetic magic, that the painter must be deploying comparable ones, which we can notice if we wish (just as we can refrain from noticing Thomas's own, if we wish). The first poem in *Between Here and Now* —'Monet: Lady with a Parasol' — will serve to show Thomas's cunning in pursuing several lines of verbal development at once. A field of flowers occupies the lower third of the Monet painting, the sky the top two-thirds. We see outlined in three-quarter view against the sky, her feet hidden in the flowers, a tall young woman carrying a parasol. The only area of considerable darkness in the painting is the underside of the umbrella, extended by the girl's dark hat. Her tanned face is in shadow from the parasol, carried under her upward-bent right arm. In his response to the painting, Thomas meditates on woman-hood (the biological state), young-ladyhood (a social construction) and femaleness (its mystery of otherness). The meditation arises from Thomas's ascribing of 'real-life' motivation to the young woman, wondering why she bothers to carry the umbrella at all:

> Why keep the sun
> from the head, when the grass
> is a fire about
> the feet? She wields her umbrella
>
> from fashion, a not
> too serious shield against
> summer's unreal missiles. She
> is brown already. What
>
> she carries is a pretence
> at effeminacy, a borrowing
> from the mystery shadow
> concocts. But that arm
>
> is sturdy, the carriage
> erect, the bust ample enough
> for a peasant to lay his
> head there, dreaming of harvest. (13)

Thomas's question-answer format tells us that his mind cannot rest content in the mere appreciation of light, colour, spatial form, painterly rhythm, and sexual appreciation. Interpretation raises its "why", and we may take what follows to be a commentary on the woman, on Monet, and on Thomas himself. Ostensibly, the

Monet: Lady with a parasol

action is ascribed to the woman ("She wields her unbrella from fashion"; "[it] is a pretence at effeminacy"). The curious notion that a woman would pretend to be effeminate makes us ascribe "her" motivations rather to the poet's idea of her (or of Monet), especially since the poet corrects himself, changing "effeminacy" to "mystery" — although he scarcely trusts the latter noun more, since shadow "concocts" this mystery. The defamatory word "concocts" is a comment perhaps on the painter; he has placed the woman's head in shadow in order to keep her from rustic openness, to keep something of mystery about her. In a revenge on both the woman's "fashion" and the painter's "concocting", the poet enters his triumphant adversative: BUT — for all her frills and mystery and self-shielding against summer's missiles of light, her tanned face and feet deep in fire reveal the underlying truth: that her arm is the sturdy arm of a peasant girl, her bust an ample extent of robust flesh, her ultimate will the drive towards sexual fruition. The poet thus conveys to us what he wants women to be — creatures not of the fashionable world of parasols or even the coy and mysterious world of chiaroscuro, but rather creatures of honest and solid naturalness, natives of a Hardyesque pastoral. Do we know the painting better, or Monet himself better, or the lady better, or Thomas better? All of the above, perhaps. The intense moment of Thomas's response has changed our own perception of the painting.

What makes this commentary a poem and not simply an essayistic meditation on a painting? What are its formal principles? It does not rhyme (in the usual sense of the word) though it is written — why? — in four-line 'stanzas'. The lines have no predictable uniformity of word-count or syllable-count, though the poet is fondest of lines made up of four words (10 out of 16). There is a strange symmetry among the words which open the lines: *from/from/from/for* (2,5,11,15); *is/is/is* (3,8,13) — as if Thomas's poetic allows a 'front-rhyme' of this sort to substitute for an end-rhyme. And there is such a plethora of internal echo that we can believe that Thomas is not only practising the usual English assonance, alliteration, and figures of speech, but is also imitating the *cynghanedd* of Welsh poetry. One phonetic group clusters, for instance, around long 'e': *keep, feet, she, wields, serious, shield, unreal, she,* effeminacy, mystery, dreaming. Another clusters around the two heads that organise the poem's opening and close, the lady's head, the peasant's head: h*ead*, al*ready*, st*urdy*, h*ead*. Yet another consists of *why, when, what*; another, *grass, fashion, carries, shadow, that, carriage, ample*; another, *brown, borrowing, shadow*. There are yet more (*sun, umbrella, summer, bust*; and, in terms of opening and closing consonants, again*st*, conco*cts*, *st*urdy, ere*ct*, bu*st*, harve*st*). These word-chains, which construct meaningful semantic clusters — and conventional alliteration and assonance in such groups as *fire/feet*, *shield/shadow*, *arm/harvest* — explain why Thomas's language arranges itself satisfactorily on the page even though rhyme as such is not present.

Thomas's line-breaks (elsewhere as well as here) tend to make us replicate the process of interpretation, with its constant hesitations and rephrasings:

```
Why keep the sun---------------------------------------------Where?
from the head when the grass----------------------------Is — what?
is a fire about --------------------------------Where? Zoom down.
the feet? She wields her umbrella----------------------------Why?
from fashion, a not ------------------------------------Not what?
too serious shield against ----------------------------Against what?
summer's unreal missiles. She ------------------Why not serious?
is brown already. What ---------------------------Look at umbrella.
she carries is a pretence -----------------------------------At what?
at effeminacy, a borrowing -----------------------------Whence?
from the mystery shadow--------------------------Confers? No--
concocts. But that arm-----------------------------How describe it?
is sturdy, the carriage ----------------------------How describe it?
erect, the bust ample enough--------------------Enough for what?
for a peasant to lay his--------------------------Match hers above--
head there, dreaming of harvest.
```

It would be tedious to go through this process (which applies to all) with respect to more than one poem, but before I leave the Monet poem, I must add that its shape is partly determined by the length of its sentences. Its sentence-shape by number of words per sentence is as follows:

```
---------------- (16)
--------------- (15)
---- (4)
```

--------------- (15)

-----------------------(23)

Or, if one prefers a syllable-count shape, it is as follows:

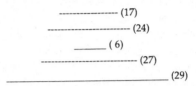

----------------- (17)

----------------------- (24)

_____ (6)

-------------------------- (27)

_____ (29)

In either case, the four-word, six-syllable central sentence, "She is brown already" is revealed to be the crucial perception. The young woman has already, so to speak, been impregnated by the summer sun, and the man to come will only reap the harvest of those first "unreal missiles" of the sun, which have awakened the imagination of sexuality in the woman's body.

Though noticing word length or syllable-length with respect to the sentences satisfactorily isolates the short third sentence, it does not serve to distinguish the four longer sentences from each other. The opening one is perceptual, the second (realistically) motivational, the final one triumphantly conclusive. The mysterious sentence is the fourth, inserting itself in the poem before the fifth sentence, which, reverting to the tonality of "She is brown already", adds, in a final confirmation of the earlier perception, that her arm is sturdy, her carriage erect, her bust ample, ready for love and bearing fruit. The mysterious fourth sentence is motivational, like the second, but not realistic, as was the representation of the umbrella as shield against the sun. The fourth sentence is an accusation. It is permissible, though venially blameworthy, to be fashionable; and it is a form of play (since there are no 'real' missiles in question) to defend oneself against unreal ones. But is it permissible to defend oneself against one's true and honest biological impulses? Not in Thomas's view. The "lady", by pretending she is not sexual, by hiding in the shadow of the umbrella, by illegitimately "borrowing" something not her own (a mystery proper to the concocting of chiaroscuro but not to young women), deliberately obscures her own robustness — she effeminises herself, pretends she is less sturdy than she is. Here we see Thomas's

own distrust of the "pretences" of art when it is being deceptive
vis-à-vis reality. There is a masculine rage here at society's insist-
ence that women veil their biology in "mystery" and "shadow",
over and above their shielding themselves in the fashionable. The
symbolic joining of the elegant "lady" to "a peasant" brings her
back from her quality as a "lady" to her quality as female repro-
ductive partner — but also to a partner in love. The peasant finds
repose on her breast, and is a dreamer as well as a rustic. The lady
will be happier fully in the sun, without her parasol, in the Law-
rentian embrace of her peasant-lover, because she is more woman
than lady, more body than accoutrements.

We are now in a position to answer our original question: why
is this continuous meditation on a painting separated into four
'stanzas'? The stanzas mark off the stages of Thomas's own lyric
states (it is a truism that every lyric is about its own author as well
as about its subject). The first stanza represents the poet's quick
intake of the subject-matter of the painting — standing lady, sun,
fiery grass, umbrella — and his querying of the necessity of the
parasol. The second stanza presents Thomas's answer to his own
question (the parasol is for fashion's sake) and his reason for the
answer (she is brown already). He is disturbed by the answer he
has been forced to by her tanned face; he dislikes fashionableness
and its "shield" against nature. By the third stanza his disturbance
has mounted; the denigratory words ("pretence", "effeminacy",
"borrowing", "concocts") betray a more serious threat to female
naturalness than the "not too serious" impact of fashion. The lyric
state reaches its greatest agitation in "concocts", but hastens to
reassure itself by its faith in nature's innate power to assert itself
against both fashion and "femininity" — "But that arm/is
sturdy". Once the poet is reassured, he can himself 'enter' the
picture and connect with the young woman, via his surrogate the
peasant reposing on her breast.

The interesting thing about the four stanzas is that each of the
latter three begins before its predecessor has finished. We have
only to rewrite the poem in a conventional way to see how much
Thomas does not want his stanzas encapsulated as self-contained
units. How different the effect of:

Why keep the sun
from the head, when the grass
is a fire about
the feet?

She wields her umbrella
from fashion, a not
too serious shield against
summer's unreal missiles.

She is brown already.

What she carries is a pretence
at effeminacy, a borrowing
from the mystery shadow
concocts.

But that arm is sturdy, the carriage
erect, the bust ample enough
for a peasant to lay his
head there, dreaming of harvest.

This is the 'same' poem, in one sense (and the way I have been
talking about each stanza as an encapsulation of a lyric state might
make it seem as though I have been talking of this 'version').
Thomas, by 'pulling' each lyric state up into the orbit of its prede-
cessor, tells us that lyric states are not separate moments of per-
ception, query, answer, reason, criticism, and reassurance, but
rather a seamless flow of responses. The modernist 'stream of
consciousness' has here found a lyric equivalent, in part imitating
the global response one must have to a non-temporal object like a
painting.

It is fair to say, I think, that we have been given more by the
poem than we might have gathered from the painting by our-
selves. The inferences Thomas has drawn from Monet's 'land-
scape with figure' would be perhaps illegitimate in an
art-historical essay; but they tell us something not only about the
Impressionists' fascination with the relations among woman, na-
ture, and culture, but also about Thomas's own conflicting views
of woman — as creature of fashion, as timid about 'heat', as a
natural body, as deceptive in 'femininity', and as a potential sexual
partner. The final trust which the poet shows in his willingness (as

peasant) to lay his head on woman's bosom and to dream of harvest suggests that he is willing to dare heterosexual contact, in spite of female fear and coyness, and his own male dislike of fashion and pretence, in the hope that it will bring blessings.

Many of the remarks I have made about the Monet-poem's stanza-form, 'rhymes', lineation, sentence-relations, and subject-matter apply, *mutatis mutandis*, to Thomas' other painting-poems. Once one has learned how to read them, they become much richer than their concise and reticent surfaces at first suggest, and they often "tease us out of thought". One might consider at length all that Thomas says about women, for example, and about non-lustful observation of them as an exigent discipline necessary to the artist; but I prefer to turn now to his general figures for the artist, which will give us some glimpses into his own aesthetic. In these painting-poems, Thomas has put to one side two powerful components of his life — his Welshness and his priesthood — and can write as artist alone (in so far as the separation of such intermingled aspects of self is possible). One of the most idyllic of his meditations on art is 'Pisarro: Landscape at Chaponval'. The painting is divided horizontally into four ascending horizontal bands: at the base grass, then houses, a hill, a sky with clouds. Framed on the left by a large tree, and on the right by a sapling, and contained entirely by the band of grass, stand a woman and a grazing cow. Here is Thomas on Pisarro's pastoral:

> It would be good to live
> in this village with time
> stationary and the clouds
> going by. The grass is a tide
>
> rising and falling. The cow
> sips it. The woman stands
> patiently by the slow udder
> as at a cistern filling. (45)

Perhaps erroneously, I am reminded by Thomas's opening of the episode of the Transfiguration, retold in all of the synoptic gospels (Matt. 17, Mark 9, Luke 9). In each version, after the vision of the transfigured Jesus talking with Moses and Elias, Peter says, "Lord [Master], It is good for us to be here." (Peter then proposes

Pissarro: Landscape at Chaponval

building three tabernacles, one each for Jesus, Moses, and Elias, not yet recognising Jesus as greater than the prophets; he is rebuked by a voice from a cloud, and the disciples are led down from the mountain by Jesus — by which it is signified that we have no permanent resting-place, even on a transfigured earth.) "It would be good to live/in this village", says the poet, but the conditional itself tells us that he knows he has no lasting dwelling in art. Borrowing one of the classic grammatical signs for the eternity of representation, the present participle, Thomas heaps up a variety of such signs: going, rising, falling, filling. Thomas 'reads' the Pisarro painting from background to foreground: the first sentence quickly covers the three rear bands (the village, the stationary hill behind it, the clouds going by above); the next three sentences (one for the grass, one for the cow, one for the woman) concentrate on the first band alone, scrutinising the import of the two creatures and their surround, the grass. The technique of the single central short sentence ("She is brown already") recurs here in "The cow sips it", itself dependent on the metaphor of the grass as a tide that (with the seasons) rises and falls. The cow takes advantage of the propitious season of rise to sip the nourishment of the earth, which is metabolised within her as her udder, like a cistern filling with water, slowly swells with milk.

We recognise the woman who stands *patiently* at a *slowly*-accruing richness as a cousin of Keats's Autumn: "[And] by a cider-press, with *patient* look /Thou watchest the last oozings hours by hours."[2] This affinity leads us to recognize the cow as an improbable yet indubitable cousin of Keats's bee of 'Melancholy'; but instead of nectar-pleasure "turning to poison while the bee-mouth *sips*"[3], the grass turns to milk as the cow *sips*, a far more benevolent transaction. Keats's pastoral is the poem of perishing earth, which includes all the things the Grecian urn suppresses — transiency, mortality, metamorphosis. Thomas's pastoral, by contrast, is Keats's 'Autumn' rewritten into the stability of the urn. The woman can be "patient" at the "slow udder" without becoming melancholy because the cistern is constantly filling; the poetry of earth is never dead. Of the three motions in the poem— the clouds going by (directed motion like Keats's "o'erbrimming"), the tide rising and falling (oscillatory motion, like Keats's gnats borne aloft and sinking), and the cistern filling (like Keats's loading and blessing and filling all fruit with ripeness) — the climactic one is the one of fullness, and there are no motions of oozing or leakage.

In this transfiguration of life accomplished by art — "It would be good to live in this village" — the figure for the artist is the patient woman who waits by the cistern of observation, meditation, and distillation as it fills. She and the cow are linked in the cycle of benevolent consumption and nutrition; the grass nourishes the cow, the cow will nourish her, she will see to the continuation of the grass for the cow. The hierarchy of benefits — grass to the cow, cow to the woman — mirrors the benevolence of the Christian providential interpretation of vegetative and animal nature: "Man is one world, and hath/Another to attend him" (Herbert)[4]. Everything in the painted scene responds to biological desire; it is a female universe of human and bovine nurturance, as c-*ow*, *wo*-man, and sl-*ow* "rhyme" in their 'overlapping' phoneme of the natural. The human, the animal, the natural, and (in the echo of the Transfiguration) the divine are here all in eternal synchrony, "with time stationary". By putting himself into the mood of the woman, by attending to his meditation as to a cistern filling, the artist transforms savage and frustrating existence into this image of yearned-for repose.

Not all of Thomas's representations of the artist are so serene. In 'Renoir: Muslim Festival at Algiers', the beast-like crowd is "rampant upon a background of/of dung": on another plane altogether, "gazing,/as at a window", is "the detached/ocean with its cerulean stare" (47). What does it know of dung? How can it see the people except as "combs and wattles"? The artist's detachment is not only interrogated here, I think, but also condemned: Renoir's distance from the crowded Muslim festival reduces human beings to anthill anonymity.

In 'Degas: Women Ironing', Thomas confronts the artist's temptation toward revulsion or boredom when he is faced with the unaesthetic spectacle of ordinary life. In the painting, two laundresses occupy most of the picture; one, holding a bottle of wine, yawns grossly; the other, hunched over her ironing, both hands leaning on the iron as she presses a shirt, is sunk in tiredness. Here is Thomas seeing them and moralising on Degas's response:

```
one hand
      on cheek the other
on the bottle
      mouth open
her neighbour
      with hands clasped
not in prayer
      her head bent
over her decreasing
      function    this is art
overcoming permanently
      the temptation to answer
a yawn with a yawn (53)
```

The women, it is clear, have been turned into statues by their nominal and past-participial verbal clothing. Insofar as the labouring second woman has any trajectory at all, her "decreasing function" bears her towards the paralysis of her yawning neighbour. We would expect a stanza-break after the description of the two women:

```
      her head bent
over her decreasing
      function

this is art
      overcoming...,
```

Among other things, we would lose by this rearrangement the 'front-rhyme' of "over her" and "overcoming"; but that alone does not account for Thomas's breaking of symmetry in beginning "this is art" on the same line as the close of his description. His overlap asserts once again (as in the Monet poem) that perception, evaluation ("her decreasing/function"), and interpretation ("this is art") happen synchronically rather than successively (as my rearrangement would imply). The present participle ("overcoming") once again evidently stands for the 'eternity' of visual art. What does the 'antiphony' of the alternately-indented lineation 'stand for'? I think it mimics the wandering of the watcher's eye, and perhaps even the trajectory of the painter's brush as the canvas is in process. We can imagine the artist, saying between his teeth as he paints the woman on the left, "One hand — yes, where — on

Degas: Women Ironing

cheek the other —where — yes, on the bottle — mouth? open —
all right, that's that one; — now for the other — her neighbour —
now where are her hands — yes, not apart, both together, clasped
— but not the way hands would be clasped in prayer, these are
one over the other, for more pressure on the iron; — now her head,
yes, bent; bent why? how? as she gets tireder and tireder —". As
we move jerkily in and out — left, pause — right, pause — we go
back and forth rather like the women ironing; and in the middle
of our soporific motion, back, forth, bent, tired, dulled with wine,
yawning — we meet the alert awakeness of the artist, shaking off
sloth, snobbery, boredom, to devote as much draughtsmanship to
laundresses as to aristocrats. Thomas redefines aesthetic 'sin' here;
temptation for the artist does not lead toward the usual vices but
to the subtler but no less destructive sin of perceptual and moral
indifference.

Elsewhere in Thomas the artist is simply a delighted eye, over-
come by the abundance of the visual world. 'Gauguin: Breton
Landscape, the Mill' ends — after an inventory of sensory riches
— with "the whey-faced cloud/agog as at a far sill" (57). This is a
benevolent version of the ocean's cerulean stare. Yet elsewhere, as
in 'Cézanne: The Bridge at Maincy', Thomas accepts the burden
of sadness endemic to the creation of art. Here, the artist returns
from "the outside world" to his vigil on the bridge, itself placed
in the painting as the middle ground between sky and water. The
traveller returns

> to his place
> at the handrail to
> watch for the face's
>
> water-lily to emerge
> from the dark depths
> as quietly as the waxen
> moon from among clouds. (49)

"With how sad steps, O Moon, thou climb'st the skies,/How
silently, and with how wan a face!"[5] The love-sick moon, the pale
face — is it the artist's own? or Wordsworth's drowned man's? —
are equally the business of the artist, poised on the isthmus of his
middle state between depths and clouds. Nothing can be forced;

he must wait for the face to "emerge", and it must happen as silently as the natural motion of moonrise. "When night is bare,/From one lonely cloud/The moon rains out her beams — and Heaven is overflowed" — that is Shelley's version of the skylark/artist's music[6]. Here, in a stiller version, Thomas's patient artist waits, not for a filling cistern, but for an emerging metamorphosis — face to flower.

In extreme cases, as in 'Guernica' — the first poem in *Ingrowing Thoughts* — the flower has to be made from the torture of atrocity:

> The painter
> has been down at the root
>   of the scream and surfaced
> again to prepare the affections
>   for the atrocity of its flowers. (9)

And Thomas does not neglect the suspicion that the artist may be other than benevolent. A macabre little poem in *Ingrowing Thoughts* called 'Two Children Menaced by a Nightingale: Max Ernst' reads in part:

> Fly, children,
>   anticipate the nightingale's
>   migration. Postpone
> the knowledge of the insects
> that are required to produce
>   its sweetness of tone.
>   Remember the babes
> in the wood who were discovered
>   with their heads buried
> in leaves that were the colour
> of the feathers of the bird
>   that had sung to them,
>   pressing sanguinely
>   its breast against time. (42)

The formal structure Thomas adopts here — his triple admonition to the children ("Fly... Postpone... Remember") — suggests, by its helpless repetitions — each time increasing in length — its own futility. The children will never anticipate the nightingale's disappearance, never recognise that they are the insects that will feed its craving for endless ingestion, never recall the minatory myth of the babes in the wood. Thomas's other formal means here is the figure of concatenation, or chains of circumstance. Once you listen to the nightingale at all, you are entrammeled in its sequence — the knowledge *of* the insects *that* are required *to* produce its tone; the babes *who* were discovered *with* their heads buried *in* leaves *that* were the colour *of* the feathers *of* the bird *that* had sung to them, *pressing* sanguinely its breast *against* time. The inescapable syntactic chain of cause and effect, ending with its origin — Time itself — enacts the eventual extinction of art and children alike.

Why has Thomas written these cycles of painting-poems? In part, as the title of the first volume suggests, to insert himself and his readers into the aura of art, which evades time and space by placing itself "between here and now". But a deeper reason may be suggested by the title of the second cycle — *Ingrowing Thoughts*. The title comes from the poem 'The Red Model: René Magritte', where it serves, in the singular, as the closing line, "an ingrowing thought". The eerie Magritte painting has an unremarkable background: the lower third is bare earth, the upper two-thirds a horizontally-planked pine wall, perhaps the side of a house. In the foreground, vertically rising through the horizontal line separating earth from wall, are a pair of laced 'boots', ankle-high, which would be unremarkable too except that they change, at the instep, from leather boots to feet of flesh. Here is the poem:

> Given the boots
> solitary against
> the boards, I construct
> the body, kneed
> and hooded, perforated
> with dark, taken
> away at dawn on
> a barrow to be provender
> of a grave.
>
>   Tall
> and shapeless, too
> (as they deemed)
> big for them, he
> left them behind,
> not for robins
> to build nests in,
> not for the dust to tell

Magritte : The Red Model

boneless time; for his out-
at-toe ghost to walk
onward for ever against
an ingrowing thought. (33)

The poem is certainly suggestive rather than explicit. It has
overtones of the graveclothes left behind after the Resurrection
(the subject of a poem by George Herbert, 'The Dawning').[7] The
vanished man seems to have been executed ("perforated" as with
bullet-holes, "hooded", as if blindfolded, trundled away on a
barrow after the "dawn" execution, carted to an ignoble burial).
Those who killed him deemed him "too big for [his boots]". The
poet speculates, having constructed "the body" upwards from
boots to knees to hooded head, on the intentions of the dead man
in leaving his feet/boots behind. After two negative speculations
(they are not to be returned to natural uses, not to be a grave-mar-
ker in the dust) he settles on a reason; the impoverished ghost of
the executed man will need them in his ongoing advance against
"an ingrowing thought". That "ingrowing thought" would ap-
pear to be any thought that militates against renewal, transforma-
tion, the resurrection. "Things thought too long can be no longer
thought," Yeats wrote, "For beauty dies of beauty, worth of
worth."[8] An "ingrowing thought" is one that, satisfied with itself,
has ceased to grow outward. No matter how beautiful the original
object of its affections, once a thought becomes "ingrowing" it can
offer no further stimulus to the moral or aesthetic nature. This
poem is Thomas's prayer to be "new, tender, quick" (Herbert),
forever reminded of the possibilities of spiritual resurrection.
Looking at paintings, thinking about them, is for Thomas a way
to turn his ingrowing thoughts outward. Married to the painter
Mildred Eldridge, he had occasion to reflect often on the dif-
ferences between his art and hers, and on the artists — nineteenth
century and modern — that are his contemporaries in aesthetic
and moral investigation.

"It is not necessarily the poems couched in conventionally relig-
ious language that convey the truest religious experience",
Thomas wrote in his 1963 Introduction to *The Penguin Book of
Religious Verse*. "Are we not coming to accept that, wherever and
whenever man broods upon himself and his destiny, he does it as

a spiritual and self-conscious being without peer in the universe which we know?" (*Prose*, 66). Thomas (like Herbert) can therefore find the elixir of spiritual intention even in work without an ostensibly religious subject matter. In fact, in 'The Making of a Poem' Thomas confesses:

> I have been guilty of propaganda, in that I have written a lot of poems pushing [my] ideas at people, which is not what a poet should do at all.... I became rather tired of the themes about nationalism and the decay of the rural structure in Wales, and one of the gifts reserved for age is that I can now think more about poetry and remember all the wonderful poems which I might have written and never will write if I had concentrated more on pure poetry and on the technique of poetry without pushing these themes and propagandas; without strutting and beating my chest and saying "I am Welsh." (*Prose*, 110-111)

This self-lacerating statement, made in 1968, represents a moment of self-reproach for "ingrowing thought". In so far as the painting-poems represent a departure from things Welsh (though not from the rural or the spiritual) they offered Thomas a way out of the dilemma of "propaganda" and a way into a realm of "pure poetry and the technique of poetry". The opulence of many of the paintings he chose to write about also offered him an alternative to the bleakness proper to poetry written "under the harsh crags of Cader Idris and Yr Wyddfa, or on the bare gaunt moorland of central Wales" (*Prose*, 31). Thomas's extraordinary catholicity of visual response let him wander far afield, in commenting on European paintings, from the themes temperamentally available to him in autobiographical verse.

When I heard Thomas read at Cambridge University in 1981, I thought of him as the poet of Wales and of Iago Prytherch, of Christianity and the *Deus absconditus*. I could not have imagined the appearance of the painting-poems — a venture that changes his place, to my mind, in literary history. We grow to know him better through these poems — to see him as possessing a wider sensibility, perhaps, than we had guessed. And perhaps — drawn to the puzzle of the correspondence of the poem with its painting — we examine his formal means more carefully in these volumes than in books governed by a more autobiographical impulse. Form calls to form; what Focillon called "the life of forms in art" takes on a second existence as Thomas leads our eye through the planes and personages of his paintings, disciplining his own structures to the arrangements of the painter. His means of conducting the eye; his strategies of arriving at a focus or point of rest; his inventions of syntactical enactments of stasis, enclosure, temporality, eternity; his interweaving of perception and interpretation; his metaphors for the artist's relation to his painting; his fine and concise rendition of the emotional import of items in the art-work; his chains of signifiers and consonant-chime — all these attract our deepest interest and respect as we study these brief poems, so much smaller than their visual partners, and yet no less arresting and enlightening.

Notes

1. Germain Bazin, *Impressionist paintings in the Louvre* (London: Thames and Hudson, 1958). Herbert Read, *Surrealism* (London: Faber and Faber, 1936). Herbert Read, ed., *Art now: an introduction to the theory of modern painting and sculpture* (London: Faber and Faber, 1948).
2. H.W. Garrod, ed., *Keats: poetical works* (London: Oxford University Press, 1966 ed.), 219.
3. *Keats*, 220.
4. F.E. Hutchinson, *The works of George Herbert* (Oxford: Clarendon Press, 1970 ed.), 92.
5. William A. Ringler Jr., ed., *The poems of Sir Philip Sidney* (Oxford: Clarendon Press, 1962), vol.1, 180.
6. 'To a Skylark', in Thomas Hutchinson, ed., *Shelley: poetical works* (London: O.U.P., 1971 ed.), 602-3.
7. *Works of George Herbert*, 112.
8. 'The Gyres', in *The collected poems of W.B. Yeats* (London: Macmillan, 1971 ed.), 337.

Rowan Williams

"Adult Geometry": Dangerous
Thoughts in R.S. Thomas

I

R.S. Thomas' two major collections from the mid-1970's (*Laboratories of the Spirit*, 1975, and *Frequencies*,1978) return several times to a particular nest of themes — adulthood, the imagery of 'emerging' from a state of tutelage and imperfect understanding (there are poems titled 'Emerging' in both collections), the significance of mathematics, the mind as 'tool', and the ambiguity of this image. The first 'Emerging' poem, which opens *Laboratories of the Spirit*, draws all these together in what is at first a quite startling way. "My life is not what it was./Yours, too, accepts the presence of/the machine?" Is there, the poem asks, a new level of spirituality that has something to do with the impersonal world of mathematical structure — and so with what, at least, underpins the world of technology? The "adult geometry/of the mind" is invoked as an acknowledgement of impersonal structure, structure in which the thinking subject has anything but a central place. The mathematics of our world tell us that we are 'thought' before we think, 'spoken' before we speak: our subjective lives are not privileged. They are at best the matter of a kind of surgical experiment on the part of a larger reality (a typically grand-Guignol Thomas metaphor here about poems, flesh and scalpel); they may, then, be construable as solutions to a formal problem, the outcome of a particular configuration of possibilities: "There are questions we are the solution/to, others whose echoes we must expand/to contain." Thus prayer is not a drama for the subject, but a suspension of the subject, the thinking ego immersing itself in the sheer process of the structured world as a means to identification with God. We and our world are internal to the mathematics of God's mind.

This is not a reconciliation with technology, however: the 'acceptance' of the machine is, I think, heavily ironic. It seems to hint at the notion that God's relation to the world is analogous to ours to machinery — whose structures are internal to our planning minds; the world is an instrumental or problem-solving mechanism. Something similar is going on in 'Rough' in the same collection (*LS*, 36): the world of death and predation is "perfect, a self-regulating machine/of blood and faeces", yet requires one thing more, the image of God himself as toolmaker or experimenter, a being whose relation to things is marked by a clinical indifference to their pain comparable to God's indifference — though the divine laughter is terminally interrupted by the "incurred stitch" of Jesus. This is, even for Thomas, a disturbingly bleak conceit, but it unquestionably represents a particular elaboration of the metaphor of God as a sort of cosmic instrumental reason. But instrumental for what? what is the divine purpose? The cosmic machine, as a self-regulating mechanism, might be its own justification, but this perfection has to be supplemented: the process looks towards the human mind. Creation culminates in God's imaging or *imagining* of himself, telling himself what he is, and incurring consequent pain himself. The creation of the divine image has issued in a "casualty" ('Dialogue', *LS*, 18), but the experiment is not over yet. Like other poems of this collection, 'Dialogue' nudges at the question of whether there may still be, in the "adult mind", a new possibility.

The casualty, of course, is instrumental reason itself as it works in the human world, the business of machine-making. The world may be imagined as a machine devised and powered by God (a "great dynamo" [*LS*, 44] writing "the instructions/the genes follow" ['At It', *Frequencies*, 15] and c.f. 'Perhaps' and 'Roger Bacon' in the same volume); yet God confronted by "the cold touch of the machine" ('God's Story', *LS*, 7, and c.f. 'The Hand', *LS*, 2) does not recognize himself. The two '70s collections do not take us very far in resolving this paradox, though they hint at what may be part of the key. The divine 'machinery' exists for the sake of the divine self-imaging; and if God cannot find himself imaged or imagined in the machine, we must conclude that human instrumental reason fails because it is not a work of authentic human self-imaging or self-imagining. God does not see his image as maker here, because technology is *ersatz* creativity. This appears more explicitly in some of the poems of the '80s (see pp. 44 and 57 in

Experimenting with an Amen, for instance); and 'Pardon' (*EA*, 29) sums up the problem (and a kind of resolution) in speaking of "homo sapiens, that cracked mirror,/mending himself again and again like a pool". But whence comes the casualty, the crack in the mirror, the "ingredient/in thought that is its own/hindrance"? 'The Gap' (*LS*, 37) shows us the rupture between 'primitive' art (presumably Lascaux and other examples of cave-painting, hands moving "in the dark") and something more bitter and ambiguous and familiar. The cave artist penetrates the interiority, the "privacy" of the animals represented, in sheer contemplation of life in them — the equivalent, perhaps, of the proper mathematical contemplation of "form and number" in 'Emerging', the salvific geometry of so many poems in the two mid-70s collections (*LS*, 1, 17, 44; *F*, 15, 24, 29, 31, 41, etc.). But now art has moved into a "forbidden" area, shaping a "mirror that life holds up/to itself" and finding in it "emptiness". "The cold acts of the machine" are the acts of frustration at the perception of this void. So is the casualty rooted in a false or destructive reflexivity? The failure of technology to be a means of human self-exploration begins, it seems, in an art that confuses self-exploration with the contemplation of interiority in oneself, the search for the inner truth of our nature — which is, in itself, nothing, no determinate content. It looks as if we image/imagine/explore ourselves only by our immersion in what's other — the life, the structure, of which the subject is neither centre nor essence.

But this takes us only so far. The fall here described is a destiny for which God has to take final responsibility. Two poems in *Laboratories of the Spirit* set this out clearly enough. 'The Hand' (*LS*, 2) has God looking at the human organ of making, seeing "As at the end/of a dark tunnel... cities/the hand would build, engines/that it would raze them with." It wrestles with him, demanding his name, so that meaning may be given to the world; but God, already crucified by this encounter (notice the careful polysemy of "feeling the nails/ in his side"), resists, shakes off the hand to go "without blessing", yet to "tell" what it makes (actions, progeny, poetry; the future?) that God is. The same imagery of Jacob's wrestling with God (Genesis 31) is, of course, developed further in 'The Combat' (*LS*, 43), with the same crucial modification of the original, that God does *not* bless as the struggle ends with the dawn.

God makes a maker, to show himself *as* maker to the world: we are brought back to Thomas' insistence on the moral cloudiness of the notion of the human as image of a God experimenting towards self-reflection. But 'The Tool' (*LS*, 11) turns the theme in a slightly different direction. The human looks Godward, seeking to overcome the absence of God in what is made:

> There was emptiness
> and a face staring, seeking
> a likeness. There was thought
> probing an absence.

God withdraws further, afraid of his nakedness being un-covered — a sharp ironic inversion of the myth of Genesis 3 — and, in that intensified absence, pain flourishes. The mind reaches out

> as though to implore
> wisdom, and a tool
> gleamed there. The alternatives
> of the tree sharpened. God
> spoke to him out of the tree's
> wholeness, but the sound
> of the tool drowned him. He came forth
> in his nakedness. 'Forgive me',
> he said, suffering the tool's
> insolence in his own body.

This is a particularly, perhaps for Thomas unusually, densely worked conceit. The wholeness of non-human life, that which is accessible to the painters of Lascaux or to the contemplation of form and number, is made inaccessible by the developed aware-ness of human pain; and that pain, or rather the consciousness, the language, of pain is somehow the fruit of a divine failure of nerve and abandonment, atoned for on the cross. God is *afraid* of the probing thought that is his image in the world: afraid (should we say?) of what he imagines and what he shows himself to be.

II

This divine anxiety is repeated but also allayed in 'The Gap', the first poem in *Frequencies*: the ascent of language threatens to deliver equality with God, but God is reassured by the persistence in language of the absence that cannot be eroded, "the equation/that will not come out". What seems to be in view here is something like the *différance*, the 'trace', of postmodern literary theory, the shadowing of language by what is never said, of the solution by the other question not asked or answered. The shadowing is both what makes language possible (because language must be committed to saying this and not that, it is always a suppression as well as expression), and also what relativises and undermines what is said (not only this could be said). And while the identification of Derrida's *différance* with the God of classical negative theology is — as Derrida himself has insisted — too facile a resolution, the Derridean model does seem to have some pertinence to Thomas' picture of the relation of God to language, and suggests a structure for holding together the complex of metaphors and myths we have so far been discussing. Language is flawed, and, in its constant effort to overcome its flawed character, it produces monstrous totalitarian projects. So for Thomas: the thinking/speaking mind, when it fails to find itself in the structures of the natural order, to participate in given form (to let itself be spoken, to borrow a familiar Derridean idiom), refuses both its own proper limits and the possibility of a truthful self-imaging — the paradoxical self-discovery or self-imagining of contemplative entry into the structure of life not its own. And in that refusal it condemns itself to the sterility and self-destructiveness of technology, whose issue is finally the weaponry of global annihilation ('Pre-Cambrian' and 'Roger Bacon' in *Frequencies*).

God, for Thomas, is what is (intermittently) shown in the mind's attempts at stillness or participation in order beyond itself, what appears only "on the innocent marches/of vocabulary", "at the frontier" ('The Combat', *LS*, 43). There is therefore no possibility of speaking directly of God with any truthfulness. Probing directly for the knowledge of God is like the "forbidden" search for one's own interiority. It will deliver only emptiness and so frustration, the frustration that engenders the turn to mastery, problem-solving, the violent fancies of technocracy. God happens when we are not looking for God. This I take to be the force of the repudiation in the *Laboratories of the Spirit* 'Emerging' of conscious or deliberate waiting on God ("Hear my prayer, Lord, hear/my prayer"), and, in the 'Emerging' poem of *Frequencies*, the similar repudiation of waiting on a "peninsula" or "promontory". In this latter poem, it is the putting together of "plain facts and natural happenings" in art, composition, that "composes" God: we should notice the risky metaphor here of "the mind's *tooling*" — given the sinister resonances of "tools" in so much of *Laboratories of the Spirit*. It would not be true to say that Thomas turns away from the conviction of God's knowability in silence alone; far from it. But somehow the deliberate preparation of the mind for divine visitation compounds the mind's ambiguity and begins to falsify. The true God cannot be prepared for.

But how does this relate to the powerful myths of God's relation to the world which Thomas so often deploys? The God "composed" in the bare fact of selfless attention, in union (mathematical or Lascaux-artistic) with the formal structures of living things, is a long way from the ambiguous and guilty maker depicted in so many of the poems in *Laboratories of the Spirit*. It is, of course, a waste of time to look for a tidy metaphysic in this or any poetry, but there is a tension that needs examination. It seems that what Thomas is struggling for is an account of the ultimate root of the guilt and danger in our speech and thought. Why is it so hard for us to return to Lascaux — indeed impossible? Because the human agent carries an over-complex programme, doomed to the lethal illusions of thinking selfhood: a secondary maker, yet called to reflect the reality of the world's primary source by being intelligent, aware of making; and, in that summons to awareness, being condemned to the tantalising knowledge of a non-negotiable horizon that frustrates and provokes, the horizon variously represented by death, time, failures of control, pain. To imagine itself, the human agent must voice these dangerous things, dangerous because they send us seeking for ways of avoidance. How can we acquit of guilt the source of this impossible vocation? Thus the myth of the guilty or even sadistic God is a way of articulating a centrally tragic quality in human awareness: the mind's dividedness is *like* the product of an already eternally divided or flawed desire. The Guilty Creator model tells us that there is no level of reality beyond flawed desire. In a rather different philosophical language, there is an irreconcilable and violent schism between Being and beings — the rupture (*Riss*) Heidegger writes of, that has been so much discussed by Derrida and his American disciples.[1] The myth of divine violence, in Thomas as in some gnostic mythologies or in Jung's *Answer to Job*, dispossesses us of any doctrine of comprehensive given harmonies. God, in other words, cannot be invoked as providing a canopy of meaning, let alone explanation. To consent to the "form and number" of the world — and thus to displace the mastering intellectual self — is to compose God in the only way possible. If the classical forms of waiting on God, so sceptically handled in the two 'Emerging' poems, still have any promise, it is of the kind splendidly evoked in 'The Answer'(*F*, 46):

> There have been times
> when, after long on my knees
> in a cold chancel, a stone has rolled
> from my mind, and I have looked
> in and seen the old questions lie
> folded and in a place
> by themselves, like the piled
> graveclothes of love's risen body.

As in other poems of this period, the vision of God is a breaking-down of the questions or need with which we come; it is what happens to us in what we could call reflective emptiness (c.f.'The Absence', *F*, 48) — not the emptiness that faces us when we try to understand our interiority, but an attention without expectation (think of *East Coker*). This is how the *Riss* ceases to tempt or torment: somehow, in the mind's immersion in the connected structures of an alien reality, in the putting together of mind and world, there is some sort of peace made — not by bridging the impossible gulf between Being and beings, for that wound is not to be healed and there is no simple path for relating things to God in a fully reconciled mutual presence, but in the refusal to project the thinking mind into the place of a God who will unite and explain things. Just as, in the theological story, atonement is made only in the vulnerability of God to the world ("suffering the tool's/

insolence"), a God dispossessed of the status of unifier and sense-maker, so for us: we refuse the temptation to reach for Being in itself (the final fantasy of power[2]), for the position above all positions, and are content to compose words, thoughts or silence appropriate to our being among beings.

> I am left with the look
>
> on the sky I need not
> try turning into an expression. (*ERS*, 103)

God 'acts' as God in the dismantling of what we take to be the life of the mind and the life of the mind's object:

> He listens in
> at the self's councils,
> planning the exercise
> that will come to nothing.
>
> He is the double agent
> of life, working for
> the continuance of it
> by its betrayal. (ERS, 113)

III

To be adult is, in this poetry, to know the danger of thought. *The Echoes Return Slow* speaks of a kind of reparation for the sins of fluent religious talk (pp.48, 55, 96, 102-3, 112, 114-5). And the temptation to such talk is intensified by our technological nimble-ness: 'Calling' (*EA*, 31) plays with the thought of telephoning God, but suggests that the very act of trying is to deny that God is already there. We hear the "purring" of the mechanism and are prompted to "experiment/with the code" that will break through this "tameness" and reach "the divine/snarl". This poem might well be read as suggesting that even the earlier poetic rhetoric of the violent or cruel God can be a seduction, trying to shatter the smooth and consensual thought of a technological and totalising era by directly invoking the divine self-alienation at the origin of things — a seduction because it is itself another kind of refusal of "the still pool" (*EA*, 43), another forced bid for presence, even violent presence. Not even by mythologising the *Riss* do we escape danger, because that fissure must be inhabited and lived through by the unselfing of attention. It is notable, certainly, that the poems of the '80s are almost without reference to the mythic constructs of the middle '70s. It is as if the focus on the guilty creator had proved to be another way of reinstating at the heart of things a troubled ego — divine in this case, but no less problematic than the human ego. The inadequacy of the troubled *ego* at the centre is, of course, already implicit in the language of impersonal communion with a mathematised God in the same collections. The metaphors of the violence of divine instrumental reason will have done their work if they succeed in weaning us from a longing directed to a place or level of being beyond ambiguity, from the search for a God to contain and order our dangerous thoughts.

Experimenting with an Amen, then, directs us far more straightforwardly to the God appearing in the connections that are produced in silence. Grace is

> '...the power which supplies
> not the maggot of flame you desired,
> that consumes the flesh, but the unseen
> current between two points, coming
> to song in the nerves, as in the telegraph
> wires, the tighter that they are drawn.' ('Revision', *EA*, 22-3)

Or, more bluntly still, in 'A Thicket in Lleyn' (*EA*, 45), encountering a flight of migrating birds, the poet is left

> to reflect on the answer
> to a question I had not asked.
> 'A repetition in time of the eternal
> I AM.' Say it. Don't be shy.

This is a poem which seems to indicate something in the poet that has to be challenged or overcome, a hesitation that must finally be laid aside: "Don't be shy." And — if I read correctly — the agenda of a good deal of the poetry of the '80s is to do with this hesitation. Dangerous thought means dangerous poetry; so a poetic rhetoric is needed that counters the danger of fluency, idolatry, mastery. This, of course, is the task of any serious religious poetry — and indeed of any serious poetry of any sort, in various ways — and it can be charted just as clearly in Herbert or Eliot. For Thomas in the '70s, the strategy is at least twofold. I think that the language of violent mythology is one part of it: as I have suggested, this serves to dispossess us of a harmonising canopy. And perhaps the other and complementary aspect of the strategy is the intensification of a practice already in evidence in the poetry of the '50s and '60s, a practice sometimes thought to be careless or arbitrary, unexpected line breaks and a consequent rather jarring enjambement. These have the effect of redistributing the sense of a statement, destabilising surface meanings, and so relativising the claim of any particular sentence (and it is interesting to note that they work *visually* more than aurally: Thomas' rhetoric is generally one of the written even more than the spoken word, and it is not in fact easy to read him aloud adequately). To take an example more or less at random from *Frequencies*:

> After Christ, what? The molecules
> are without redemption. My shadow
> sunning itself on this stone
> remembers the lava.

And later in the poem,

> ...less permanent
> than these waves. Plato, Aristotle,
> all those who furrowed the calmness
> of their foreheads are responsible
> for the bomb. I am charmed here
> by the serenity of the reflections
> in the sea's mirror.   ('Pre-Cambrian', 23)

What each sentence 'actually' (grammatically) says is shadowed by the way the lines are divided, so that the collocation of words in one line, or even the apparent sense of a line standing alone, somehow nags at the reader's awareness, setting up a counterpoint of meaning. "After Christ, what? The molecules", standing alone, is an evocation of some kind of stark reduction, which hangs over the following line's more 'orthodox' (if no less despairing) conclusion. "Redemption" and "shadow" are pushed together in this next line: the words (the poet) are shadowed by the possibility that there is no atonement. Further on, "waves" and "Plato, Aris-

91

totle" are juxtaposed, reinforcing the scepticism about intellect that is at work in the whole poem; and the more startling colloca-tion of "bomb" and "charmed" points to the seduction/enchant-ment/spurious protection (a charmed life) promised by the bomb, so that the return to "serenity" in the next line is a jolt. Nor do we learn immediately that these serene "reflections" are not thoughts but literal reflections in the sea: or *are* they thoughts of another kind, the ambiguous thoughts of the whole poem so far, sharing in the corrupt but alluring intellectuality that breeds violence?

Such an analysis could be pursued with the vast majority of Thomas' poems of the '70s and '80s, and many from earlier as well. It suggests not so much a tug of contradiction, *hostile* subversion, within the text, but a diffusion of sense beyond syntactical struc-ture, and thus an effort to pre-empt the temptations of formal closure at the level of propositional order and intelligibility. If this is how it works, then here too, as in the overall 'anti-metaphysics' of the poetry, Thomas has some affinities with literary post-mod-ernism, in his attention to the visual qualities of the written word and its consequent underdetermination by a 'present' speaker /author; as if he said, "I know that what I write as continuous sentences will set up uncontrollable chains of resonance, and, by breaking up and redistributing the building-blocks of 'my' meaning, I license the reader's meanings and warn the reader of the danger of poetic rhetoric — even the rhetoric of anti- rhetoric".

But it brings us back to 'A Thicket in Lleyn'. "Don't be shy": the skilful self-relativising of the poetry can have the paradoxical effect of making us look more, not less, closely at the authorial ego (a familiar problem of literary post-modernism). There is a reluct-ance to risk a statement claiming some of the force of 'atonement', to risk a mending of the rupture between Being and beings ("a repetition in time of the eternal/I AM").[3] To *say* 'atonement' is, for Thomas, almost inevitably to court shipwreck, to claim something for thought or language and so to deny their danger and to take a step towards the ravages of ignorant technocracy. Yet suspicion is not enough: "Escape from your mortal cage/in thought. Your migrations will never/be over. Between two truths/there is only the mind to fly with" (ibid.). Imagination, constantly renewing itself by its own fecundity, is also — it seems — mind, thought determined *not* to arrive at a point of mastery and closure, but abiding in the tension or flight "between two truths" (or "between two points", as in 'Revision'). The implication is that there might be a legitimate word or thought, an utterance beyond suspicion, if it held to a point of pure tension, articulated in a way that *showed*, rather than imposing, the co-presence of God and world — a true unity-in-otherness, not reductive reconciliation (the world speaks to me of God) nor a cataloguing, whether orderly or despairing, of the plurality and contingency of things (the world is too manifold for meaning).

IV

"Say it"; but how? It is outside anything that could be called poetic *strategy*. We are not here talking about a way of describing the world in poetry that avoids obvious seductions, but about the possibility of a poetic language (never mind the ostensible 'subject') exhibiting grace, authority, reparation, God and world held together; in other words, it is conceivable that the achieving of a certain kind of *formal* perfection (as in music, to reiterate what has become something of a cliché) does this job. But such finishedness of form cannot be planned; there are no rules for its attainment — which is why such an attainment can produce what Eliot memorably called "a moment of exhaustion, of appeasement, of absolution, and of something very near annihilation".[4] This theme is explored with typical subtlety by Geoffrey Hill in his essay on 'Poetry as "Menace" and "Atonement"':[5] the poet must understand the ambiguity of the modern poetic craft, poetry after the loss of unselfconscious innocence — the proudly and resourcefully rhetorical attack on rhetoric, the posture of self-castigation, pre-empting criticism or dismissal, even the "stylish aesthetic of despair, that desire for the ultimate integrity of silence, to which so much eloquence has been so frequently and indefatigably devoted".[6] The poet must see and be appalled by the flawed *morality* of the acts of writing. Yet to look for an inner purity that will offset such 'menace' is to compound the moral seductions of romanticism still further. There is an "ambiguous hope"[7] in the possibility of true vision and "carnal blundering" being brought together in some verbal/formal structure that softens neither and so articulates repentance and (Eliot's word again) absolution. It may not be effective for the poet's subjectivity; but the *poet's* absolution is not quite what is at issue here, so much as the formation of words for absolution in a language constantly pulled towards unseriousness, a language without moral weight and moral grief. Criticisms of Hill, incidentally, that focus on his alleged evocation of an élitist pre-modern social order, a malign and mythical nationalism, seem to me to be extraordinarily deaf to the significance, the *political* significance, of all this in a culture unable to cope with the possibilities of public articulations of provisionality and penance; Hill's rhetoric can better be read as an education in suspicion of language without a vital idiom for loss and desire and the recognition of pain, given and experienced. But that would need another essay to spell out.

Does Thomas absolve? I am not sure. 'A Thicket in Lleyn', along with several of the later pages of *Echoes* (106-7,119,120-1), *points* as clearly as could be to absolution in Hill's sense, most movingly at the very end of *Echoes*, where the dual presence of the sea and a loved and dying woman imports for the poet a forgiveness buried below furrowed and unstable surfaces (and a good deal could be said about the presence of the sea in his most recent work as a powerful metaphorical vehicle for something other than violence; 'West Coast', *EA*, 19, brings this into sharp focus). The poems have a good many epiphanic moments (like 'The Bright Field', *LS*, 60, and *Echoes*, 107), but these are commonly placed in very conscious and overt opposition to the flawed mind, the unabsolved speaker. 'The Bright Field' *alludes* to a moment unrealised *in* the poem: phrases like "I realize now", or even "Life is not hurrying//on to a receding future, nor hankering after/an imagined past" distance the poem itself from epiphany by generalisation (though the latter passage, with a stanza break between "hurrying" and "on", is a particularly good example of Thomas' enjambement strategies). I suspect that Thomas' nearest approach to Hill's "absolution" is in the numerous poems that end with reversals, metaphoric jolts, aphoristic closures: he is as remarkable a craftsman of endings as George Herbert. 'Mediations' (*LS*, 17), 'Pre-Cambrian', 'Dialectic', 'Roger Bacon' and 'After Jericho' (*F*), 'Fable', 'The Bank', 'Sarn Rhiw', 'Their Canvases Are' and 'Reply' (*EA*), all exhibit this feature with particular power, though there are countless other instances, early and late. It is as if the poetic rhetoric attains its authority and finality, its absolving quality, only literally on the edge of silence. The effect is something like the "glancing blow" of vision Augustine speaks of in Book IX of the *Confessions* (ch.10). The language is trusted and transfigured precisely in the moment of its being thrown away. I am not, of course, talking about endings that resolve, let alone console, in terms of content or idea, but about a quality of unselfconscious 'fit' in the rhetoric itself. While 'unselfconscious' here does not mean naive, innocent or un-reflective, the quality in question is whatever establishes the words used at a sort of saving distance from the unreconciled or struggling poetic ego.

That this is something associated with Thomas' endings is, in the light of all that has so far been said, unsurprising. Language has authority when it projects us directly into silence; thought is absolved of its dangerous taints when confronted with the verbal jolt of these conclusions. The poet achieves saving distance by the sheer abrupt abandonment of words, and that abrupt cessation, by leaving words on the frontier, "unattended", catches some-thing of the fusion of vision and "blundering" that Hill speaks of. But a certain uneasiness remains. Thomas' 'absolutions', if they do indeed belong primarily on this frontier, seem not to be quite what Hill has in view, insofar as they *depend* on the silence they introduce for their integrity and authority. The question remains of whether there could be a language of absolution that worked *within* the rhetoric and movement of the verse, not in what might be unsympathetically read as a violent/heroic gesture of abnega-tion.

It is arguable that some of Hill's own work (especially the *Tenebrae* collection of 1978) effects such 'internal' absolution: a kind of formal closure that, in the very act of drawing attention to its finishedness, proclaims a distance from both poet and world.[8] In the distance achieved by formal perfection, the 'matter' of the poet's subjectivity and the world's unreconciledness is shown transmuted; not cancelled or resolved but (precariously) con-tained, in a way that, because it is not founded in an appeal to reconciled subjectivity, escapes the trap of claiming privilege for the poetic stance, the poetic self. Now what this effectively says is that poetic absolution, the loss or silencing of the ambiguous thinking (manipulating) subject, happens not beyond but within the frontier of what is said. The still unpublished work of Maggie Ross and Vincent Gillespie of Oxford on 'apophatic images' in the writing of Julian of Norwich has great pertinence to this issue of how a collocation of words carries a kind of silence and suspension of analytic subjecthood or consciousness within them. And, if my reading is correct, Thomas' idiom finds its maximal authority *on* the frontier, by its evocation of the silence beyond (let me refer again to 'The Combat' in *Laboratories of the Spirit*).

Has he then found a way of realising *in* the poetry the adult geometry to which he looks? This seems to me still largely unresolved; there is no new Lascaux in the poet's words, no consistent distance from the unreconciled ego, except in a few places in the most recent volumes. The creation mythologies of *Laboratories of the Spirit* and *Frequencies*, even when no longer explicitly deployed, still haunt the poetry, suggesting that there is no true undoing of the primordial catastrophe because it is rooted in the fractures of God's own will or desire. Beyond the vigilant self-suspicion and self-subversion of the poetry is something very like a theological option, an acceptance of the "foundational violence" identified in much modern and postmodern thought by John Milbank in his recent *Theology and Social Theory*[9] — the assumption that conflict and rivalry (and thus *ressentiment*) are somehow native to our being, because, explicitly or implicitly, the relation of beings to their final origin is itself a kind of flaw, 'wound', violence. The particularity of the world of the multiple and contingent is at odds with the peace or self-coherence of 'Being'. Between origin and actuality, then, must be some kind of tragic fissuring, capable of being healed only in the fissures, the gaps, of language. Silence negates the negativity of a contingent world. Somewhere in this area also lie complex issues to do with the masculinity of the troubled ego in view here, with its fascination with and horror at separation, which is yet seen as the price of rationality and identity. Thomas is himself clearly not unaware of this dimension to his world.

This should certainly not be taken to mean that Thomas would be a 'better' poet if he had a better doctrine of creation. As already indicated, his creation myths are essentially ways of denying access to a vantage point beyond the violence of creation as it is — access for the thinking/speaking mind, that is: there is always silence and there may be (as in 'A Thicket in Lleyn') something else as well, out of the covenant of thought, thought 'escaping' as it receives answers to what it has not sought. But it is just this hint of grace (absolution) that makes the entire project so tantalising. Poetry cannot quite be shut out from the possibility of speaking with authority, even in contexts other than the direct springboard for silence that is Thomas' technique of endings. And if it cannot, the mythic language of *Laboratories of the Spirit* and *Frequencies* leaves more to be said, and the making by God of a making creature need not be irredeemably under the rubric of flawed desire and rupture. Another theology — never wholly silent for Thomas — intimates itself: an act of creation bestowing both otherness and participation.

Well, yes; but Thomas remains unapologetically alert to the ease with which the *articulating* of such a theology by the dangerous mind risks false and easy closures. Some things must not be said, they must occur, they must surprise and overtake. And meanwhile a truthful poetry must resist the saying, go on insisting upon the guilt of the craft and the non-reconciliation of the speaker. A few years ago, reviewing D.Z. Phillips' study of Thomas' religious themes,[10] I borrowed another term from Geoffrey Hill, "exemplary failure", to characterise Thomas' work. This is easily misunderstood: but for Hill, who applies it to the moral philosophy of T.H. Green, it is a way of categorising writing that is "creative in [its] distress"[11] because it persists faithfully in holding to a problem that the reader is morally and aesthetically obliged to labour at as well. This is, I believe, the sense in which Thomas' poetry is "exemplary failure" — exemplary and deliberate, even *homiletic* failure, a poetry dramatising resistance to verbal seduction. Yet the result is also to dramatise the ego's reluctance to abandon its own drama: this is a poetry that enacts sin and repentance simultaneously, compounding the sin with each step of penitent self-exposure, repenting each word as it is uttered. It remains deeply suspicious of verbal enactments of atonement, and it is no use saying that these 'should' be there, since their planning is their corrupting. If this makes for an almost obsessively discomfiting rhetoric, a compulsive 'distress' in the writing, Thomas is content, poetically and theologically, with this: "'Let it be so', I say. 'Amen and amen'" ('The Priest', in *Not That He Brought*

Flowers, 29). But, the latest poems insinuate, shouldn't distress itself be sometimes "distressed", overtaken ('Self-Portrait', *LS*, 27)? "Say it. Don't be shy"? No "shouldn't" about it; but sometimes it is given.

> '...Am I not
> also in the debt of love?' (*ERS*, 119)

Notes

1. See especially Mark C. Taylor, *Tears* (New York: State University of New York Press, 1990).
2. Because the final liberation from the constraints of language and its supposed indirectness, its 'mediated' quality; thus the liberation from what is distinctively human.
3. The phrase echoes Coleridge's celebrated dictum in *Biographia Literaria* about art as the repetition in time of the eternal.
4. *On Poetry and Poets* (London: Faber and Faber, 1957), 98.
5. *The Lords of Limit* (London: Deutsch, 1984), 1-18.
6. Ibid., 9.
7. Ibid., 16.
8. A point elaborated in John Bayley's essay, 'Somewhere is such a kingdom: Geoffrey Hill and contemporary poetry', in Peter Robinson, ed., *Geoffrey Hill: essays on his poetry* (Milton Keynes: Open University Press, 1985).
9. John Milbank, *Theology and Social Theory* (Oxford: Oxford University Press, 1990).
10. *R.S. Thomas; poet of the hidden God* (London: Macmillan, 1987). Reviewed in *Philosophical Investigations* 11.4 (1988).
11. *The Lords of Limit*, 120.

William V. Davis

"The Verbal Hunger": The Use and Significance of 'Gaps' in the Poetry of R.S. Thomas

Today, gaps speak as loudly as presences, and no story is complete without its absences. — John W. Kronik*

R.S. Thomas, like all great poets, is a poet of obsessions — even, we might say, an obsessed poet. His obsessions (beyond the typical ties and tricks of language which are part of every poet's fingerprint on the page), his quintessential themes (as he turns them through his mind and through his spare and characteristic lines, as he holds them fixed but freely lets them flow), have, we find in reading and rereading him, become, subtly and quite quickly, our own obsessions too, and, indeed, finally, our own possessions as much as they are his.

One reason Thomas is so obsessed, and so possesses us, is that he has had, throughout his life and art, a singly dominant theme. This theme has come to climax twice: first, and most importantly for his literary work, in *Frequencies* (1978); second, in terms more turned towards Thomas's own personal life, in *The Echoes Return Slow* (1988). These books are two of his strongest individual collections and, taken together, they contain some of his finest work as well as much of what we need to know about him personally, as man and priest and poet.

The Echoes Return Slow is much the more personal of the two books and, in some ways, the most unique of all of Thomas's books, both structurally and thematically. The prose-poem paragraphs which face the lined poems page by page provide a running commentary on Thomas's life (they need to be read along with his autobiographical *Neb*)[1] while the accompanying poems in lines are some of the most beautiful of all of Thomas's lyrics (is there any poem in his canon, for instance, more lovely than "There are nights that are so still"?). This book may also be the most demanding of Thomas's books from a critical point of view since it requires a more thorough understanding of his biography than is yet available, or may ever be available.[2] The nuances in *Echoes*, as indeed the title itself suggests, will no doubt take years.

Frequencies, on the other hand, both because it may be Thomas's single strongest volume of poetry *per se* and because it contains the clearest evidence of his constant, continuing obsessions, the dominating theme that runs throughout his work, is the book I want to concentrate on here.

However, before turning to the poems in *Frequencies* themselves, let us look briefly at Thomas's title and its significance for the theme of this book as well as for his work *in toto*.

No reader of Thomas can have failed to notice how often, how *frequently*, he uses a single word as title for one of his poems, or for one of his books. Four of his most important books (*Tares, Pietà, H'm*, and *Frequencies*) have one word titles, and hundreds of his individual poems have single word titles (some of these title words being used more than once!).[3]

Frequencies, like many of Thomas's titles, and certainly all of the single-word ones, is an immediately suggestive word, title, and title word. Thomas plays on all of the meanings of this word. A simple mention of only the most obvious meanings of the word will serve to suggest the wide-ranging use Thomas makes of it. As an adjective 'frequent' suggests the regular, the persistent, the habitual, the constant; an almost addictive association of things recurring in close association or at short intervals. As a verb it means to busy oneself with or familiarise oneself with, to visit or revisit often, to practise or habitually repeat, to celebrate or honour, to resort *to* (in terms of a person) or *unto* (in terms of a place). And if we add to these basic meanings of the word the newer nouns built upon the basic meanings, we can find in Thomas's poems metaphors of his major themes. Perhaps the definitions alone will do to start the waves of metaphoric meaning so frequently at work in these poems to begin to mixin our minds:

frequency distribution — "an arrangement of statistical data that exhibits the frequency of the occurrence of the values of a variable"
frequency modulation — "modulation of the frequency of the carrier wave in accordance with speech or signal"

frequency response — "the ability of a device to handle the frequencies applied to it."[4]

All of these 'meanings' reverberate through *Frequencies* — and through much of Thomas's work. To take only two examples from elsewhere, we might mention 'Revision' and 'One Way'. In 'Revision' Thomas speaks of "the unseen/current between two points, coming/to song in the nerves" (*EA*, 23). In 'One Way' Thomas speaks of "a frontier/I crossed whose passport/was human speech."

> God,
> I whispered, refining
> my technique, signalling
> to him on the frequencies
> I commanded. (*BHN*, 95)

And now, to use an archaic meaning of 'frequent', let us look at *Frequencies*, R.S. Thomas's "song in the nerves", somewhat more systematically.

Thomas begins his book abruptly. The first poem, 'The Gap', suggests, at once, both the basic theme and the dominant metaphor which will run throughout the book, a theme and metaphor which run throughout much of Thomas's work.

'The Gap' begins, "God woke, but the nightmare/did not recede" (*F*, 7). These lines, here at the outset of both poem and book, indicate a shift from one state to another, from sleep to waking, from an unconscious to a conscious knowledge of reality. Even so, the transition, the 'gap', between the physical states of sleep and waking and the epistemological states of conscious and unconscious knowledge has not fully been bridged ("the nightmare/did not recede"). Perhaps more importantly, God's dream was a "nightmare", a nightmare which even in an awakened world will not now go away. Thus, this 'gap' in consciousness has been bridged by God's 'awakening', in both a literal and an epistemological sense, but, even so, the nightmare He dreamed remains, beyond this bridging of the 'gap'.

And God's 'nightmare', of course, is man.

Man has been trying to reach God with words, his "tower of speech". This phrase suggests a kind of human babel growing upwards like a tower towards God, seeping into His subconscious in sleep. And where are words more reminiscent of "towers" than in the columns of words which are poems? Are man's prayers poems? God, "reclining" on the air as if in a fresco by Michelangelo, watches in horror as this tower of words rises towards him: "One word more and/it would be on a level/with him; vocabulary/would have triumphed." It is something to be feared, this metaphysical, indeed almost physical, proximity which man has with God through words:

> He
> measured the thin gap
> with his mind. No, no, no,
> wider than that! (*F*,7)

God measures the gap between himself and man not with His hand as we might expect — since this is clearly an anthropomorphic God who sleeps and dreams — but with "his mind." God hopes that the gap is wider than He imagines, that man and his words are farther away than they seem to be. "But the nearness/persisted." God begins to wonder how He can continue to "live" with the "feat" of this "fact" of man's increasing closeness, how He can "take his rest/on the edge of a chasm a/word could bridge." God, clearly, is uncomfortable; His "repose" has been disturbed. The second 'stanza' of this broken column of words effectively suggests, visually and rhythmically, both the presence and the absence of this 'gap' between God and man and his words, which, ironically, as they are written 'down' in the columns of lines continue to accumulate and thus push themselves 'upward' towards Him. There is no space, no 'gap', between lines 16 and 17 and yet the white space and the indentation of the line before the beginning of the new sentence suggest the presence of a traditional stanzaic 'gap' — one which is further indicated, if not 'closed', rather neatly by the use of the word "bridge" at the end of line 16, the last word before the spatial 'gap', and by the fact that the rhythm of the gapped line 16-17:

> word would bridge.
> > He leaned

is both maintained and simultaneously 'broken' by the white space. We are told (apparently from God's point of view) that He "leaned/over" (the line itself leaning over) to look into man's dictionary in an attempt to discover whether He had as yet been defined. He finds that "There was the blank still/by his name" (another 'gap') and He thinks or believes that this blank is equivalent to "the territory/between them", a void which suggests the "verbal hunger" for a relationship through words, for meaning and identification. This relationship, He seems to see, is one that man wants to have with Him — but which, apparently, He does not share in nor wish to have with man in return. Indeed, God cannot 'rest' easy on the edge of such a "chasm/a [single?] word could bridge."

The final eleven and one half lines of the poem are one long complicated sentence in which "the darkness" (like the night in which one dreams? or in which things are shrouded in mystery?) "that is a god's blood" swells and is "let" (spilled, like ink?) to "make the sign in the space/on the page" (i.e. fill up a 'gap'?). This ambiguous bloodily signed message, written "in all languages/and none", is a "grammarian's/torment", "the mystery/at the cell's core" (like the mystery of life itself) and "the equation/that will not come out" (an equation as in the association or identification of two related but not identical entities which share in a single process). It is, finally,

> the narrowness that we stare
> over into the eternal
> silence that is the repose of God.

Here at the end of the poem (the line breaks working extremely effectively) the point of view seems to shift to man's perspective, as he, in his own version of a waking nightmare, also sees "the narrowness" of the 'gap' between himself and God, and as — perhaps even more terrifyingly — he realises the "eternal/silence" which greets his tower of words — these words, this poem become prayer, in which he has attempted to reach and meet God on his own terms. Here at the end of the poem, God, in "repose" (with all the meanings of this word at work at once), seems to mock man's feeble attempts at communication. If it was man's word which awakened God from his nightmare sleep at the beginning of the poem, and even perhaps briefly terrified Him, here at the end of the poem the enigma of God's "eternal/silence" provides little hope beyond the torment of continuing the attempt to reach Him through more mere words.

But there is another suggestion which might be drawn from the enigmatic final line. The "repose of God" implies sleep (literally, 'repose' is 'eternal or heavenly rest'). If, at the end of the poem, God has gone back to sleep, this would account for (even if it would not finally, fully justify) the shifting of the point of view, and it would also account for God's lack of response to man's appeal, to his "tower of speech". It would also, perhaps, imply that God's actions *are* His words, that, indeed, His only 'action' is through words. If this is so, then God, like the poet, can only work through words. Therefore, the "verbal hunger" would apply to God and man equally, reciprocally, and the only way which man could meet God would be through his words — just as the only way God can meet or has ever met man is through His words. This poem, then, or at least the end of it, might be thought of as an exegesis of the famous opening sentence of the Gospel According to John: Ἐν ἀρχῇ ἦν ὁ λόγος, καὶ ὁ λόγος ἦν πρὸς τὸν θεόν, καὶ θεὸς ἦν ὁ λόγος. ('In the beginning was the Word, and the Word was with God, and the Word was God.'). If God is Word, and can only be met through words, then, even if He never responds, the 'gap' between God and man can only be closed (if it ever can) through words sent back and forth through prayers and poems. These words, then, would be as the Greek text literally states it, a beginning.

Beyond this, and perhaps even more importantly for Thomas, every poem itself fills in a gap in knowledge and experience. In so filling-in a space where otherwise there would have been nothing, the poem becomes the means of voiding the void, of closing the gaps — both between God and man, and between man and man. Thus, the poem communicates by its structure and its statement, both by its being and by its saying. And, furthermore, it fills up this gap, this void, even if, before it was, the void had gone unnoticed. Thus, the poem becomes the necessity for a need as quickly as the need is noticed.

But, of course, one poem is not enough.[5] If the gap between God and man is ever to be bridged, it must be bridged, as we now know, by man alone — since the period of God's overt action, the sending of His son, is long since past. And so Thomas, again and again, presents us with one man, alone, lonely for and before God, calling across this gapped void between them, hoping beyond hope, that, somehow, God will hear his "verbal hunger" and be moved, if not to respond, at least to listen. This is Thomas's constant theme, expressed and explored throughout his work, but insisted on in *Frequencies*.[6] Indeed, as Thomas has recently said, "Granted that a certain kind of religion has made capital out of a God of the gaps, this does not mean that each closure of a gap is a kind of erosion of the reality of God".[7]

The second poem in *Frequencies*, 'Present' (*F*, 9) has an ironic, punning title. In a 'present' which is both immediate moment and a kind of gift, Thomas, "at the switchboard/of the exchanges of the people/of all time", continues to "engage with philosophy", and to present in poems the 'gap' he has already discovered in 'The Gap', the presence of God's absence and aloofness.

'The Porch' (*F*, 10) begins with questions and answers:

> Do you want to know his name?
> It is forgotten. Would you learn
> what he was like? He was like
> anyone else, a man with ears
> and eyes....

Here we see deity, "like/anyone else", on a "church porch on an evening/in winter", "driven/to his knees...for no reason/he knew." And without the power to pray, He "kept his place/...on that lean/threshold" and "looked out on a universe/that was without knowledge/of him". This "lean threshold" which Thomas tells us is "neither outside nor in" is of course another 'gap'. Even God, leaning, almost lounging, in the church's threshold, with "His back turned on the interior", seems simultaneously both stopped in this gap and stopping it up, even as He uses this temporary (stopgap?) measure to attempt His failed communication with man.[8]

In short, the gap between man and God remains.

This litany continues throughout *Frequencies*. The fishermen in

'Fishing' (*F*, 11) "wait for the// withheld answer to an insoluble /problem". In 'Henry James' (*F*, 20) there is "the eloquence of the unsaid/thing, the nobility of the deed/not performed", "the significance/of an absence". 'Adjustments' (*F*, 29-30) begins, "Never known as anything/but an absence, I dare not name him/as God", and goes on to talk of the "invisible structures/he builds" and that "There are no/laws...other than the limits of/our understanding." In 'The Possession' (*F*, 33) the "religious man","looking around him with his worried eyes/at the emptiness", says, "There must be something", but he has nothing to hold on to but "infinite darkness between points of light." The protagonist of 'The Film of God' (*F*, 47), with his camera "as sensitive to/an absence as to a presence", wonders "What language/does the god speak?" Finally, in a poem intriguingly entitled 'Balance' (*F*, 49), the poet wonders, "Is there time/on this brief platform for anything/other than mind's failure to explain itself?"

But if the theme of this obsession with the gaps between man and God runs throughout *Frequencies* in many subtle ways, it is treated in substantial detail in a number of the most important poems in the second half of the book. And if it is the case that Thomas, in this book, has forced furthest this the most crucial theme and thesis of his life and work, then an analysis of these poems is inevitable for any full understanding of that life and work.

'Dialectic' (*F*, 24), placed at almost the exact centre of the book, has at *its* centre the thematic issue of the complete book: "the mind swinging/to and fro over an abysm/of blankness." The title is immediately interesting. A 'dialectic', a discussion via dialogue between two parties, an intellectual exchange or investigation of (historically, in Plato's dialogues for instance) the eternal ideas, immediately suggests 'gaps' and the crisscrossing of 'frequencies' back and forth over them. Man speaks, God listens (like "a spider spinning its web") but He does not answer except "as of old with the infinity/I feed on". Thus, even though He "delights in" man's attention and acknowledges that once "there were words" between them, even if "they could not understand" them, now men must be left alone (in the lurch, with their gapped knowledge?), on their own with the "truth/...born with them" but that truth to be shed, "sloughed off like some afterbirth of the spirit." The poem

'At It' (*F*, 15) seems to suggest Thomas's response to this God: "I would have/things to say to this God/at the judgement". But, he acknowledges, "there will be/no judgement" other than "that abstruse/geometry that proceeds eternally/in the silence beyond right and wrong".

The 'dialectic' then is to take place in a shadowy world, as the next poem, 'Shadows' (*F*, 25), makes clear.

> I close my eyes.
> The darkness implies your presence,
> the shadow of your steep mind
> on my world. I shiver in it.
> It is not your light that
> can blind us; it is the splendour
> of your darkness.

God's metaphysically mystical presence is only 'visible' as a mental shadow, and, at that, it is only an implied presence. This meeting, mind to mind, across the gaps of thought, creates a shiver of recognition so dark in splendour that it can "blind us". This is a kind of mental groping in the dark, as Thomas has earlier suggested in the poem 'Groping' (*F*, 12). Here, hearing the interior calling, the speaker begins the inward journey towards this silent source of sound deep in the dark of the mind where, even there, strangely enough, "sometimes a strange light/shines" (*F*, 12). Such 'journeys' are quintessential to the mystical tradition Thomas has always been attracted to and often follows in many of his most important and interesting poems, a tradition which perhaps first comes to climax at the end of his lovely poem 'Sea-Watching', where we read:

> There were days,
> so beautiful the emptiness
> it might have filled,
>   its absence
> was as it presence; not to be told
> any more, so single my mind
> after its long fast,
>   my watching from praying. (*LS*, 64)

We need only mention Dionysius the Areopagite, Thomas's most obvious source in the substantial body of the mystical literature, to see the immediate significance of this tradition for his work, here and elsewhere, but especially so here in the middle of his career. Dionysius describes the essence of the 'negative way' in terms of the metaphor of light and darkness:

> Unto this Darkness which is beyond light we pray that we may come, and may attain unto vision through the loss of sight and knowledge, and that in ceasing thus to see or to know we may learn to know that which is beyond all perception and understanding....
> ...we strip off all qualities in order that we may attain a naked knowledge of that Unknowing which in all existent things is en-wrapped by all objects of knowledge, and that we may begin to see that super-essential Darkness which is hidden by all the light that is in existent things.[9]

This is "the language/of silence" heard in 'Shadows', the "sentence/without an end" that runs throughout the rest of *Frequencies*.

The next poem, 'Abercuawg' (*F*, 26-27), asserts that "An absence is how we become surer/of what we want." And Thomas describes himself as "a seeker/in time for that which is/beyond time.../...always/about to be; whose duration is/of the mind..." (*F*, 27).[10]

It is, perhaps, a time, now, for 'adjustments'. Thomas's poem 'Adjustments' (*F*, 29-30) begins, "Never known as anything/but an absence, I dare not name him/as God." Yet, "Patiently with invisible structures/he builds" (*F*, 29) across the gaps of our comprehension, and "we are forced/into the game, reluctant/contestants" (*F*, 31).

The next important poem in *Frequences* is 'Waiting' (*F*, 32). Indeed, it is almost as if Thomas has been waiting for 'Waiting'. Waiting for this meeting here in the middle of these 'frequencies'. The poem begins with the obvious question, which has been echoing through all the ages: "Face to face?" And the speaker immediately answers his own question, "Ah, no/God; such language falsifies/the relation." Thomas knows that God's name, "vouching for you, ubiquitous/in its explanations" and throughout time, needs only to be "pronounced" to echo back to man. Therefore, he finds himself,

> ...leaning far out
> over an immense depth, letting
> your name go and waiting,
> somewhere between faith and doubt,
> for the echoes of its arrival.   (F, 32)[11]

"Somewhere between faith and doubt". Such vacillation is an accurate description of Thomas's position. It has, indeed, become a 'possession', as the next poem 'The Possession' (F, 33) asserts. Here, the speaker, "nothing/religious", dreams his "fused prayers" and wakes to find the "reflection" (obviously both a physical and a metaphysical phenomenon, and obviously as well another play on the word 'frequencies') of "infinite darkness between points of light." The main difference is that his 'waiting' has here become noticeably more impatient.

'The Empty Church' (F, 35), appropriately enough, follows 'Gone?' (F, 34). 'The Empty Church' plays on another kind of echo, a shadow. The poem begins:

> They laid this stone trap
> for him, enticing him with candles,
> as though he would come like some huge moth
> out of the darkness to beat there.   (F, 35)

"*They*". Who? In the second stanza the speaker invokes himself, "Why, then, do I kneel still...?" His answer is only another question, "Is it in hope" that a "spark" of prayer, struck from his "stone/ heart" will "ignite" and throw a "shadow" on the empty walls of the stone church? Thomas here hints, beyond his question, at another poem, 'Passage', where we find the metaphor extended and further complicated as poem and church become conflated: "I stand now, tolling my name/in the poem's empty church" (LP, 192). And, finally, one cannot help but think that Thomas's poems are, if not "stone traps" like churches, perhaps verbal traps for such a "fast/ God", as he calls Him in the last poem in *Frequencies*, "always before us and/leaving as we arrive" ('Pilgrimages' F, 51-52).

But all is always tentative, as 'Perhaps' (F, 39) with its questions and answers (that seem to be further questions) indicates. 'Perhaps' comes to its final question ("To believe.../...in the ubiquity of a vast concern?") through a series of questions and 'answers' or 'answers' which elicit further questions:

> His intellect was the clear mirror
> he looked in and saw the machinery of God
> assemble itself? It was one that reflected
> the emptiness that was where God
> should have been. The mind's tools had
> no power convincingly to put him
> together. Looking in that mirror was a journey
> through hill mist where, the higher
> one ascends, the poorer the visibility
> becomes. It could have led to despair
> but for the consciousness of a presence
> behind him, whose breath clouding
> that looking-glass proved that it was alive.
> To learn to distrust the distrust
> of feeling — this then was the next step
> for the seeker? (*F*, 39)

But poems, for Thomas, seem always to end in questions — demanding more poems. Finally, something seems to be 'Emerging' (*F*, 41):

> Well, I said, better to wait
> for him on some peninsula
> of the spirit. Surely for one
> with patience he will happen by
> once in a while. It was the heart
> spoke. The mind, sceptical as always
> of the anthropomorphisms
> of the fancy, knew he must be put together
> like a poem or a composition
> in music, that what he conforms to
> is art.

"He must be put together/like a poem...". Only through "the mind's tooling", through words put down in poems, can man hope to discover God. God, as elusive as a rare bird or a white tiger, only "breathes within the confines/of our definition of him" (*F*, 45). God, that is, only lives within our words about Him (in poems) or directed towards Him (in prayers). And then, as if the whole "tedious argument" of the book has led us "to an overwhelming question",[12] here, late on, we come to a poem called

'The Answer'.

'The Answer' (*F*, 46) begins with a twilit setting. It is here where "even the best/of minds must make its way". "And slowly the questions/occur..../They/yield, but only to re-form/as new problems". Sometimes, finally, "after long on my knees/in a cold chancel", Thomas tells us, "a stone has rolled/from my mind, and I have looked/...and seen the old questions lie/folded and in a place/by themselves, like the piled/graveclothes of love's risen body" (*F*, 46). This is a most intriguing 'answer'. First of all, we notice that the questions "lie". Does this mean that they are bad or inappropriate questions? That they are false, inaccurate, intended to deceive? Whatever, they are there still, "folded and in place" like the "graveclothes" on Easter morning. The questions are there and they remain. But the answer is absent. And thus although the title of the poem asserts 'the answer', the poem itself ends with the absence of any definitive answer — indeed it ends in yet another question. Right questions, in Thomas, are always more important than wrong answers. And, as he seems to be suggesting here, *the* answer is only a sequence of correct questions.

'The Answer', with its lack of answer, leads, appropriately enough, to 'The Absence' (*F*, 48), where "this great absence/that is like a presence... compels/me to address it", even though, Thomas knows, there is no "hope/of a reply." Indeed, Thomas finds himself caught in a kind of metaphysical gap: "It is a room I enter//from which someone has just/gone, the vestibule for the arrival/of one who has not yet come." Acknowledging that "he is no more here/than before", that nothing, seemingly, will call Him forth — and that nothing ever has, not "genes and molecules" nor "the incense of the Hebrews//at their altars" — Thomas comes again to another question: "What resource have I/other than the emptiness without him of my whole/being, a vacuum he may not abhor?" Unable to avoid the seeking, but only to come, again and again, to a void — both a physical and an epistemologically draining gap as large as an abyss — what can one do save to acknowledge the "emptiness" and hope against hope that such a "vacuum" may not be "abhorred"? Is this definition by negation? Does the presence of absence suggest or demand bounds to absence bordered by presence? The poem seems to circle on itself, going back to its beginnings, to assert that "this great absence", the essential essence of our first and final knowledge, is finally, "*like* a presence" (my italics).

Such a state, teetering on the edge of gaps as large as these, such deep abysses, demands the kind of intricate balance that perhaps only poems and philosophy can have. The next poem, inevitably it seems entitled 'Balance' (*F*, 49), invokes Kierkegaard, theological gap-leaper *par excellance* and one of Thomas's frequent sources of reference.[13]

'Epiphany' (*F*, 50), the penultimate poem of *Frequencies*, plays on the meanings of ἐπιφάνεια, "manifestation", in several senses. The poem begins with a question ("Three kings?") which alludes to the Church festival of January 6th commemorating the coming of the Magi as a manifestation of Christ to the Gentiles. The tradition, in England, of the King bringing the symbolic offerings of gold, frankincense and myrrh to the Chapel Royal on the feast day is also apparently alluded to in the first several lines of the poem. But, rather quickly, rather typically, Thomas leaps (here fully in keeping with the kind of sudden manifestation appropriate to epiphanies) back and forth across the 'gaps' of ancient tradition and historical precedent to present practice, then back again, across time and the span of the life of a man, collapsing Christ's life from birth to death to birth and bringing it up to date, even if ironically, at the centre of the poem. "The child/has become a man."

At the end of the poem the Christ, both child and man, out of place in time and place ("Far//off from his cross in the wrong /season") comes to sit "at table/with us with on his head/the fool's cap of our paper money." This final image is rather elaborate. Christ, out of place in every way in our day, has become a kind of fool, jester or dunce (even the traditional three flaps of the fool's cap mocking the Trinity) who wears a cap of counterfeit (paper) money, not real gold as of old. And, finally, this 'epiphany' is a watermark (another meaning of "foolscap") indelibly present, even if invisible, on the stamped writing paper typically used in Britain (formerly called "foolscap") — the paper Thomas no doubt used to write this poem on.

Christ is the indelible, invisible 'gap' manifest only in His present absence.

The Use and Significance of 'Gaps'

The final poem of *Frequencies* is, appropriately enough, entitled 'Pilgrimages' (*F*, 51-52). Of course, the title is significant. Like the others before him, and after his 'epiphany', journeying towards sacred places "the way/the saints went", Thomas finds himself arrived at a "stone altar and the candles/gone out". Kneeling, lifting his eyes, he wonders, "Am I too late?", and "Were they too late also, those/first pilgrims?" How can one catch "such a fast /God, always before us and/leaving as we arrive" — this God of the gaps whose presence constantly eludes us, who is known to us only as longing and absence?

The place of pilgrimage in this poem is an "island", a place surrounded by the sea. Literally, the island of the poem is Bardsey Island (*Ynys Enlli*), a tiny island off the tip of the Llŷn peninsula across the strait from Aberdaron, where Thomas served his final years as a priest, from 1967 to 1978. (Today, in retirement, he lives nearby, at Sarn-y-Plas Rhiw, on the bay of Porth Neigwl, the Mouth of Hell.) Bardsey Island, also known as the 'Isle of 20,000 Saints', was the site of the earliest Christian settlement in Wales. Founded by St. Cadfan in the 6th century, it became a famous place of pilgrimage in the Middle Ages. In one of the prose poem meditations in *The Echoes Return Slow* Thomas refers again to this place, both defining it and his purpose for being there:

> A bough of land between sea and sky with the clouds for apple-blos-
> som, white by day, pink towards evening. This is where he had
> crawled out, far as he could go, repeating the pilgrimages of the
> saints. (*ERS*, 68)[14]

But, for Thomas, "repeating the pilgrimages of the saints", this "place" is truly a "peninsula/of the spirit" (*F*, 41), a metaphysical, more than a physical, place: "There is no time on this island", "the events/are dateless" (*F*, 51). It is, therefore, a place, surrounded by 'see', where an 'I', through vision, 'lands'. It is where R.S. Thomas has come to.

His book and his quest end with a question:

> Was the pilgrimage
> I made to come to my own
> self, to learn that in times
> like these and for one like me
> God will never be plain and

out there, but dark rather and
inexplicable, as though he were in here?

(F, 52)

The answer is obvious, but it is beyond words.

Notes

* John W. Kronik, 'Editor's Column', *PMLA*, 107:1 (1992), 9.
1. *Neb* was written in the third person, in Welsh, and it has not been translated into English. However, rather surprisingly (and somewhat curiously) a sizeable portion of it, in the first person, appeared in Adele Sarkissian, ed., *Contemporary Authors: Autobiographical Series*, Vol. 4 (Detroit: Gale Research Inc., 1986), 301-313. (For alerting me to this English version of the essay I am indebted to Tony Brown of the University College of North Wales, Bangor.)
2. See footnote 1 above as well as Thomas's comments in a recent interview: "I was asked to write *Neb*. It would never have occurred to me to write an unsolicited autobiography, because I am of no importance as a person and have never been at or near the centre of so-called important events.... If there be such an unwise person in the future as to undertake to write a biography of me, he is welcome to enter the morass of trivia which may or may not be open to him. I don't consider it of any importance. Hence the title I gave the short account which I wrote myself. I was approached some while ago for permission to write such by a professional biographer. He did not consider his lack of Welsh an impediment, but how else could he have found out my size in shoes?" (Ned Thomas and John Barnie, 'Probings: An interview with R.S. Thomas', *Planet* 80 (1990), 36.)
3. Thomas's habit of using a single word as title more than once, along with his practice of failing to reprint some of his strongest poems in the several selections he has made of his work (and, one suspects, of keeping some strong poems out, even, of the various individual volumes as they have appeared), make for complex bibliographic and critical complications. More than for most contemporary poets a complete edition of Thomas's poems and a definitive bibliography are needed.
4. *Webster's Nineth New Collegiate Dictionary* (Springfield, Massachusetts: Merriam-Webster, Inc., 1985), 492.
5. At least two of Thomas's earlier poems need to be remembered in terms of the larger context of 'The Gap' here at the beginning of *Frequencies*. First, and most immediately, there is that other, earlier poem, also entitled 'The Gap', in *Laboratories of the Spirit*. This poem begins with a description of an Edenic world: "The one thing they were not troubled/by was

perfection...." In this paradise, "Their hand" (as if Adam and Eve are truly one, singular) "moved in the dark/like a priest's, giving its blessing". And then, "their work/finished", they "withdrew.../leaving the interrogation of it/to ourselves". This, of course, "was before/the fall." And "Somewhere between them and us/the mind climbed up into the tree/of knowledge, and saw..." (my italics) (LS, 37).

And, in an even earlier poem, 'The Gap in the Hedge', we find Thomas's peasant paradigm, Iago Prytherch, "framed in the gap/Between two hazels with his sharp eyes,/Bright as thorns, watching the sunrise" (SYT, 53). This vivid image of Prytherch has remained in the speaker's mind: "he's still there/At early morning, when the light is right". There is a double frame here. First, the title of the poem, 'The Gap in the Hedge', (note that 'hedge' contains the word 'edge') provides the initial frame or vantage point for the vision of Prytherch, who is first seen through a gap of hedge. Then, a second frame, Prytherch is described as being "framed in the gap/Between two hazels". The symbolic suggestion, and even the double remove (which deepens the distance as it accentuates the image), clearly implies a parallel between Prytherch and Christ, each of whom is here 'framed', in memory and imagination, between two trees. But beyond *that* framing and behind this poem Thomas surely has in mind, and wants us to remember, that greater 'gap' between God and man, filled and framed by Christ on his cross. (In spite of the Welsh tradition of *cynghanedd*, it is, of course, no accident that the poem is written in rhymed couplets, approximately like the Welsh *cywyddau*.)

Furthermore, if this obsession with 'gaps' has been obvious since the beginning of Thomas's career, it is equally evident in his most recent work. For instance, in 'Bleak Liturgies', one of Thomas's most recent poetic sequences, we find the line, "The gaps in belief...." (MHT, 61). Clearly, this word 'gaps', and the various literal and metaphoric meanings it suggests, continue to obsess Thomas.

6. The Welsh words *adwy* and *bwlch* can both be translated as 'gap' or 'pass'. In addition, the feminine *adwy* can be translated 'breach' and the masculine *bwlch* as 'notch'. The connotative differences between a 'gap' and a 'pass', a 'breach' and a 'notch' are, no doubt, important to Thomas as well as to his readers — even in English. This is, of course, only a small instance of the much greater problem Thomas has faced throughout his life as an 'Anglo-Welsh' poet. Thomas has often commented on the complexities of his life and poetry in terms of this issue, but in this specific instance it is perhaps most important to remember his comments in his essay 'Words and the Poet' and in a recent interview: "One of the problems of an Anglo-Welsh poet...is that of having to try to transpose the raw material of his imagination and experience into the alien medium of English speech which has no exact equivalents for *mynydd* [mountain]

115

and *bwlch, cwm* [valley] and *hafod* [upland farm]; poetry being, as all will allow, in the last resort untranslatable. I mention that as personally applicable" ('Words and the Poet,' *Prose*, 80-81).

7. Ned Thomas and John Barnie, 'Probings', 45.

8. 'The Porch', set "in a church porch", may well be indebted to George Herbert's 'The Church Porch'. Thomas has long been interested in Herbert and there are many connections between them. In the 'Introduction' to his selection of Herbert's poetry, Thomas, in defining Herbert's dominant theme, defines his own dominant theme: "What he [Herbert] had was an argument, not with others, nor with himself primarily, but with God...." See R.S. Thomas, *A Choice of George Herbert's Verse* (London: Faber and Faber, 1967), 12.

9. Dionysius the Areopagite, *The Divine Names and the Mystical Theology*, trans. by C.E. Rolt (London: SPCK [Translations of Christian Literature], 1940), 194, 196.

10. Thomas's poem 'Abercuawg' has its obvious parallel in his essay with the same title, originally delivered at the Eisteddfod in 1976. The original essay, in Welsh, can be found in Sabine Volk, *Grenzpfähle der Wirklichkeit: Approaches to the Poetry of R.S. Thomas* (Frankfurt am Main: Verlag Peter Lang, 1985), 259-273. Volk (her work revised by Thomas himself) has translated portions of this essay. A translation of the complete essay is included in *Prose*, 163-174. For additional details concerning the translation of 'Abercuawg' see Volk, 68, note 3.

In terms of our present purposes here it is interesting to note that 'Abercuawg' is itself a kind of 'gap'. In searching for it "[w]e are searching...within time, for something which is above time, and yet, which is ever on the verge of being... ...we can never become conscious of absence as such, only that what we are seeking is not present". (See *Prose*, 171-172.) As Volk indicates, 'Abercuawg' is a "key symbol" for Thomas "since it is almost an empty form..." (69). In talking about Abercuawg, she refers to the "gap between the word and the fact" (70) and quotes Thomas, "For such a place I am willing to sacrifice perhaps even as much as my life" (71). The Anstey version translates this passage, "For such a place I am ready to make sacrifices, maybe even to die" (166). Finally, as Thomas himself says, "Welsh is perhaps superior to English in this matter. 'Nothing is nothing' is an ambiguous proposition, to say the least. But 'Dim ydyw dim' is quite clear and final. What the English suggests is: 'Nothing is without existence'. And in the light of this it would be possible to assert that Abercuawg exists. But a Welshman can say 'Nid yw Abercuawg yn bod'" (See *Prose*, 167-168).

11. In one of the prose poems in *The Echoes Return Slow* Thomas asks, "is the meaning, then, in the waiting?" (*ERS*, 42). Later, in the same book, he seems to answer himself: "You have to imagine /a waiting that is not

impatient/because it is timeless" (*ERS*, 81). Rather obviously, Thomas might well agree with his fellow cleric Paul Tillich, in whose sermon 'Waiting' we find the following sentences: "Waiting means *not* having and having at the same time." "The fact that we wait for something shows that in some way we already possess it." "If we wait in hope and patience, the power of that for which we wait is already effective within us." "We are stronger when we wait than when we possess." "Let us not forget, however, that waiting is a tremendous tension. Waiting is not despair. It is the acceptance of our not having, in the power of that which we already have." (See Paul Tillich, *The Shaking of the Foundations* [New York: Charles Scribner's Sons, 1948], 149-152.) Cf. Thomas's poem 'Emerging' (*F*, 41) discussed below.

12. Thomas knows Eliot's poetry and criticism equally well, and the echoes and direct references to Eliot (and, indeed, to Yeats, Wordsworth, etc.) in his work are numerous, and have been increasingly frequent.

13. Thomas has often had Kierkegaard in mind and has directly referred or specifically alluded to him on several occasions both in his poems and in his prose works. The two most significant specific references in the poetry, before 'Balance,' are 'Kierkegaard' (*P*, 18) and 'A Grave Unvisited' (*NBF*, 9). In the former poem Kierkegaard, "wounded", "crawled/To the monastery of his chaste thought/To offer up his crumpled amen", (i.e. like Thomas, already "experimenting with" his "amen"). 'A Grave Unvisited' is even more explicit and makes clear several parallels between Thomas and Kierkegaard. Thomas notes at the outset of the poem that he has "Deliberately not" visited Kierkegaard's grave in Copenhagen, although he has been in Denmark. Even though the Danes have done "What they could do to anchor him/With the heaviness of a nation's/Respectability" (like Wales has Thomas?), Thomas asks, "would he have been/There to receive this toiling body's/Pilgrimage....?" What is important for Thomas is to "go /Up and down with him in his books,/Hand and hand like a child /With its father, pausing to stare/As he did once at the mind's country." And, although its occasion and Thomas's thesis are clearly removed from the context of these particular poems, in 'The Creative Writer's Suicide', a lecture he delivered in 1977, Thomas refers specifically to Kierkegaard's *The Present Age*, the thesis of which he wants, he says, to use "as a springboard" for his address. In *The Present Age* Kierkegaard speaks of "the infinite freedom of religion" and "the religious courage which springs from...individual religious isolation" and argues that "in the reality of religion and before God" each man must learn "to be content with himself", "to dominate himself, content as priest to be his own audience, and as author his own reader". (See Søren Kierkegaard, *The Present Age*, translated by Alexander Dru [New York: Harper & Row, 1962], 53, 54, 57.) Clearly Thomas has taken much of

Kierkegaard to heart. Kierkegaard, Thomas notes, "defined a poet as one who suffers. It is in his anguish that he opens his mouth" (*Prose*, 178).
14. C.f. 'Retirement' (*EA*, 38, lls. 1-4) where Thomas, in the first person, uses almost identical imagery.

Marie-Thérèse Castay

The Self and the Other: the Autobiographical Element in the Poetry of R.S. Thomas

There is very little doubt that R.S. Thomas's poetry, in the early collections at least, bears an obvious relation to his life as a priest in the Welsh countryside. The themes developed in these volumes are by now familiar, be they the celebration of the Welsh land through which he walks frequently on his way to the distant farms of his first parishes, or the presentation of the form of life practised there, the emblem of which is to be found in the much antho-logised 'A Peasant'. In these poems, the tone hovers between admiration for the farmers' patience and strength (as at the end of 'A Peasant') and bitterness, a bitterness which can no doubt be explained by their materialism, but also and above all by the disillusionment of the young poet who came to the countryside with his head full of romantic ideas. A particularly telling example of this love-hate relationship is to be found in 'A Priest to His People' (*SYT*, 29-30). But the closeness of his poetry to his life experience is also revealed by the use of places familiar to him, as for example Manafon church described in 'Country Church' (*SYT*, 27). 'Ninetieth Birthday (*T*, 23), for its part, presents a walk up a hill above Eglwys-fach which R.S. Thomas himself must have taken often, pausing "for breath and the far sea's signals" as in the poem, on his way to the isolated farm. One could also mention the 'No through road' sign heading the final poem in *Song at the Year's Turning* (115) devoted to the dilemma of the poet who wishes to "cease now/ [His] long absorption with the plough" and turn to other themes. The same road sign is to be found at the bottom of the track leading to the farm of 'Ninetieth Birthday'. In all these examples, the borrowings from his life experience are handled as objectively as possible and the emotion is always under control, the aim of these poems being to express and convey the essence of a given world and way of life, the life of the Welsh hill farmers in the fifties, and not to display the emotions of the poet.

The same emotional restraint characterises the few poems which have members of his family as their subjects. The first of these chronologically is 'Song for Gwydion' (*SYT*, 48) in which the personal touch is to be found in the title, in the name of his own son. The poem no doubt relates an episode of family life, for it is more than likely that R.S. Thomas must have often fished for trout for his son, if only in the river Rhiw flowing just beneath the rectory at Manafon. But the treatment of the theme is both objective in the description of the trout and highly symbolical in the comparison of the boy to "A young god, ignorant of the blood's stain", which refers to a constant preoccupation of the poet's, namely the cruelty and insensitivity of nature. With 'Ap Huw's Testament' (*PS*, 29) is introduced the whole family, his parents, his wife and his son, but without bringing us nearer lyrical emotion. Significant features like his mother's possessiveness and his father's past life as a sailor are alluded to, but they are framed and enclosed within evocations of his wife and son which are sketchy, and almost allegorical in the case of the wife described as "her of the immaculate brow". In this way a structural pattern is created in which the abstraction of the wife's and son's descriptions which open and close the poem serves as a screen to cover up and restrain the emotion. And even though the devices used may be different, the same wish to hold the affective level in check is evident in all the personal poems of this early period, be they like 'Anniversary' (*T*, 18) — a celebration of his nineteenth wedding anniversary in which the repetition of "nineteen years" and of "opening", together with the progression "friend", "stranger", "the one son", tends to introduce a formal dimension linking the poem to the Welsh tradition of praise poetry — or like 'Sorry' and 'Welsh' (*BT*, 12 & 15), in which the poet uses his own relationship to his parents as the starting point of a much wider debate. In 'Careers', opening *Not That He Brought Flowers*, we may feel that the author is now able to overcome his self-consciousness and use personal events as a poetical theme. He uses elements of his life which are more identifiable than has so far been the case, and 'Careers' is first of all an assessment of his own existence. But it is also a more general reflection on what goes into the building of a man's life and personality. The writer no doubt gives the age he was when he wrote the poem, and "the broken elbow" of the first stanza belongs to his own infancy, as we learn from his autobiography *Neb* (7), but the handling of the theme aims at universality, and the personal implication is both present and highly controlled.

There are in fact two notable exceptions to this set pattern. The first of these is the poem 'The Way of It' which gave its title to a collection (30), and in which Elsi, his wife, is so movingly recognisable, in her talent as a painter, her love of flowers and her skill at growing them, and also her birdlike aspect, diminutive and volatile. The second is the evocation of his father, allusively in some poems like 'The Survivors' (*BT*, 15) or 'The Boy's Tale' (*BT*, 36), more transparently in 'Sailors' Hospital' (*NBF*, 24-5) which expresses his feelings at his father's death, and lastly explicitly and at some length in 'Salt' (*LP*, 159-63), which is a sort of poetical biography. This long poem, broken up into stanzas of unequal lengths and shapes and suggestive of the technique of the fugue at times, with its variations, echoes and oppositions, follows his father's life from the Cardiganshire churchyard adjoining the Teifi where he used to fish in his youth to the Holyhead graveyard where he now lies buried. The use of these two burial grounds to frame the narrative is highly significant of the part played by oppositions in this text. We first note the contrast between his father's youth as a sailor of the deep seas, and the shallows of his married life; and a second contrast is found between the "bones/splintered" in the accident back in his youthful sailing days and the "bone's anchor" of the dead body at the end, which in its turn is reversed into the opposition between the possible "fall /of the soul /from favour" in the accident and the hope expressed in the last two lines that the "child spirit" will "haul on and be up and away". There is another kind of opposition, in the tone, which goes from an almost childish admiration in the opening line, "The centuries were without/his like", to a more matter-of-fact, more truthful attitude in the evocation of his father "fishing/in a hurrying river,/the Teifi". The same dualism of tone is to be found in the next sentence, with the opposition between "ideas" and "thoughts", lending the father elevation, and the "toy boats" to which these ideas are compared; and likewise in the final stanza, the refusal of the son to accept that his father's voyages "are done", a refusal which frames the whole stanza, is made to counterpoint the sordid evocation of the paraphernalia of burial in "this mean shoal of plastic /and trash". The poem would merit a much more thorough study (of the modulation of the various modes in particular), but in the perspective of this essay this structure of opposites appears to be highly significant of the tension between objectivity and subjectivity, aesthetic distancing and emotional involvement, and the choice of a complex, music-like structure can be seen as a means to deflect emotion and make it usable aesthetically.

As has been pointed out earlier, the dramatisation of the life story of a member of R.S. Thomas's family is exceptional. More often than not, the autobiographical element is reduced to passing allusions whose biographical origin is not always evident. Thus the search for mushrooms in 'Song' (*SYT*, 62) is a veiled echo of a youthful pastime, as he tells us in the autobiographical radio talk *Y Llwybrau Gynt* (12) that he gave in 1972. Again, the metaphysical poem 'The Porch' (*F*, 10) is, as he reveals in his autobiography *Neb* (87), based on an impulse he had had as far back as his Manafon days to kneel on the very threshold of his church; and we could also refer the allusion to "deaf men" in 'Adjustments' (*F*, 29) to his father's deafness and his prayers for him to be cured (*Neb*, 92). The description given in *Y Llwybrau Gynt* (23) of an ashtree at the bottom of the rectory lane in Manafon, which kept its leaves unusually late one autumn and shed them all one morning, "like a golden fountain"[1] after a night of frost, reappears in two images. One can be found at the end of the poem 'The Bush' (*LP*, 194), and the other comes at the end of 'The Prayer' (*LS*, 10): "Let leaves /from the deciduous Cross/fall on us, washing /us clean, turning our autumn/to gold by the affluence of their fountain". And therefore, the overall impression one forms of R.S. Thomas from these early poems is that of a secretive or self-conscious poet who either shrinks from using his private life as a matter for poetry or else handles it in such a distanced manner that the personal implication is either barely visible or made to serve as a mere pretext or illustration for a much wider theme.

This makes the publication of *Y Llwybrau Gynt* in 1972, of *Neb* in 1985 and of *The Echoes Return Slow* in 1988, three productions of a primarily autobiographical nature (the first two in Welsh prose,

the last one in English, half in prose and half in verse), all the more
surprising and unexpected. *Y Llwybrau Gynt* was conceived as part
of a series of half-hour radio programmes of reminiscences (what
a thrill it was one evening to recognize the even cadences of R.S.
Thomas's voice made more lively by the use of the Welsh lan-
guage, on Radio Cymru!), and therefore the scope and range of
the episodes was necessarily limited. Three major aspects of the
author's life come out in this text. The first and possibly most
appealing concerns his exhilaration as a little boy, running about
the cliffs and fields and lanes around Holyhead; the second fo-
cuses on his encounter with the farming world in Manafon and
the clash between his expectations at his arrival in a rural parish,
and the down-to-earth reality of money-minded peasants await-
ing him there; and the third shows the determination and efforts
of the young poet-priest to learn Welsh. This is certainly not a full-
length autobiography, but it gives us in a nutshell what R.S.
Thomas himself deems essential in his life (or at least what he
deemed essential in 1972), and, in any case, the vividness of the
evocations and of the descriptions of nature makes it a delightful
piece.

Neb is a fuller-bodied autobiography, since it spans his whole
life, from his birth in Cardiff, the wanderings of mother and child
from port to port to welcome the father home on his returns from
long distance voyages, the settling of the family in Holyhead, his
youth there, his studies in Bangor and Llandaff, his first years as
a curate, his married life (and it could be noted that while his son's
name Gwydion is given, his wife's, Elsi, is not), the various stages
of his career as a clergyman (with a particular emphasis on the
differences in the atmospheres of the three parishes he spent most
time in, Manafon, Eglwys-fach and Aberdaron), his travels to
Scandinavia and Spain, and on to his retirement at Sarn-y-Plas.
Throughout these pages, his wish clearly is to present himself as
an ordinary person, a child and student whose performances were
average, a rugby fan who shouted himself hoarse when Wales beat
the All Blacks (28), a naive young man not very well prepared to
face life. A man of strong likes and dislikes, he stresses his diffi-
culties in integrating himself not so much into the farming world
of his first parish, as into the conventional circles and sherry
parties of the second (81). But he also pays tribute to his friends,

the Keating sisters (54), who were to provide him with his retire-
ment cottage, Bill Condry (56) who was instrumental in his mov-
ing from Manafon to Eglwys-fach, Hubert and Patricia Mappin in
Eglwys-fach (77) — and it is highly revealing of his extreme
kindness that he went so far as to jeopardise his move to Aberda-
ron, where he very much wanted to go, in order not to abandon
Hubert Mappin who was extremely ill — and Jack and Siani
Roberts in Aberdaron. But *Neb* is not a mere life story. There is first
the use of the third person to speak of himself, which some may
have considered as typical of his sense of humour, or as a mere
gimmick given that *Y Llwybrau Gynt* was written in the first person
and one really cannot speak of greater self-distancing in the port-
rait he gives of himself in the second work than in the first. As a
matter of fact, the reason behind this choice is more metaphysical
than aesthetic. For if the bulk of *Neb* is indeed taken up by his
memories and is thus similar to any other autobiography, wider
perspectives are implied right from the start. The text opens with
an ironical comment on man's propensity for reproducing himself
and covering the earth with his brood. This is R.S. Thomas's brief
concession to the label of misanthropy that some like to give him.
But a bare few lines further down, the more serious and authentic
tone comes to the fore, as each new birth is not only proof of man's
fecundity, but also means "an addition to the sufferings of the
world". The general theme of the first paragraph, together with
the third person as subject of the narrative and the anonymity of
'Neb' ('No-one'), is therefore meant to place him within the fold
of suffering human kind. And thus is introduced, from the very
start, one of the major concerns of R.S. Thomas's work, one of the
guiding threads in fact from the early descriptions of farming life
to the later explorations of the significance of the universe. In this
opening page, the theme of suffering is quite naturally seen in
relation to birth, the labour pains of the mother, the cries of the
baby, and the diseases awaiting him in those days when infant
mortality was much higher than it is now. Later, in his curate days,
this is also the first problem which confronts him (30) through the
sick and the aged of the parish he is sent to. It is a practical issue,
as he strives to comfort those in pain, but it is also the incentive to
reading and meditation as "he came to understand that this is one
of the major problems which has troubled man since he started

The Self and the Other

using his brain".

Alongside suffering, other preoccupations appear, such as why it is that memory retains some events and forgets others (9). And when an answer to this is offered (77), through the example of artistic creation feeding on forgotten, unconscious things, it is clear that his standpoint is not really a psychological one. Likewise with the problem of identity and personality on which he ponders on several occasions (13, 22, 81-2): what he has in mind relates more to man's social status and to related aspects of his life, such as the influence of professional and social success or failure on his attitude to others, than to a more psychological approach which, for example, would look for a narcissistic wound incurred in infancy and seeking compensation in adulthood. But it is only with his arrival in Aberdaron in 1967 that the metaphysical quest becomes obvious and paramount. Confronted with sixty-million-year-old pre-Cambrian rocks on which his shadow falls as he walks past, he is indeed challenged by the discrepancy between the formidable age of those formations and the fleetingness of man who, in this light, is little more than nothing, nobody, "neb" (87). We thus come to understand the full significance of the title which has nothing to do with false pretence at humility, but is a lucid statement of man's importance and place in the universe.

Some of these pages too (87 and 88 in particular) throw invaluable light on the poems, although the tone and standpoint are slightly different. A fair number of the poems written at Aberdaron can indeed be read as expressions of violence, doubt and rejection. The God portrayed in them (as in 'Rough' [LS, 36]) sometimes appears as a cynical monster who relishes the sufferings he is inflicting on his creatures, a deity far removed from the fatherly figure of the New Testament. Such excesses are to be related to the poetic process: each poem is an individual unit made to interact with its companions and the aim is not so much to form the coherent image that the prose is striving after, as to attempt to reproduce the changeable moods of life and meditation. Extreme language and situations are therefore part and parcel of this interplay between poems within the framework of the collection. In *Neb*, on the other hand, the thought is coherent and deeply rooted in the Christian message, to the extent that some paragraphs would not have been out of place in his sermons. Thus, after looking back on the evolution of his poetry from the portrayal of the life of hill farmers to the religious verse of his later years, he states:

> At the end of the day, there is nothing more important than the relationship between man and God, and nothing harder to establish than such a relationship. Who has ever seen God? Who has heard Him speak? We have to go through the whole of our life almost in the presence of an invisible and dumb God. But this has never prevented anyone from trying to make contact with Him. This is what prayer is all about. (124)

The message is perfectly orthodox, and the tone akin to pulpit oratory with its repetition of words ("perthynas"/relationship) and patterns (negations first, questions next). As for the moral lesson, it is given on the next page: "In the face of all that, the only wise attitude for man is humility". And it appears again, in the very last words of the book: "Is there anything better for man to do than to repeat, day after day: Miserere me Deomine [sic]".

In spite of this ethical emphasis at the end, *Neb* is in no way a sermon. It is very much a life story, but a life story informed by a progressive discovery, that of man's insignificance, hence the title and the overriding use of the adjective "pitw" ("tiny" or "negligible"); and this also explains why, as has been noted earlier, psychology has so little room here, for the explorations of the subconscious workings of the psyche tend to magnify man out of all proportion, while, on the contrary, R.S. Thomas's aim is precisely to show how unimportant and puny he is.

But while the poet-priest was thus reminiscing about his past life, he was also producing volumes of poetry, and if we consider the dates of publication of the prose autobiographies (*Y Llwybrau Gynt* 1972, *Neb* 1985) on the one hand and the books of poetry on the other (*H'm* 1972, *Laboratories of the Spirit* 1975, *Frequencies* 1978, *Between Here and Now* 1981, *Later Poems* 1983 and *Experimenting with an Amen* 1986), we realize that he was simultaneously engaged on two different tasks. To put it (a little too) sketchily, on the one hand, on the prose front, there was an inward pull towards himself through these reminiscences and assessments of his life and ideas, even though, as this essay has tried to show, this inward bent has to be qualified by the growing sense he has of his own unimportance. And, on the other hand, on the poetical front, he had given himself whole-heartedly to an outward-bound metaphysical quest for God. Much critical attention has already been paid to the poems of this period, with in particular D.Z. Phillips's very perceptive study *R.S. Thomas: Poet of the Hidden God*, and for the purpose of this essay it may be enough to state a few major points and conclusions.

As D.Z. Phillips has forcefully pointed out, the confrontation with suffering and particularly with arbitrary suffering, displayed not only among men but also in nature, seems to have been the determining factor in R.S. Thomas's metaphysical quest. For how can such suffering be reconciled with the conventional image of a benevolent, loving God? The next stage in the meditation is marked by 'Abercuawg', both the literary lecture Thomas gave at the National Eisteddfod in Cardigan in 1976, and the poem bearing the same title and largely the same message, first published in the *T.L.S.* (30.5.75) before its inclusion in the 1978 collection, *Frequencies* (26). Both the poem and the lecture focus on the way in which the ideal is always elusive and its materialisation always a betrayal of it, which posits the necessity for the ideal to remain always absent, always beyond man's reach: or to put it in more theological terms, God is defined by His absence, for if He was present and accessible, eavesdropping behind the door, He would not be a transcendent, infinite Being, but a finite man-like one. The third ingredient, so to speak, in this quest is the world of science and technology which, especially in the twentieth century, has enabled man to reach almost godlike power and dimension, and which is related to the tree of knowledge of Good and Evil in the Garden of Eden and the snake's promise "You shall be as gods" (Genesis, III, 5).

From these premisses, conclusions gradually emerge; some obvious and explicit, others less so. Thus the problem of suffering will elicit two opposite responses, a straightforward, unambiguous attitude of acceptance and resignation, as in the very poignant poem 'Petition' (*H'm*, 2), or, on the contrary, an absence of definite answer. Instead of pointing, as he does in 'Petition', to a desirable form of behaviour, he builds up an evocation of God as a cynical being who finds his joy in the sufferings of his victims, and leaves it to the reader to formulate his own response: a straining of resignation and acceptance beyond what is humanly bearable, a violent rejection of, and rebellion against, a Deity who could treat His creatures so wantonly, or a realisation that, because of the Cross, suffering is a common point between man and God, possibly the only real common point. An example of this implicit, ambiguous manner could be the poem 'Rough' (LS, 36). The quest for God is articulated between poems of illumination like 'The Bright Field' or 'Llananno' (LS, 60 and 62), conveying the miraculous, God-given grace of those scarce, fleeting moments, and much more numerous poems expressing the absence, the silence of God, as in 'That' (NBF, 44), 'Via Negativa' (H'm, 16) or 'The Film of God' (F, 47). The mood alternates between near despair as in 'Senior' (BHN, 97) and serenity in the knowledge that, given God's and man's respective natures, it cannot be otherwise, as in 'Abercuawg' (F, 26-7). The only possible attitude, as D.Z. Phillips has particularly well underlined, is one of self-withdrawal, of dying to the self:

> Knowledge is only possible through a sacrifice, a dying to the self, so that God can come in at the right place.... But there is much in us that rebels against such knowledge and so the task of sacrificing ourselves to God is a never-ending one.[2]

This approach finds its clearest expressions in 'The Absence' (F, 48):

> It is this great absence
> that is like a presence, that compels
> me to address it without hope
> of a reply ...
>   My equations fail
> as my words do. What resource have I
> other than the emptiness without him of my whole
> being, a vacuum he may not abhor?

and in 'The Presence' (BHN, 107):

> There is nothing I can do
> but fill myself with my own
>   silence, hoping it will approach
>   like a wild creature to drink
> there, or perhaps like Narcissus

128

to linger a moment over its transparent face.

With *Experimenting with an Amen*, a more abstractly contempla-
tive attitude emerges, in which the perspective that God may
come to fill the vacuum recedes still further. It is merely suggested
at the end of 'Bequest' (43), with the allusion to John V, 3-4, in "sit
down by the still pool/in the mind, waiting for the unknown/visi-
tant's quickening of its surface". *Counterpoint* goes as far as advo-
cating a Buddhist-like form of mute stillness devoid of wish or
intention: "Wiser/the Buddha who, though he looked/long, had
no name for the packed/bud never to become a flower" (13). The
major stress is now on the meaninglessness of movement, as at the
end of 'Strands' (*EA*, 32) or the beginning of 'Approaches' (*EA*, 55),
("Moving nearer I found/he was further off, presence/being re-
placed by shadow"), and on the valuation of motionlessness (as
in 'This One' [*EA*, 58]). The language has reached an unpre-
cedented level of abstraction and instead of the sunlight illumi-
nating the bright field, we now find "the brightness over/an
interior horizon, which is science/transfiguring itself in love's
mirror" (*EA*, 14). And yet, paradoxically, alongside these poems
expressing the highest possible form of self-withdrawal, *Experi-
menting with an Amen* is noteworthy for its autobiographical evo-
cations, such as the graphic autobiography of 'A Life' (52), the
celebration of the house he now lives in ('Sarn Rhiw', 26), and the
assessment of his present life in 'Retirement' (38). In other words,
we witness a pattern somewhat symmetrical to the one we had
noted at the level of the prose autobiography. While focusing on
the self had indeed led to a growing feeling of its unimportance,
it now appears that the striving after a withdrawal of the self in
the end calls up signs of its re-emergence. And therefore the
tension, the dialectic at the heart of R.S. Thomas's work, seems to
lie not so much between contrasted images of God as within an
antithetic pull towards the self on the one hand, towards God on
the other, and to aim at a synthesis that we shall attempt to find
in *The Echoes Return Slow*.

This collection, published in 1988, is quite remarkable for its
presentation. It is made up of a sequence of short prose extracts
alternating with poems on the facing pages, and these two modes
of expression combine to unfold R.S. Thomas's autobiography in

chronological order. Such a manner of suggesting a dialogue between facing pages is no novelty for Thomas. Both *Between Here and Now* and *Ingrowing Thoughts* used much the same technique, but in a more obvious way, since the dialogues there were between reproductions of paintings and poems expressing the responses that the paintings evoked for the poet. In an interview that R.S. Thomas gave to the magazine *Planet*[3], he draws a comparison with the glosses S.T. Coleridge wrote in the margin of 'The Rime of the Ancient Mariner' for the *Sibylline Leaves* edition. And there is no doubt that the prose pages in *The Echoes Return Slow* provide useful information for the understanding of the poems, especially for such readers as may not have been able to read *Neb*: but they also stand as texts in their own right, in a way Coleridge's glosses hardly do, and so the comparison he makes, in the same *Planet* interview, with Geoffrey Hill's *Mercian Hymns* is more convincing. In both cases, we find both the fragmentation of a man's life story into individual sections in chronological order, and an atomisation of the continuous flow of prose into separate, loosely co-ordinated units, elliptic sentences and noun phrases for the most part, as in:

> Coins handsome as Nero's; of good substance and
>   weight. *Offa Rex* resonant in silver, and the
>   names of the moneyers. They struck with accountable
>   tact. They could alter the king's face.
>   (Mercian Hymns, XI)

and

> A scrubbed door-step, clean enough to be defiled by the day's
> droppings, circulars, newspapers. A threshold of war, unbeknown
> to the young couple, the child-planners, choosing the capital of a
> fake nation to be their home. (*ERS*, 4)

The link with *Mercian Hymns* however remains a purely formal one, if only because the time gap between the life events and their poetical evocation is much shorter in Thomas's collection and does not call for the anachronisms which are a distinctive feature of *Mercian Hymns*. More important, the emphasis that such a mode of writing puts on continuity (the various sentences within the prose texts generally bear upon the same subject) and discontinuity (through the already noted double fragmentation) is to be related to the combination of permanence and transience in man's life. This has already been encountered in 'Careers' and challenges the author at the beginning of *Neb* as he wonders why memory retains some incidents and forgets others.

In fact, the primary function of the prose texts is to be a double mirror reflecting in two opposite directions, backwards to the memories and life story of *Neb* and *Y Llwybrau Gynt*, and forward to the poem on the facing page. The vast majority of the prose pages — especially in the early and middle sections of the book — bear a close link to *Neb* and more occasionally to *Y Llwybrau Gynt* (the episode of gathering mushrooms before dawn narrated there [12] is echoed twice in the poetry [*ERS*, 10 and 74]). Both *Neb* and *The Echoes Return Slow* lay stress on the same features in R.S. Thomas's life, his exhilaration as a little boy in the midst of nature, his nostalgia for Wales, his disappointment in his first parish, the difficulties encountered in the second, the sense of homecoming in Aberdaron with the return to landscapes of his childhood and his retirement to Sarn-y-Plas at the end, all of which forms the background and sometimes the starting point of his inner struggles and self-questionings. But within this general similarity, a few differences appear in the emphasis given to this or that aspect of his life. A very striking example is the handling of the first and second world wars, which are far more forcefully insisted upon in the poetry than in *Neb*. In *Neb*, R.S. Thomas's prime concern is to give as faithful an account as possible of the infant, and then of the young man, as he was at the time. Thus in *Neb*, he forbears to comment upon the coming of the first world war as he was totally unaware of it, and when he is ultimately confronted with the blackout, he does not even experience fear as he does not understand what is going on (7). The outbreak of the second world war coincides more or less with his getting married. Therefore, although he does insist on his pacifist ideas (32) and his disagreement with his vicar and the Church at large for not being faithful to Christ's message of peace, these pages are understandably more full of his own personal life and preoccupations, particularly his wish to prove to himself and to his future wife that he too can be a creative artist in his own field, his trips to Scotland and Ireland, and eventually his wedding. Whatever may have been his pacifist ideas at the time, they remain largely subdued and the text insists more on practical problems like the rationing of food and petrol. The concern for biographical accuracy has far less importance in *The Echoes Return Slow*, and rather than attempting to reproduce the past as he lived it then, he now offers a distanced interpretation, an image of the past coloured by the present. Indeed, the second world war is dealt with at some length, for six pages (18-23), but more crucially in relation to himself in the two middle pages (20 and 21). These juxtapose two distinct images of himself. The first one, on the prose page, reverberates backward to the passage in *Neb* in which he alluded to his pacifist ideas, but now develops his qualms in a "conscience doth make cowards of us all" manner (except that 'conscience' is replaced by 'imagination' and 'cowards' by 'not brave'). This is in its turn echoed in the facing poem in which the theatrical dimension now comes to the fore, as does the cowardice. One can feel the fervent pacifist he now is judging his former self somewhat critically.

The influence of the distance from the past is also noticeable in the way in which he considers people and events. This is particularly obvious in the presentation of his parents. In *Neb* , he insisted on his mother's possessiveness displayed (19-20) when he left the family home to go to university; later (91), he alludes to her domineering, sulky attitude which makes her difficult to live with, and explains his greater closeness to his father (92). In *The Echoes Return Slow* (76), the standpoint clearly is beyond their deaths, which seem to have levelled out the differences between the two, as is suggested by the parallel between his father's deafness and his mother's inability to speak at the very end. Paradoxically, this time, it is the facing poem which provides the more faithful echo of the autobiography, with the description of the mother's final illness while, at the same time, bringing the life-long relationship between mother and son into perspective, through the progression from "not out of our affection/for her", alluding to the strains and difficulties, on to the gesture of the final sentence: "Yet I took her hand/ there and made a tight-rope/of our fingers for the mis-shapen/feelings to keep their balance upon", thus restoring peace and harmony.

Not all the "external problems" (to use the phrase he himself employs, [48]) of life are smoothed out. And both *Neb* and *The*

Echoes Return Slow put a particular emphasis on the difficulties encountered at Eglwys-fach with the middle class snobbery and bossiness of ex-Army officers living there. Allusions to this recur like an undercurrent in the autobiography (24, 27, 60, and 64), while in *The Echoes Return Slow* six pages are devoted to it. The tone now is one of sharp criticism as in the terse "Education is the refinement of evil" (*ERS*, 46), the alternation of metaphors like "His china-eyed children/with their crêpe-de-Chine hair" and "reputations congealing about their mouths/cutlery after the prandial remarks", and the direct punch of "nastiness", "envy, malice" (47). The hilarious parody of the cocktail party neatly framed by "these sparrings" and "exchange/insults civilly" is closely followed by the ironical impersonation he makes of those selfsame people in church "telling Him what he is like" (55). The same metaphor of clothing is used, so as to stress the painfulness of the confrontations with the hardness of his Manafon parishioners in the first place, and with the social cruelty and hypocrisy of the Eglwys-fach set in the second. But while in the first experience, the professional role of the priest enabled him to achieve the contact which was refused on the human level ("Often, / when I thought they were about/to unbar to me, the draught/out of their empty places/came whistling, so that I wrapped/myself in the heavier clothing/of my calling, speaking of light and love/in the thickening shadows of their kitchens" [25]), not even that is possible in the second case. The "heavier clothing" has now become "the patched-up charm in humanity's/wardrobe, draughty habiliment/this for the candid heart that would keep itself warm", and "would" conveys the unfulfilled wish. And so, we can conclude that, apart from some already noted shiftings in the perspectives, as far as the contents are concerned the reflection of the autobiography in *The Echoes Return Slow*, and more precisely in the prose pages, is faithful enough to be recognisable. And yet the new image produced is completely different from the one conveyed by the autobiography.

A comparison between the prose text alluding to R.S. Thomas's arrival in Manafon (*ERS*, 24) and the corresponding pages in *Neb* (38-9) might prove interesting. Three main themes are developed in the four sentences composing the text. The first half of the first sentence ("What had been blue shadows on a longed-for horizon, traced on an inherited background") focuses on his attraction to the Welsh hill country, the blue hills as he could see them in the distance from Maelor Saesneg, and his feeling that this was where he belonged. It is therefore a graphic summary of pp. 38 and 39 from *Neb*. The last sentence in the text ("The young man was sent unprepared to expose his ignorance of life in a leafless pulpit" [*ERS*, 24]) heavily underlines the unpreparedness of the young priest for his new task, and but for the metaphoric "leafless" may be seen as a condensed expression of what is suggested many times in the pages of *Neb* about his early manhood. "Leafless" announces and prepares the image of draught and cold to be developed in the facing poem in relation to the already mentioned metaphor of clothing and so it offers a transition from the prose message to the poem. But the most significant section of this page is the middle one. It begins with a very sketchy description of the place ("this valley, this village and a church built with stones from the river, where the rectory stood") and the echo of earlier texts is obvious: "a church built with stones from the river" is the exact translation of the Welsh from *Neb* (43), but it sends us back as well to 'Country Church' from *Song at the Year's Turning* (27). This extreme simplicity in the presentation is soon belied by the passage from the merely factual, disconnected notations just quoted to an obviously metaphorical language: "plangent as a mahogany piano. The stream was a bright tuning-fork in the moonlight. The hay-fields ran with a dark current". The opening musical comparison is slightly ambiguous as it can be applied both to the rectory (this is what is suggested by the order of the words in the sentence, the shape of a piano and the possible use of the rectory as a sounding board for the river in spate — a not too infrequent happening as *Neb* indicates [42]) and to the river (it is the source of sound and "mahogany" refers to peat). This ambiguity underlines the ubiquity of the sound of water in the place. The next sentence again takes up a musical image, thus creating a pattern of continuity in an evocation which has so far consisted of a mere juxtaposition of elements; but the metaphor of the tuning-fork now highlights the ruling function of the river and no longer stresses the purely sonorous element as it is now framed by two notations of light ("bright" and "moonlight"), that are opposed to the "dark currents" of the hay-fields in the following sentences.

And thus the double sidedness of Manafon is gradually suggested, the brightness and beauty of nature symbolised by the river and the darkness (the uncouthness?) of the farming world represented by the "hay-fields". These are messages that the earlier poems have made us familiar with, and as for the importance of the river, source of stones and source of sounds, *Neb* has also stressed it, but with a telling difference. Unlike the musical metaphor of *The Echoes Return Slow*, the two comparisons in *Neb* (respectively page 41, "It sounded in the night like the blood running in their veins" and page 42, "like a living thing as changeable as a girl") relate the stream to the human field. This seems to suggest that if the message is the same, the perspective is different, basically human in *Neb*, and aesthetic in *The Echoes Return Slow*. And thus we come to the conclusion that if the prose pages are, as R.S. Thomas claims in the *Planet* interview, comparable to Coleridge's glosses, it is not only through the light they throw upon the individual poems, but also and above all for the progression they pinpoint in the process of poetical elaboration in the passage, the transmutation of the human material into the poem. As the confrontation between *Neb* and a prose page from *The Echoes Return Slow* has just shown, the first stage in this process consists of a summing up as well as a fragmentation of the message, together with a more markedly metaphorical and symbolical use of the language. But as we said earlier, as well as mirroring the autobiography, the prose pages also interact with the facing poems and it is to this second stage that we shall now turn.

Let us take two examples, an argumentative one in the confrontation between pages 28 and 29, and a more purely lyrical one with the last two pages of the collection. In keeping with what has already been seen, continuity and discontinuity characterise the prose text on page 28. It is composed of eight seemingly unconnected short sentences. But behind this surface incoherence, a very neat pattern soon emerges. Within the frame created by the first, second and last sentences focusing on the self-questionings of the priest (as the repetition of the word "question" underlines), the middle portion of the text develops an opposition between peace and traditional subsistence agriculture on the one hand, and war, technology and profit on the other. The superiority of the forces of war and technology is asserted quantitatively through the greater number of words referring to them ("machine — tractor — technology — infiltration — Mars — profit" as against "horse — age-old quietness — Ceres — subsistence") and qualitatively through their position at the outset of the contest ("machine") and at its outcome ("profit"). There is also the contamination of such a value as reason which is "open to the blandishments of the machine", but the presence of pain in the old world, with the horse serving as a "reservoir of blood" for the horse-fly, justifies the modernisation of agriculture which brings an alleviation of suffering. The language is double. It is concrete and metaphorical in the middle two sentences (four and five) which mention the replacement of the horse by the tractor, and include the comparison of the horse to a "reservoir of blood" and the use of a war metaphor in "invaded": but it is abstract and predominantly Latin in the rest, with such words as "reason, technology, infiltration, allegiance, subsistence, profit". This enhances the dualism of the text, the concrete situation being part of a wider, general one which, as the piling up of abstractions and the reference to classical mythology suggest, is in fact a far more distant reality. The autobiographical element is here reduced to bare allusions in the framing sentences ("the remotest backwater" in the opening line suggesting the isolation of Manafon and "the priest again questioned his vocation" relating to the sense he had of his inadequacy in his new parish) and contributes to the overall pattern of opposition. This is shown in the parallel positions of "the farmer" and "the priest" at the beginning of the last two sentences. The farmer has "changed his allegiance from Ceres to Mars", while the priest is "conscious that peace is transitory" and therefore is aware of its value.

The facing poem is made up of two stanzas of nine lines. But within this balanced presentation, we note a discrepancy in the distribution of the sentences, since the first stanza contains three sentences focusing on the various aspects of the land that the speaker perceives, while a single sentence dealing with his own predicament forms the whole of the second stanza. In other words, the self-questionings of the priest which formed the frame of the prose page have now moved to the centre and acquired as much importance as the world in which he finds himself. The three sentences of the first stanza are each characterised by a key word or phrase calling up a host of cultural and religious echoes. The first of these key expressions is "waste-land" in the second line, which not only evokes T.S. Eliot's poem, but also (and more probably) the third Branch of the *Mabinogion*, as the antithetic notion of harvest in the next line would suggest. And if we take up that association and relate it to the message of the prose page, the first sentence shows that technology (represented by "computed") has destroyed — or at least replaced — the cultural past of Wales. The second sentence is a parody of the Gospel scene of the stilling of the tempest (Mark IV, 39), and the emphatic negative ("no/saviour's voice") is meant to point to the disappearance from Wales of the Christian message and its replacement by false values ("false calm"). In the third sentence appears a familiar feature of Thomas's rural poetry, the scarecrow. It is here compared to "an old totem of the soil", which has also been destroyed, thus implying that the primitive, possibly pre-Celtic past of Wales has also been obliterated. And quite significantly, in the last line of the stanza is to be found the only abstract word of the poem, "irreverence", thus strategically positioned in order to point out that, in opposition to the threefold literary, religious and primitive cultures of Wales which are now denied and forgotten, the present times are characterised by "irreverence", by their lack of respect for these old values. For this threefold destruction no reasonable justification is possible as still seemed the case in the prose page, and to the abstractions which made the infiltration of technology appear a little unreal or at least distant, has now succeeded a single, but how much more telling and evocative word "computed". Man is evoked only by means of the pun on "breakers" ("And a voice, that was no/saviour's voice, had said to the breakers:/Be still"), to the extent that one is left to think that the voice could be a synthetic, computerised one, and the "false calm" could be that of the absence of life and man.

The second stanza is a direct consequence of the first. Given the drastic transformation of the rural world described in the first stanza, it follows that the speaker — who may be the poet-priest of the prose page but could also be anyone not accepting the modern way of life — is confronted with two equally unacceptable choices. He can opt either for the "conveyor-belt/of the traffic", most effectively combining two of the blights of urban technology, or the transformed (as "another" and "different" underline) countryside which looks as if it had given itself a new god who, with "his human rags", evokes the scarecrow at the end of the first stanza and is denied transcendence. No real possibility of identifying this god of modern times is given, and a certain amount of vagueness surrounds him for the initial "as though" ("as though at the foot of another/cross with a different saviour/on it, and one never to come/down, because of his human rags") suggests that he may not even exist, and if he does, unlike Christ, he cannot be incarnated, precisely because he is not transcendent to man. Like T.S. Eliot's 'The Waste Land', this truly is a poem about the spiritual death brought about by modern civilization, and whatever autobiographical implications remained in the prose page (albeit in a not very accurate manner since, as he says in *Y Llwybrau Gynt* [18] "When I arrived there in 1942, there was not a single tractor in the area. The men worked with their hands" and the situation cannot have altered as much as he claims during the war) they have now subsided. In spite of the first person pronoun and the familiar attitude at the beginning of the second stanza ("And I waited there at the gateway/on the uncertain boundary between/road and field, not sure of where/I belonged"), the poem has lost all anecdotal, personal dimension and truly reaches universality. And so, after the summing up and atomisation characterising the passage from the autobiography to the prose text, the second stage in the poetic process now consists of a complete transformation. A notation, an idea, a theme in the prose page (here the invasion of the countryside by technology) is selected and developed in a new perspective (here a spiritual one, while the prose page insisted more on the material and economic level). This involves the incorporation of new elements (for example, the scarecrow/Cross identification or the fusion of Incarnation with a pietà scene) so as to produce a new synthesis, a new image which bears some relation to the prose page but is also vastly different from it. Even the tone has changed, since the argument has given way to despair.

The last two pages of *The Echoes Return Slow* deal with the two greatest loves in R.S. Thomas's life, his wife and the sea. The prose page (120) is composed of three elliptic sentences following a rapidly expanding progression, as the first is made up of two words, the second of ten and the third of twenty five. But alongside this disjointed style which is a frequent characteristic of the prose texts (as if to suggest that they are unfinished drafts), continuity is achieved through the presence of "both" in the three sentences and of the sea vocabulary in the second and third sentences. In fact, the passage is built on a double opposition. On the one hand there is the contrast between the game of seduction played by the two unidentified female characters, towards whom he adopts the anti-feminist stance so typical of his sense of humour, with the cliché of woman as the archtemptress, self-centred, changeable and difficult to manage, and the (presumably true) love felt by the male character introduced as a mere object, diluted in the generality of men at first ("us"), and so obviously full of good will, perseverance ("lifetime's apprenticeship in navigating their surface") and humility ("nothing to hope for"). On the other hand there is an antithesis between the playful tone of the major part of the text, which reads like a puzzle as we have to guess the identity of the two unnamed "both" through the combination of human and naval terms, and the more serious turn of the last line. The last word indeed sends us to the prayer of supplication closing *Neb* (Miserere me Domine), and this, with the allusion to the Gospel equation between love and forgiveness (Luke VII, 47,"Her sins, which are many, are forgiven; for she loved much"), introduces a religious dimension in what had so far appeared mere banter. And so we are left to wonder whether, as the very exaggeration in the terms of the human opposition leads us to think, the text is merely a clever joke on the similarity between women and the sea, or whether it aims at putting into some kind of perspective the difficulties in a love relationship.

Different from what we noted on pages 28-9, but similar to the pages on his mother's death, the facing poem is both far more personal and far more straightforward than the prose text. The sea is identified right from the start (the very last word in the first line) and the poem is a tribute to his ageing wife, troubled for many years by health problems. In fact, the poem effects a reversal of the prose page: instead of the rapidly expanding progression of the elliptic sentences of page 120, we now note a slowly decreasing one (the first sentence taking up the whole of the first quartet, the second sentence two and a half lines and the third one and a half), as if to point to the gradual waning of his wife's existence. Instead of the fusion of the woman and the sea in a continuous, indistinct "both", there is now a clear dissociation of the two. The sea is only mentioned in the opening line and then disappears from the poem, and an obvious contrast is drawn between its timelessness and the heavy weight of time on human life, skilfully conveyed by the interplay of the extended metaphor of the calendar ("calendar/to time's passing, who is now open/at the last month, her hair wintry") with the two allusions to his wife framing it ("the head of one...her hair"). Here the repetition of the semi-vocalic sound (w), culminating in the disphoric combination of "who is now open" and the fragmentation of the sentence into shorter units, brings out the contrast between the continuous, even flow of the sea and the shortness of breath of a human existence drawing near its end.

In the second quartet, the simplification of language and style is even greater as the syntactical pattern of prose is now strictly adhered to, but it is here that the reversal of the facing page is manifested most fully. The critical overtones and exaggeration are now replaced by praise of her courage and dignity ("Am I catalyst of her mettle that,/at my approach, her grimace of pain/turns to a smile?"), and the change in the sequence of the personal pronouns (from a gradual passage from "they" to "he" in the prose page, to two parallel progressions from "I" to "she" in the poem) is meant to give her the last word, the prominent position that was his at the end of the prose page. Above all, the last line (" 'Over love's depths only the surface is wrinkled' ") takes up again the notion of "surface" opposed to "depths", echoing "fathoms" precisely in order to reverse it. For while the alluring, "crystal-eyed" surface concealed "unstable fathoms", now "only the surface is wrinkled", thus suggesting that the depths are stable. As for "love", now linked with "depths" (thus the very opposite of the seduction game), it is associated with the woman, and if we relate this to "navigating their surface" that described the man's attitude, it now appears that of the two the man's love was the more shallow. The last line is so memorable and felicitous that it offers a particularly good illustration of the definitions of poetry R.S. Thomas gave in the *Planet* interview[4] as "language at its highest level of articulation", and as "deploying language at a higher tension, in a more concise and memorable way than....prose". It offers two possible readings according to whether the pause is before "only" or after, but both are equal proofs of the depth of her love. At the same time, the impersonal proverb-like formulation suggests that, together with the limited, personal significance, the sentence can have wider more general implications, namely that when love reaches certain depths, the problems, the wrinkles are only superficial ones. In any case, as in the previous example (28-9), the prose page has provided a word, a phrase (here the opposition between the surface and the depth of the sea and of love) from which to build a new synthesis which, this time, offers an opposite message to the one of the original text.

A sort of middle term is suggested by the confrontation between pages 74 & 75. As was the case on page 120, the prose text reads a little like a riddle. In the first three sentences we are confronted with a particularly developed lexical field of death ("skulls — oily — cemetery — grave-stones — angel") totally at odds with what is alluded to, a childhood memory of himself picking mushrooms at the crack of dawn and mistaking stones for them (*Y Llwybrau Gynt*, p.12). The aim of such a vocabulary is to prepare for the final mushroom scene, the spectre of nuclear war made more startling by its juxtaposition with such a peaceful, homely pastime. In the facing poem, the same two scenes are evoked but in exactly reversed order. The first three stanzas allusively refer to the atomic bomb, in a careful progression through various forms of weaponry from the bow, beams, gases, ultimately reaching the nuclear ("radio-active"), while the childhood episode appears in the final stanza. Whereas the prose page evokes man's life in a loosely chronological order from the child to the adult, forty years later, the poem on the contrary stresses the opposite time scale, with the old man in the first stanza, Byron, the mature poet in the second, and the child in the third and fourth stanzas. In this last stanza, the shift from the perspective of the prose page is also underlined by the proximity of "dew" and "mushroom" ("there was dew on the early-morning/mushroom") bringing together the first ("White skulls, oily with dew in the late moonlight") and last ("the mushroom-shaped cloud") lines of the facing text. "Early-morning" in the last but one line of the poem echoes and opposes "the late moonlight" at the beginning of the prose page. Such a reversal does not amount, as in the last poem in the volume which was previously discussed, to a change in the message but it certainly contributes to highlighting the nostalgia of the youthful scene. At the same time, as on page 29, a totally new perspective is introduced, that of poetic creation. From the sense of failure conveyed by the direct speech at the beginning of the first stanza and heavily underlined by three adjectives "old", "bent" and "broken", the poet is then confronted in the second stanza with two poetic possibilities, either the antiquated one represented by the Romantic poetry and its cult of the Middle Ages, or a resolutely modern form of verse, using the language of contemporary technology. This is the one he adopts and it apparently gives him some sense of achievement ("Ah/me" being also suggestive of a certain amount of self-irony). But, as the juxtaposition of the youthful episode implies, he nevertheless fails to recapture the life ("dew") he knew and throve in as a child, even though the poems he composed then (c.f. *Neb*, 13) were little more than plagiarism, but it was plagiarism which was "innocent" compared with the harmful imitation of the mushroom produced by man with the atomic bomb. And so, the end-product of the poem is both akin to and very different from the human scene, be it the one portrayed in the Welsh autobiography or the English prose page. We are reminded of the transmutation effected by Yeats in the Byzantium poems, to transform "the unpurged images of day" into "a miracle, bird or golden handiwork", and it appears that the aim of *The Echoes Return Slow* is to illustrate this passage from the individual life experience to the abstraction and universality of the aesthetic recreation.

But, at the same time, one cannot but note that the transformation operated is to be related to two particularly meaningful words. The first of these is the verb "return" to be found in the volume's title. The poem from which the title is taken (63) evokes the visits the priest used to pay to his sick parishioners (here decrepit old ladies) and compares the difficulties he experienced in communicating with them to sonar echoes of his own life returning to him as he is getting old: in both cases, this centripetal movement is laborious and imperfect (hence the process of atomisation, juxtaposition and summing up) and is to be opposed to the centrifugal motion of the other keyword "recession". "Recession" appears twice. The first time (49), it is the last word of the poem ("with such stars over him / as were like love only / in the velocity of their recession") and relates either to the stars only, if we pause after "only", or to both the stars and love if we pause before that word. In the second example ("So we learn / something of the nature / of God, the endlessness / of whose recessions / are brought up short by / the contemporaneity of the Cross" [83]), it refers to a notion of God as the eternally evasive being that the volumes from *H'm* to *Experimenting with an Amen* have made us familiar with, and which is also to be found here, in the more homely context of his infant son (41). Thus the juxtaposition of "return" and "recession" is a graphic expression of the double, antithetic pull, towards the self on the one hand and towards God on the other. The message of *The Echoes Return Slow* is thus metaphysical as well as aesthetic, as it illustrates the passage from a situation in which "the ego / renews its claim / to attention" to a self-renunciation echoing God's and thus likely to enable communion with Him, as "At times / in the silence between / prayers, after the Amens / fade, at the world's / centre, it is as though / love stands, renouncing itself" (117). The last two poems in *The Echoes Return Slow* however do not focus on such a spiritual experience, but on the relationship with other men (119) and with the beloved (121). This suggests two possible readings: given the stress on love in both these poems, they can be read as examples of self-effacement on a human level, of humility (119), of the effort to see things no longer from one's own standpoint but from that of the other, or of the beloved (121), which of course is to be related to the Gospel equation between the love of God and the love of one's neighbour. On a more purely aesthetic level, they suggest Yeats's poem 'Byzantium', at the end of which "That dolphin-torn, that gong-tormented sea" reasserted itself after the flight into perfection. The reintroduction of a more personal and human level at the end of *The Echoes Return Slow* could thus be a reminder that however desirable the ideal of self-sacrifice on a spiritual level, poetry cannot survive in abstraction, but needs tension in order to exist and deploy itself, tension between flesh and spirit in Yeats's poem, tension here between love of God and self-love. And it is in this double sense, of illustrating a possible passage from self-centredness (in the autobiography) to self-effacement (in the aesthetic or universal value of the poem), as well as pointing out the limitations of man's capacity to sacrifice himself, that *The Echoes Return Slow* appears as the synthesis of the dialectic of the self and the other at the heart of this poetical adventure.

All this is illustrated in fact by a key-image in R.S. Thomas's poetry, that of the mirror. Introduced as early as *Song at the Year's Turning*, this trope is then a representation of the interaction between man and nature; and if in the initial example (*SYT*, 36) man's world is shown as a possible mirror for nature ("the floor unscrubbed/Is no mirror for the preening sun"), the more usual situation is that of nature mirroring man. With *Tares* and the poem 'Judgment Day' (20), the metaphor acquires a deeper significance. Starting from the Biblical assertion of man's likeness to God in the Book of Genesis, R.S. Thomas visualises man's creation as God breathing on a mirror, and his death as God breathing again, blurring that first image into mist. Quite significantly in the same volume, the mirror becomes an image of human love, which in fact appears as a form of self-love, with "in his eye/The light of the cracked lake//That once she had propped to comb/Her hair in"(22); and it can also reveal a strained mother-son relationship as in "Let me go/Beyond the front garden without you/To find glasses unstained by tears,/To find mirrors that do not reproach/My smooth face"(37), a probable autobiographical allusion, as we remember his mother's tears (*Neb*, 19) when he left home to go to university. With *The Bread of Truth*, the metaphor expands again and becomes more complex and original. In 'Strangers' (*BT*,32), the poet walking past houses now lived in by strangers (presumably English) evokes the Welsh people who lived there before ("memory of a face/For ever setting within the glass/Of windows about the door"). To the watcher outside, now that the previous dwellers are dead (as "for ever setting" implies) the reflection of the moon on the window pane is reminiscent of their faces looking out of the window, and the same image reappears in *Not That He Brought Flowers* ("There is a house with/a face mooning at the glass/of windows [7]) and again in *Later Poems* (165). The metaphor has now become double, and works in two opposite directions, gradually appearing to be related to the author's major concerns. Thus as he makes explicit in his description of the sea in *Neb* :

> There are two sides to the sea, the outside and the inside. Or if you
> prefer, there is the mirror and the window. In the mirror, you can
> see all the beauty and glory of creation: the colours and shapes of
> the clouds and the birds on their eternal migrations. But using it as
> a window, you can see the constant warfare, one creature for ever
> ruthlessly devouring another. (87-88)

or as he puts it in *The Echoes Return Slow* :

> Both window and mirror. Was he unique in using it as a window of
> an asylum, as glass to look through into a watery jungle, where life
> preyed on itself, ferocious yet hushed as the face of the believer,
> ambushed in a mirror. So much easier for the retired mind to lull
> itself to sleep among the reflection. (72)

In view of all this, the temptation is to withdraw into narcissistic
self-contemplation, as in 'Present' (*F*, 9) in which "I would be the
mirror/of a mirror, effortlessly repeating/my reflections". Such a
position is however not tenable on the human level: it destroys
love as is made clear in 'All Right' (*H'm*, 29) in which "you" behave
"as/Though you were your own mirror" and the end of the poem
clearly shows that such a narcissistic attitude cannot but lead to
the destruction of the relationship ("A finished performance").
More generally, 'Present' emphasises man's position and func-
tion, which are to relate to other human beings ("I am at the
switchboard/of the exchanges of the people/of all time"[*F*, 9]) and
this forbids yielding to such temptations of self-centred withdra-
wal.

But it also appears untenable on the metaphysical level. God
being likened on two occasions (*Later Poems*, 182 and *Counterpoint*,
12) to "two mirrors/echoing one another", anything, any creature
intruding upon this endless self-reflection, cannot but shatter it,
so that, as appears in 'The Presence', "There is nothing I can
do/but fill myself with my own/silence, hoping it will ap-
proach/like a wild creature to drink/there, or perhaps like Nar-
cissus/to linger a moment over its transparent face"(*BHN*, 107).
The only valid position, both on the human and metaphysical
levels, is therefore to put the mirror away, in an attitude of
self-denial. But is it always humanly possible? The self, unlike
God, is unavoidable, always present, as appears in 'Looking
Glass': "Like one eternally/in ambush, fast or slow/as I may raise

my head, it raises//its own, catching me in the act,/disarming me by aquaintance,/looking full into my face as often/as I try looking at it askance"(*EA*, 40); or as he puts it in *The Echoes Return Slow* , "He could not escape from his looking glass"(*ERS*, 108). But what he sometimes sees in it is not himself only, since "There are //times even the mirror/ is misted as by one breathing/over my shoulder"(*EA*, 38). Looking at himself, he is led to evoke the first human being seeing his own reflection in a pool of water (*ERS*, 108), and this indicates that, unlike *Neb* which is a personal life-story, *The Echoes Return Slow* aims at a wider, more general human significance. A more thorough self-analysis ("the refinement of the mirror") will bring us no nearer the solution; it will merely give a greater awareness of the problems ("There occurred only the refinement of his dilemma") and possibly reveal unsuspected levels of complexity, since "behind//the mirror is the twin helix/ where the dancing chromosomes/pass one another back/ to back to a tune from the abyss"(*ERS*, 109). And thus the mirror is not destroyed, and self-analysis not condemned if it is an incentive to go "behind the mirror" or, like Alice, through it and view life from a different perspective, no longer personal and self-centred, but as universal and comprehensive as possible.

Counterpoint suggests a similar attitude, but on a moral and theological level this time. God and man being presented in equally narcissistic terms, with on the one hand God's mind visualised as "two mirrors echoing/one another"(12) and on the other self-infatuation appearing as the Original Sin ("The tree's fruit was a mirror,/its temptation reflection..../ /The self looks at the self/only and tenders its tribute" [11]), it follows that an encounter between the two would be impossible, but for the Crucifixion which alters this set pattern. Here again, the familiar image reappears, as R.S. Thomas pictures the darkness of Christ's countenance on the Cross as "a reflection of the three days and nights/at the back of love's looking-/glass even a God must spend"(36). In other words, in the same way as Christ was prepared to go to "the back of love's looking glass", that is to die for the love of mankind, so too must man attempt to do the same: not to shatter the looking glass (that would mean suicide), but to go behind it, that is to sacrifice himself, to die to himself for the love of God. And one can see how central and pregnant the metaphor is, in relation both to the theme of introspection and to the evolution of Thomas's views and poetry.

As has been repeatedly noted, R.S. Thomas's poetry is characterised by a great reluctance to speak about himself and even when he does the emotion is always under control. But what could at first be ascribed to self-consciousness or restraint has gradually developed into a philosophy of life sustaining the tension at the heart of these poems, tension between God and the ego which, to use Claudel's quotation in epigraph to *Neb*, is "indestructible" and always ready to reassert itself and claim attention and also tension between the self and the "néant" (again to use Claudel's phrase), the consciousness of being nothing but a shadow falling over the sixty-million-year-old pre-Cambrian rocks at Braich-y-Pwll.

Notes

1. Introduction to *R.S. Thomas, Selected Prose*, ed. Sandra Anstey (Bridgend: Poetry Wales Press, 1983), 7.
2. D.Z. Phillips, *R.S. Thomas: Poet of the Hidden God* (London: Macmillan, 1986), 83.
3. 'Probings, An interview with R.S. Thomas', *Planet* (80, April/May 1990), 50.
4. ibid., 48.

Tony Brown

"Over Seventy Thousand Fathoms": The Sea and Self-definition in the Poetry of R.S. Thomas

My dark thought upon that day
That brought me from Arfon's bay,
From the low shores of Malltraeth and its sand,
Far inland, far inland.

For I remember now at the growth of night
The great hills and the yellow light
Stroking to softness the harsh sweep
Of limb and shoulder above the quiet deep....

Autumn shakes out the thistle's curse
On the grey air, and my leafless house,
Picked clean by the frost and rain,
Cowers naked upon the plain;

But there Caergybi, Aberffraw
And holy Llanddwyn are wearing now,
Like the rich cloak of old royalty,
The wild purple of the sea. (*SF*, 34)

The poem from which these stanzas are taken, 'Hiraeth', appeared in R.S. Thomas's first volume, *The Stones of the Field*, published in 1946, when Thomas was rector of Manafon, though the reference to a house "upon the plain" suggests that it is likely that the poem had its origins in his period (1940-2) as curate at Maelor Saesneg (Hanmer) in "the flat country of Flintshire".[1] The poem expresses the poet's longing from "far inland" for the seascapes of Anglesey, where he had grown up: "The running of the sea under the wind,/Rough with silver, comes before my mind". It was clearly a longing which was deeply felt; in an essay in Welsh entitled 'Dylanwadau' ('Influences'), in which he writes of the influence of Anglesey upon him, he writes of his "two dreadful years" far away at Hanmer, while in a recent interview he spoke of the "terrible longing for the sea" he had previously felt while a curate at Chirk, on the Welsh border.[2] The poet describes his childhood in the countryside and along the shores of Anglesey in almost Wordsworthian terms, as a place of freedom and natural beauty — "I was a boy with the energy of a young colt, and would race the wind and sing out in front of the waves, trying to catch the salt snowflakes as they rose off the sea"[3] — while the town of Holyhead itself, where the Thomas family lived, was a place dominated by the sea and its moods:

> The sea became part of the life of the child too, its sounds, its smells, and its roughness on windy days. It could be seen from his bedroom. In the evening the flashes of the lighthouse would flit through his room like the sails of a windmill. (*Neb*, 11)

Even after the move to Manafon, it would seem, plangent memories of Anglesey were never far below the surface — "A savour would rise off the wet soil that would remind him of Holyhead, when he was a boy there" (*Neb*, 46) — and when Thomas came to describe the harsh life of the Montgomeryshire hill farms, a life he found shockingly different to his earlier idealistic visions of the rural world, his poetry consistently drew on images and associations which clearly have their origins far from the bare hills of mid-Wales:

> There he goes, tacking against the fields'
> Uneasy tides...
>   ...while the noisy surf
> Of people dins far off at the world's rim.
>   ('The Labourer', *SYT*, 70)

> Dewi is out paddling in the grass.
> Ianto, he is doing the same.
>   ('Brothers', *P*, 40)

Iago Prytherch is

>   ...alone, exposed
> In my own fields with no place to run
> From your sharp eyes. I, who a moment back
> Paddled in the bright grass... ('Invasion on the Farm', *SYT*, 102)

The Page's Drift: R.S. Thomas at Eighty

In 'Memories', the poet asks Iago

> Do you remember the shoals of wheat, the look
> Of the prawned barley...
> Or the music of the taut scythe
> Breaking in regular waves upon the lithe
> Limbs of the grass?   (*SYT*, 45)

Another, unnamed, labourer

> ...wades in the brown bilge of earth
> Hour by hour...
>   ('A Labourer', *SYT*, 18)

This is, of course, the most characteristic scene in R.S. Thomas's early poetry, the rural labourer isolated on an expanse of bleak hillside, engaged in grim monotonous work, watched from a distance by the poet. But equally recurrent is the nexus of images employed:

> He was far out from the shore
> Of his four hedges, marooned there
> On the bare island of himself.
> I watched him from the main road
> Over the currents of a sea
> Shallow enough for me to cross,
> Had I the time, the will...
>   ('The Figure', *BT*, 44)

The poet, despite his "strange calling" ('The Figure') as a priest, remains at a distance, a distance born of cultural and temperamental differences, and one which can result in an anguished sense of incapacity.[4] In 'Evans'(*PS*, 15), the imagery we have been indicating recurs as the poet leaves the remote farm of one of his parishioners — "into the cold/Dark to smother in the thick tide/Of night" — "appalled" at the darkness, the nothingness of death, which faces the man whom he has left and whose sense of spiritual aloneness the poet has apparently been unable to alleviate,

> ...the dark
> Silting the veins of that sick man
> I left stranded upon the vast
> And lonely shore of his bleak bed.

Again and again the lonely battle for survival of the moorland farmers and labourers, a battle against the elements and against the inexorable processes of time and change, is expressed in terms of another elemental world:

> Life's bitter jest is hollow, mirthless he slips
> To his long grave under the wave of wind,
> That breaks continually on the brittle ear.
> ('Peasant Greeting', *SYT*, 28)

In 'Green Categories', Iago's house, a "landmark in the moor's deep tides", is subject to the processes of the natural world; while he sleeps "the dark moor exerts/Its pressure on the timbers" (*PS*, 19). Not just individuals but whole communities are subject to the inexorable pressures of the tides and changes of time; an isolated village, for example, is

> ...eaten away
> By long erosion of the green tide
> Of grass creeping perpetually nearer
> This last outpost of time past.
> ('The Village', *SYT*, 98)

As he walked the hills of Montgomeryshire, R.S. Thomas repeatedly came across the ruined farmhouses which are silent monuments to those who struggled for survival but who finally went under:

> The grass
> Wrecked them in its draughty tides...
> That was nature's jest, the sides
> Of the old hulk cracked, but not with mirth.
> ('Depopulation of the Hills', *SYT*, 52)

The forces pressing in upon these hill farmers are not, of course, simply those of natural process, but the additional pressures of social, cultural and economic change, eroding the will and energy of those farming the Welsh hills. In such a context, the metaphorical pattern becomes even more insistent. 'Those Others' (*T*, 31-2) engages these issues in, it would seem, very personal terms. There is a strong sense in the poem of the way in which the poet's period at Manafon was — after his exile in Flintshire — a time of self-definition, of a focussing of his own identity and values:

> This was the cramped womb
> At last took me in
> From the void of unbeing.

It is a place, it seems, which, after the initial shock to an imagin-
ation shaped by library, lecture-room and bourgeois upbringing,
allowed Thomas to reflect on and articulate some of his most
deeply-felt impulses, a response not merely to the natural world
but to the spare, the simple,

> ...the brute earth
> That is strong here and clean
> And plain in its meaning.

The hatred expressed in the poem for those who value this land
only in material terms, and see Wales only in terms of realisable
assets, is, clearly, all the more deeply-felt because of this growing
identification with it. And hence his affection, movingly expressed
here, for those with the inner resources, the resilience, to remain
resolute in the face of the cultural and economic forces pressing in
on them, a resilience expressed once again in metaphors which
seem to have particular resonance for the poet:

> There are still those other
> Castaways on a sea
> Of grass, who call to me,
> Clinging to their doomed farms;
> Their hearts though rough are warm
> And firm, and their slow wake
> Through time bleeds for our sake.

But the plight of these survivors is an increasingly desperate one
and by the late 1970s the landscape has changed beyond recogni-
tion; in 'Gone?' (F, 34) the poet looks in vain "over the flogged
acres/of ploughland" for any sign that "This was Prytherch
country". "Flogged" in more ways than one, for this is a country
in which the values of those who have "learn[ed] what to sell"
('Those Others') have triumphed. The hedgerows and trees have
been uprooted, the seas of grass tamed; the image here, somewhat
paradoxically perhaps, being drawn from a bygone age of sailing

ships:

> ...a forest of aerials
> as though an invading fleet invisibly
> had come to anchor among these
> financed hills.[5]

The tone of several of these poems in the late 1970s which look back for a last time at the Welsh hill country is essentially, often movingly, elegiac. In 'Drowning' (*WA*, 38) the stubborn but doomed survivors of 'Those Others' have finally succumbed — "I looked on and/there was one less and one less and one less" — the imaginative link with the earlier poem being explicit in the metaphor used:

> A rare place, but one identifiable
> with other places where on as deep a sea
> men have clung to the last spars of their language
> and gone down with it, unremembered but uncomplaining.

There are, in fact, in R.S. Thomas's work a number of poems not often remarked upon, in which the human struggle against the sea is portrayed directly, not metaphorically. In 'Schoonermen' (*P*, 43), for example, the Welsh sailors who manned ships which plied the routes between North Wales and South America in the late nineteenth century are seen in heroic terms:

> Great in this,
> They made small ships do
> Big things, leaping hurdles
> Of the stiff sea, horse against horses
> In the tide race.

Despite the harsh conditions which these Welsh sailors have to confront — shipboard disease as well as the wildness of the sea itself — they are seen as remaining vigorous, even youthful, and true to their origins, to what and who they are:

> From long years
> In a salt school, caned by brine,
> They came landward

With the eyes of boys,
The Welsh accent
Thick in their sails.

While in poems about the Welsh hill country qualities of resource-fulness, endurance, being true to one's own vision of life are, as we have seen, expressed repeatedly in terms of confrontation with the pressures of tides and hostile seas, here that confrontation is a literal one. Moreover, one might suggest, we are closer here to the source of the metaphorical associations which these qualities have for R.S. Thomas. 'Schoonermen' was first published in 1965, the year in which the poet's father, T.H. Thomas, died ("Memory aches/In the bones' rigging").[6] Mr. Thomas had been sent to sea, under sail, as an apprentice at the age of sixteen, his father having died at a relatively early age, leaving eleven children but little money.[7] Mr. Thomas's father had also been a seaman, earlier in the nineteenth century. 'Schoonermen' might be seen, then, as a tribute to both men and the way of life they represented, based on his father's stories of the sea ("If tales were tall,/Waves were taller"). 'The Survivors' (*BT*, 19) — a story about a literal ship-wreck this time — would seem to have the same origin ("He told me about it often"). One of R.S. Thomas's few narrative poems, it is again, even more than 'Schoonermen', a story of endurance, a desperate clinging to life, as the survivors suffer for six days in an open boat before reaching land. Such stories of the sea, told by the poet's father, can only have endorsed the feelings for the sea — adventure, freedom, but also the need for resilience and mental and physical robustness in the face of adversity — with which the sailor's son would have become familiar as he grew up in Holy-head.[8]

R.S. Thomas has published two poems specifically about his father. 'Sailors' Hospital' (*NBF*, 24-5)[9] is an elegy and ends with a moving expression of affection as his father slowly slips away into death:

...he drifted
Away on the current
Of his breath, further and further,
Out of hail of our love.

In the poem, Holyhead, the town where his father dies, is seen as a shabby place; founded, the poet surmises, by some sailor who fetched up there long ago — "found women/To breed from— those sick men/His descendants" — the town is seen as "That refuse: time's waste" and contrasted with "the clean sea" which lies beyond it. It is here that his father, too, has run aground, a view made explicit in 'Salt' (*LP*, 159-63).[10] The opening stanzas of the poem evoke, again, the adventurous life of Welsh seamen in the age of sail and seem to mingle stories of Mr. Thomas with memories of his own sailor father, the poet's grandfather.[11] The vision is of a hard but heroic life, the imagery echoing that at the opening of 'Schoonermen': "'...teach me to ride/in my high saddle/the mare of the sea.'" R.S. Thomas's father gave up his life as an ocean-going seaman after the first world war and, now having a wife and child to support, took a job instead on the ferry between Ireland and Holyhead, though he apparently disliked Holyhead itself (*Neb*, 10). Thus, in 'Salt', the heroic sailor is perceived as being drawn home from the freedom of the sea, to be constrained and domesticated:

> Was he aware
> of a vicarage garden
> that was the cramped harbour
> he came to?[12]
> .....The deep
> sea and the old call
> to abandon it
> for the narrow channel
> from her and back. The chair
> was waiting and the slippers
> by the soft fire
> that would destroy him.

This perception of the father as being trapped by wife and mother, enveigled home and tamed, recurs in Thomas's poetry. In 'The Boy's Tale' (*BT*, 36) the sailor comes home from Port Said and takes "a girl" from the Welsh valleys; she "Caught him in her thin hair,/ Couldn't hold him". But, ultimately, the child is used to draw the father home:

> She went fishing in him;
> I was the bait
> That became cargo,
> Shortening his trips,
> Waiting on the bone's wharf.
> Her tongue ruled the tides.

Again, in 'Ap Huw's Testament' (*PS*, 29) — one notices the greater ambiguity of the status of the narrator in these early poems than in the later ones — we are told

> My father was a passionate man,
> Wrecked after leaving the sea
> In her love's shallows. He grieves in me.

'Salt' is the expression of that grief. By the time that his son was in his late teens and ready for university, Mr. Thomas had had to give up even his work on the ferries, due to the onset of deafness.[13] He is portrayed in the poem not only as removed from the way of life he had known for so many years, but as isolated by his deafness, increasingly removed from what is going on around him, lost in memories of his sea-going life:

> While the house founders
> in time, I must listen to him
> complaining, a ship's captain
> with no crew, a navigator
> without a port...
> Out of touch
> with the times, landlocked
> in his ears' calm, he remembered
> and talked.

The old sailor, beached and domesticated, is seen as having lost any real identity, as lacking any effective purpose:

> What was a sailor
> good for who had sailed
> all seas and learned wisdom
> from none, fetched up there
> in the shallows with his mind's
> valueless cargo?

But before this, and it is perhaps the most telling moment in the poem, the poet writes

> I take his failure
> for ensign, flying it
> at my bedpost, where my own
> children cry to be born.

The erosion and final defeat of his sailor father's independence, ultimately even of his identity, the defeat of a life of freedom and endurance by the insidious entrapment of domesticity, appears as a chastening and instructive example to the son, it would seem, making resolute his own efforts towards freedom and integrity. An uncollected poem, 'Autobiography' (published, like 'Salt', in 1973),[14] specifically engages the issue of the growth of identity, in the context of familial relationships. The poem traces the parents' early relationship — "two people cast up/on life's shore" — and the poet's own conception:

> And I am not present
> as yet.
> Could it be said, then,
> I am on my way, a nonentity
> with a destination?
> What do they do
> waiting for me? They invent
> my name. I am born
> to a concept, answering
> to it with reluctance.

The hesitant, tentative lineation here, and throughout the poem, is perhaps expressive of the emotional ambivalences and uncertainties which the poet is uneasily seeking to articulate. The impulse towards self-definition and freedom expressed in the poem is, inevitably, not without guilt, nor does the struggle end with the first leaving of home. The images employed here, at the end of the poem, are both striking and, in the context of 'Salt' and the other poems we have been considering, almost inevitable:

> Nothing they have they own;
> the borrowed furnishings of their minds
> frays. I study to become the rat
> that will desert
> the foundering vessel

of their pride; but home
is a long time sinking. All
my life I must swim
out of the suction of its vortex.

Here the poet himself becomes the resilient survivor, guilty esca-
pee from the constraints of the familial and the domestic, from
received opinions and conventional attitudes.[15]

Such tensions, the emotional ambiguities of the son or daughter
whose very realisation of parental hopes and aspirations takes
him/her into an intellectual or social context wholly beyond the
parents' understanding, have, of course, become familiar since the
second world war. But what is striking is the vehemence with
which that "ensign" has been flown, the resoluteness with which
the poet holds himself separate both from "the world's nets" ('Ap
Huw's Testament') and from what are perceived as the snares of
the domestic and the intimate. Identity is defined, it would seem,
not in relationship but in apartness, in resolute and solitary con-
frontation, as we have seen, with the elemental world and also
with the stresses of the mind's inner region. A central poem here
is 'The Untamed' (*BT*, 33), a poem which, one notes, is placed
opposite 'The Boy's Tale' in *Selected Poems*. By now we realise that
the imagery the poet uses to evoke the wild realm with which he
identifies has specific and personal resonance:

My garden is the wild
Sea of the grass. Her garden
Shelters between walls.
The tide could break in;
I should be sorry for this.

There is peace there of a kind,
Though not the deep peace
Of wild places.

The garden in the poem is a place of nurturing, of specifically
female nurturing, of a domesticity which the poet is on occasion
content to share. But the garden is also a place of temptation; again,
the comforts of the domestic and the female are portrayed as a
threat to the self's resolution and integrity:

The old softness of lawns
    Persuading the slow foot
Leads to defection; the silence
    Holds with its gloved hand
    The wild hawk of the mind.

But not for long, windows
    Opening in the trees
Call the mind back
    To its true eyrie; I stoop
    Here only in play.

M. Wynn Thomas notes that this final stanza is reminiscent of Kierkegaard's emphasis in *The Present Age* on the need to safeguard one's individuality and he points out that in the 1960s R.S. Thomas wrote two poems concerning Kierkegaard.[16] This is a connection to which we shall return, but it is already apparent why, by virtue of temperament and experience, R.S. Thomas would have been responsive to the Scandinavian philosopher's emphasis on individual integrity and authenticity which refuses to concede to easy compromise or social fashion.

In 1967, R.S. Thomas was appointed vicar of Eglwys Hywyn Sant, Aberdaron, a church set on the shore at the tip of the Llŷn peninsula and filled with the sounds of the sea; Thomas seems to have felt it almost as a homecoming: "Years ago...in Manafon, I would look towards the north-west, in the direction of Anglesey and Llŷn, longing for them. And here I am now, having arrived".[17] This new environment, perhaps reviving, too, thoughts of his deceased father, almost inevitably finds expression in the poetry of the late 1960s and early 1970s. The first collection which Thomas published after the move to Aberdaron was *Young and Old* (1972), a volume which has not received much critical attention since it is ostensibly a volume of poems for children.[18] But the volume makes few concessions to the youth of the intended reader either in the bleakness of its vision or, for example, in poems like 'Text', 'Circles', and 'Lost Christmas', in the complexity of its themes; some of the poems had, in fact, previously been published in journals like *Poetry Wales* and *Dublin Magazine* with no indication that these were intended in any way as poems for children.[19]

The twenty-eight poems in the collection include poems entitled 'Boatman', 'Harbour', 'Castaway', 'Seaside', 'The Sea', and, as

John Ward has noted, the sea is a central symbol in the collection.[20] Once again those individuals who battle heroically with the violent moods of the sea are celebrated, as in 'Boatman'(*YO*, 9), here quoted in full:

> A brute and
> Unconscionable. He would beat,
> If he had them, all
> Wives, wallowing in their slopped
> Kisses. Whips are too good
> For such. But when I see
> The waves bucking and how he sits
> Them so, think this man
> A god, deserving the flowers
> The sea women crown him with.

The man is "a brute", capable of violence against women, although the capacity is not acted upon, since he has no wife. Again the women are apparently seen as a potentially disabling distraction from the man's more heroic, self-realising actions, a view endorsed by the weight of "wallowing" and "slopped"; even as the boatman is adjudged "a brute", there is more than a whiff of the misogyny we find in 'Salt' ("Are all women/like this? He said so, that man,/my father, who had tasted their lips'/vinegar, coughing it up/in harbours he returned to with his tongue/ lolling from droughts of the sea").[21] As in 'The Untamed', it would seem that the maintenance of (masculine) integrity involves a hardening of self, a sacrifice of some areas of human feeling. 'Relations' (*YO*, 13), on the other hand, more sensitively engages the issue of human resilience and heroism. The poem again has autobiographical associations, in that the story told appears to concern the death by drowning of one of the poet's father's brothers, a story presumably told by Mr. Thomas.[22] The concern here is, ultimately, with the potential for heroic dignity of even one of "An ordinary lot". While his brothers and sisters live quietly at home, "as though dullness/And nonentity's quietness/Were virtues" after the wild drunkenness of their father (we notice he squanders his money "to drown in drink"), the son, one of the family's seamen, confronts his fate in a manner which is far from ordinary. The rescuers, prevented by the wild sea from approaching the sinking ship, can only watch as

> ...men lined up
> At the rail as the ship foundered,
> Smoking their pipes and bantering. And he
> Was of their company.

The poem ends, however, not with the sailor, but with the poet; in paying tribute to his (unknown) sailor forebear, he implicity measures himself, and his own capacities, against this man who had the inner resources to become more than a "nonentity", to transcend his seeming ordinariness: "his tobacco/Stings my eyes, who am ordinary too".

In 'Young and Old' (*YO*, 7) aircraft "Domesticate the huge sky", but ultimately such attempts at domestication are futile, since in the poem as a whole, as so often in this volume, human endeavour is seen to make little lasting mark on a natural universe which is hostile or at best indifferent to humankind's pretensions to order and control: "The great problems/Remain, stubborn, unsolved./ Man leaves his footprints/Momentarily on a vast shore.//And the tide comes..." Human vulnerability and mortality — we notice the volume's title — are recurrent themes in the book, both in those poems which relate to the sea and those which do not (amongst the latter, 'Sub-Post Office' portrays the plight of an ageing spinster post-mistress, 'Circles' concerns man's dreams of transcending the endless cycle of birth and death, and 'Headline' evokes human violence). In the poetry of the Welsh hill country, as we have seen, time and process are repeatedly imaged in metaphors of tidal erosion; in *Young and Old*, and in the volumes which succeed it, the sea itself becomes the dynamic embodiment of a natural universe which is both beautiful and violently predatory. The sea's "surface/is all flowers, but within are the//grim inmates" ('Fishing', *F*, 11); the sea

> ...scrubs
> And scours; it chews rocks
> To sand;
> ...Mostly
> It is a stomach, where bones,
> Wrecks, continents are digested.
> ('The Sea', *YO*, 28)

The islandmen, "crusted men/Of the sea", carrying their sheep from mainland to island (the poet has in mind, presumably, the small boats plying the dangerous channel between Aberdaron and Bardsey) embody, once more, the resilience and single-mindedness necessary to confront the treacherous uncertainties of the sea:

> They are lean and hard
> And alert, and while our subjects
> Increase, burdening us
> With their detail, these keep to the one
> Fact of the sea, its pitilessness, its beauty.
> ("Islandmen', *YO*, 15)

If the sea emblematises the complexity of the natural universe, "its pitilessness, its beauty", the determined struggle against the sea for survival becomes in R.S. Thomas's poetry in the 1970s and 1980s an image of the necessary resilience of the believer, struggling to maintain his faith in a supposedly loving God who is also capable of creating such a seemingly merciless world. Gazing at the sea at Aberdaron, Thomas seems to confront such issues with a new directness and urgency:

> To him who thinks, there are two aspects to the sea, the outer and the inner. Or if you wish, it is a mirror and a window. In the mirror can be seen all the beauty and glory of the creation: the colours and the shapes of the clouds, with the birds going by on their everlasting journey. But, using it as a window, one sees perpetual warfare, one creature swallowing another, pitilessly and unceasingly. Beneath the deceptively innocent surface, there are thousands of hideous things, like the creator's failed experiments. And through the seaweed as through a forest the seals and the cormorants and the mackerel hunt like rapacious wolves. What sort of God created such a world? A God of love? (*Neb*, 87-8)

Thomas professes to have become "obsessed"[23] with the concept of the sea as mirror and window in the years after his arrival at Aberdaron and not only the repetition of the image but the power with which the horrific visions glimpsed through that window are portrayed suggest the intensity of Thomas's spiritual meditation in this period:

> I am charmed here
> by the serenity of the reflections

> in the sea's mirror. It is a window
> as well. What I need
> now is a faith to enable me to out-stare
> the grinning faces of the inmates of its asylum,
> the failed experiments God put away.
>
> ('Pre-Cambrian', *F*, 23)

That struggle for faith in R.S. Thomas's later poetry is seen as a solitary pilgrimage across a dark landscape of unscalable cliffs, and terrifying abyss across which the lonely believer reaches out, longingly, uncertainly, to a God who, if He exists, is unseen:

> ...leaning far out
> over an immense depth, letting
> your name go and waiting.
>
> ('Waiting', *F*, 32)

> The best journey to make
> is inward...
> For some
> it is all darkness; for me, too,
> it is dark.
>
> ('Groping', *F*, 12)

> Ah,
>
> what balance is needed at
> the edges of such an abyss.
> I am alone on the surface
> of a turning planet. What
>
> to do but, like Michelangelo's
> Adam, put my hand
> out into unknown space,
> hoping for the reciprocating touch?
>
> ('Threshold', *BHN*, 110)[24]

But the central and recurring metaphor for the quest for God, the sometimes desperate struggle to maintain one's faith, is the struggle of the lone voyager against the threatening immensity of the sea. That "immense depth" ('Waiting') is, repeatedly, the vertiginous depth of the sea, "the precipice/of water" ('In Great Waters', *F*, 37) and the drowning which awaits the voyager whose faith fails. Thus, in 'Correspondence' (*BHN*, 85), one of Thomas's bleaker poems of the period, ("You ask why I don't write./But what is there to say?"),

> The waves are a moving staircase
> to climb, but in thought only.
> The fall from the top is as sheer
> as ever.

While in 'Coda'(*LS*, 59) the ocean is

> ...the gallery
> of the drowned, the staircase
> we may not climb.

The pilgrims crossing from Aberdaron to Bardsey thus epitomise the vulnerability of all believers, as they travel in their small boat

> ...the way
> the saints went, travelling the gallery
> of the frightened faces of
> the long-drowned...
> ('Pilgimages', *F*, 51-2)

The God they seek is elusive — "always before us and/leaving as we arrive" — but the real significance of the pilgrimage, the poet suggests, is not the achievement of a vision of God but the assertion of faith that the hazardous journey represents, the effort of overcoming doubt and the arrival at fuller realisation of the nature of God, and of self. The poet's attention moves from the pilgrims' geographical voyage to his own spiritual one:

> Was the pilgrimage
> I made to come to my own
> self...?

'Farming Peter' (*LP*, 64) is reminiscent of Thomas's poetry of the Welsh hill country in that, "deaf" to the scepticism of the great world beyond his fields, "the voices calling from/the high road", the farmer walking the "brown breakers" of the ploughed land remains true to his way of life, to his own vision; the poet links the man's determined faith with that of Simon Peter struggling across the rough surface of the Sea of Galilea, responding faithfully to

Christ's call, in the Gospel of St Matthew (14:24-32):

> ...the man went
> at his call with the fathoms
> under him and because
> of his faith in the creation
> of his own hands he was
> buoyed up floundering
> but never sinking...

'Synopsis' (*F*, 44) connects this image of the lonely figure struggling with his faith over terrifying fathoms to the author whose writing frequently colours the world of R.S. Thomas's later poetry. In a post-Humian, post-Romantic world, we are left with a notion of self stripped of any certainty of a transcendent reality, of any divine order; the self we are left with is

> ...that grey subject
> of dread that Søren Kierkegaard
> depicted crossing its thousands
> of fathoms...

In 'Balance' (*F*, 49) we are again in Kierkegaard's fear-filled universe:

> No piracy, but there is a plank
> to walk over seventy thousand fathoms,
> as Kierkegaard would say, and far out
> from the land. I have abandoned
> my theories, the easier certainties
> of belief. There are no handrails to
> grasp. I stand and on either side
> there is the haggard gallery
> of the dead, those who in their day
> walked here and fell.

For Kierkegaard, authentic existence is derived only from faith born of constant and strenuous spiritual struggle with doubt in a world where nothing is certain; as Walter Lowrie, Kierkegaard's editor and translator, summarises:

> The Christian...has to renounce the comfort of calm assurance bolstered upon objective proofs, and must be content with a fighting

certainty. He constantly lies over a depth of seventy thousand fathoms.[25]

The search for truth, for God, involves risk, confrontation with adversity, anxiety and fear. But individual *faith*, by definition, cannot rest in the safety of objective "proofs":

> The truth is precisely the venture which chooses an objective uncertainty with the passion of the infinite. I contemplate the order of nature in the hope of finding God, and I see omnipotence and wisdom; but I also see much else that disturbs my mind and excites anxiety. The sum of all this is an objective uncertainty...But the above definition of truth is an equivalent expression for faith. Without risk there is no faith. Faith is precisely the contradiction between the infinite passion of the individual's inwardness and the objective uncertainty. If I am capable of grasping God objectively, I do not believe, but precisely because I cannot do this I must believe. If I wish to preserve myself in faith I must constantly be intent upon holding fast the objective uncertainty, so as to remain out upon the deep, over seventy thousand fathoms of water, still preserving my faith.[26]

"Objective thought", based on shared logically- or scientifically-arrived-at "proof", denies authentic selfhood for Kierkegaard: "...objective thought translates everything into results, and helps all mankind to cheat, by copying these off and reciting them by rote".[27] As Ned Thomas has recently pointed out,[28] this is precisely R.S. Thomas's objection to the modern technological world; it is a world which is, like the machines themselves, the product of a limited mind-set, accepting of the banal. The individual is tempted to escape from the stress of imaginative and spiritual striving into the safety of the certain and the proven, but thereby surrenders his/her selfhood, becomes less than fully alive. Ned Thomas refers to Thomas's attack on the "tameness" of technology, a point which takes us back to poems like 'The Untamed' and also to those aircraft in 'Young and Old' seeking to "domesticate" the sky. Ned Thomas quotes 'Calling' (*EA*, 31) in which the poet rejects "that smooth sound that is technology's/purring", technology again being associated with contented domestication (that "smooth" is repeatedly used pejoratively by R.S. Thomas),[29] and is moved to seek contact instead with "the divine/snarl at the perimeter of such tameness".

In contrast to such tameness, Kierkegaard's vision is of a self-hood that is never finite, but in constant process:

> The principle that the existing subjective thinker is constantly occupied in striving, does not mean that he has, in the finite sense, a goal toward which he strives, and that he would be finished when he had reached this goal. No, he strives infinitely, is constantly in process of becoming...This process of becoming is the thinker's own existence...Existence itself, the act of existing, is a striving.[30]

This is a vision of life we have seen become increasingly clearly-focussed in Thomas's own work; its fullest statement, perhaps, comes in his essay 'Abercuawg', first published in 1976. "Abercuawg" is not a place, nor is its vision of purity and natural beauty even an achievable ideal; its value lies in the spiritual and imaginative effort which the individual makes in struggling to achieve the ideal:

> Abercuawg...has to do with the process of becoming...But in accepting the process of becoming, man realises that he is a created being. This is man's estate. He is always on the verge of comprehending God, but insomuch as he is a mortal creature, he never will. Nor will he ever see Abercuawg. But through striving to see it, through longing for it, through refusing to accept that it belongs to the past and has fallen into oblivion; through refusing to accept some second-hand substitute, he will succeed in preserving it as an eternal possibility. (*Prose*, 162, 164)

In its refusal to accept the unimaginative mundanity of the contemporary world, the struggle for intimations of the eternal, of God, is also the stuggle for authenticity of self. "It was never easy", Thomas writes in 'Strands' (*EA*, 32): "There was a part of us,/ trailing uterine/memories, would have lapsed/back into Eden, the mindless/place." The alternatives, though, are more terrifying:

> Must we
> draw back? Is there a far side
> to an abyss, and can our wings
> take us there? Or is man's
> meaning in the keeping of himself
> afloat over seventy thousand
> fathoms, tacking against winds

coming from no direction,
going in no direction?

What is notable is the consistency of the imagery with which R.S.
Thomas has articulated those values to which he gives his pro-
foundest assent: endurance, resilience, the struggle for faith and
authenticity of being. Thus, in a late poem praising the faith of
another of his spiritual heroes, Ann Griffiths, personal associ-
ations are interwoven with Kierkegaardian imagery. The poet
who poignantly remembers his father in his later, domestic years
as "a ship's captain/with no crew, a navigator/without a port"
('Salt'), recalls the sculpture of Ann's head in the Memorial Chapel
at Dolanog[31] as the "figure-head of a ship/outward bound" and
sees her

> like one apprenticed since early
> days to the difficulty of navigation
> in rough seas. She described her turbulence
> to her confessor, who was the more
> astonished at the fathoms
> of anguish over which she had
> attained to the calmness of her harbours.
> ('Fugue for Ann Griffiths', *WA*, 51-2)

Such calmness, though, is rare in R.S. Thomas's own writing; more
usual is the continued, lonely imaginative struggle to remain true
to one's own spritual bearings. "To a hero", he writes, "a/harbour
is that which he sets out/from" ('Selah', *LS*, 49).

Notes

1. 'R.S. Thomas' in Adele Sarkissian, ed., *Contemporary Authors: Autobio-
graphy Series*, vol. 4 (Detroit: Gale Research, 1986), 305.
2. See R.S. Thomas, 'Dylanwadau', *Y Faner* (7 November 1986), 12, and 'Y
Bardd yn erbyn y Byd?' *Golwg* (5 April 1990), 24. C.f. *Neb*, 29. Translations
from the Welsh are my own.
3. 'Dylanwadau', 12.
4. On this point, see Tony Brown, 'Language, Poetry and Silence: Some
Themes in the Poetry of R.S. Thomas', in W.M. Tydeman, ed., *The Welsh
Connection* (Llandysul: Gomer, 1986), 159-64.
5. In *Neb*, 11, R.S. Thomas describes how, in his boyhood at Holyhead,
before a storm the harbour would "fill with sailing ships of all kinds, till

it became more like a forest"; the same image is recalled in *The Echoes Return Slow*, 8.

6. See *Neb*, 91.

7. On the circumstances of Mr. Thomas being sent to sea, see the interview 'Probings', *Planet*, 80 (April/May 1990), 28-9, and *Neb*, 10. *Neb* also reprints a photograph of Mr. Thomas, in Merchant Navy uniform, opposite a photograph of the sea breaking over rocks near Holyhead, a photograph taken by R.S.Thomas when a student. (See also *Contemporary Authors*, 301, 303).

8. One of the poems R.S. Thomas (under the pseudonym 'Curtis Langdon') published in a College magazine while at university in Bangor, 'The Derelict', uses the dereliction of a ship "Far out on Life's cruel sea" as emblematic of moral failure: "There is no helmsman at the stern/To bring the ship safe home to land.../But see, how in the vessel's womb,/Life's scavengers have eaten well,/And in the skipper's dirty room/The ghost of former days might tell/How that his virtues all have fled,/And vices guide his course instead", *Omnibus* (Summer 1934), 80. On the identity of the author, see 'Probings', 30.

9. The poem originally appeared in *Critical Quarterly*, 10 (1968), 10, as 'The Sailors' Hospital, Holyhead — In Memory of my Father'.

10. The poem originally appeared in *Anglo-Welsh Review* in 1973, after the death of the poet's mother. (C.f. *Contemporary Authors*, 311).

11. The episode of the fall from the mast and the weeks of recuperation in Romania echoes the story told in *Neb*, 10, about R.S. Thomas's grandfather.

12. Mrs. Thomas, an orphan, had been brought up by a relative who was an Anglican vicar (*Neb*, 17; *Contemporary Authors*, 302).

13. See *Neb*, 18; *Contemporary Authors*, 302. The striking image in 'The Survivors' describing the seamen straining to hear the sounds of the shore — "The boat became an ear/Straining for the desired thunder/Of the wrecked waves" — perhaps takes on added, and poignant, significance, given that the poet's father may have provided the story.

14. See *Wave*, No. 7 (1973), 36-7. I am grateful to Dr. Sandra Anstey for providing me with the text of this poem.

15. It is clear from *Neb* that the poet's relationship with his mother was a very close one, the father being often away at sea when R.S. Thomas was a boy. He tells of her grief at his leaving home to go to university (*Neb*, 19-20), even accompanying him to Bangor, "ostensibly to see that my lodgings were all right, but really loth to relax her hold until the last minute" (*Contemporary Authors*, 302). See, too, *Neb*, 91-2, and *The Echoes Return Slow*, 14: "He tasted freedom in a parent's absence".

16. 'Agweddau ar farddoniaeth y chwedegau' in M. Wynn Thomas, ed., *R.S. Thomas: Y Cawr Awenydd* (Llandysul: Gomer, 1990), 29. See 'Kierke-

gaard' (*P*, 18-9), and 'A Grave Unvisited' (*NBF*, 9).

17. R.S. Thomas, *Blwyddyn yn Llŷn* (Caernarfon: Gwasg Gwynedd, 1990), 12.

18. *Young and Old* (London: Chatto & Windus, 1972). The volume appeared in a series entitled 'Chatto Poets for the Young'. The cover illustration shows a sailor rowing sturdily towards two fishing boats.

19. 'Castaway' (*YO*, 27) was published in *Dublin Magazine*, 6, Nos. 3/4 (1967), 38-9; 'Headline' (*YO*, 16) in *Poetry Wales* 5, No. 1 (1969), 38; 'Astronauts' in *Critical Quarterly*, 11, No.1 (1969), 6.

20. J.P.Ward, *The Poetry of R.S.Thomas* (Bridgend: Poetry Wales Press, 1987), 136.

21. C.f. also 'Captain Cook's Last Voyage' (*IT*, 46), where the sculpted female torso in the painting apparently represents "...the flesh that is the iceberg/on which we are wrecked".

22. On the identity of "that huge man, their father" and his purchase of a "Welsh hotel", see 'Probings ', 29.

23. *Contemporary Authors*, 311.

24. Interestingly, when reflecting in *Blwyddyn yn Llŷn*, 24-5, on the irrational urge to jump over the edge when walking along cliffs and on societies in which young men are tested by climbing over cliff edges, Thomas thinks of his father as a young man, high in the rigging of a sailing ship in stormy weather.

25. David F. Swenson and Walter Lowrie (trans.), *Kierkegaard's Concluding Unscientific Postscript* (Princeton: Princeton U.P., 1941), xviii. On Thomas and Kierkegaard, see 'R.S.Thomas talks to J.B. Lethbridge', *Anglo-Welsh Review*, No. 74 (1983), 54: "*Concluding Unscientific Postscript*...— every few years it does one good to tackle it, I suppose".

26. *Concluding Unscientific Postscript*, 182.

27. *Concluding Unscientific Postscript*, 68.

28. Ned Thomas, 'R.S.Thomas: The Question about Technology', *Planet*, 92 (April/May 1992), 56-7.

29. See, for example, 'The Fair'(*H'm*, 37), 'Gone?'(*F*, 34), 'Portrait of a Young Woman' (*BHN*, 21), 'Directions' (*BHN*, 81).

30. *Concluding Unscientific Postscript*, 84.

31. A photograph of the sculpture appears as the frontispiece to A.M. Allchin, *Ann Griffiths* (Cardiff: University of Wales Press, 1976).

Walford Davies

Bright Fields, Loud Hills and the Glimpsed Good Place: R.S. Thomas and Dylan Thomas

I

There are moments in poetry when, if we pause, the apple of the poem seems as if bitten into. An inner 'face' reveals the *kind* of poetry it is. Sometimes the poet himself arranges the insight for us. Eliot's Prufrock protests that "It is impossible to say just what I mean!/But as if a magic lantern threw the nerves in patterns on a screen... "[1] and suddenly we see that his odd logic is something the poem itself mimes. Once focused, the lines free us from expecting only *narrative* sense.

As well as interjections there are intersections. James Smith wrote penetratingly of Wordsworth's 'Michael', cutting into it at a mean point:

> The verse of the poem is a delicate thing. It has almost ceased to beat, and seems maintained only by the flutter of tenuous hopes and sickening fears.

> > the unlooked-for claim
> > At the first hearing for a moment took
> > More hope out of his life than he supposed
> > That any old man ever could have lost.

> Wordsworth, who was so often an imitator, here speaks with his own voice; and the verse is the contribution he makes to prosody. [2]

"It has almost ceased to beat": Wordsworth is in any case concerned with stasis ("the stationary blasts of waterfalls", "the central peace subsisting at the heart of endless agitation"), though always sensing "something evermore about to be".[3] R.S.Thomas relishes the same paradox, asking of a changeable landscape "yet

what eye...ever saw/This work and it was not finished?" (*PS*, 27)
— itself the end of a poem about change. What James Smith
crystallises in 'Michael ' is the deep syntax of such watchfulness.

As well as intersections there are recesses. I have in mind a
particular moment in Edward Thomas. And since I want to say
something about the two most Welsh Thomases, this third — more
English, but equally attractive — is welcome. It was Edward
Thomas's *Wales* that started R.S. meditating on the 'Abercuawg'
of the Llywarch Hen cycle — "*Yn Aber Cuawc yt ganant gogeu*" ("In
Abercuawg the cuckoos sing") — a focus for what R.S. calls "the
longing to make the glimpsed good place permanent".[4] Other R.S.
images for the sudden place are less literary: "the bright field", for
example, glimpsed as "the one field that had/the treasure in it"
(*LS*, 60) — Seamus Heaney's "far hill in a freak of sunshine".[5] But
the literary tap-root went deep quickly: it can now be shown that
Edward Thomas's reading in Welsh texts had been specifically
guided by O.M. Edwards.[6]

But first, a *textural* glimpsing. Edward Thomas's 'October' ends:

> But if this be not happiness, who knows?
> Some day I shall think this a happy day,
> And this mood by the name of melancholy
> Shall no more blackened and obscured be.

That final couplet is distinguished poetry. But 'distinguished', not
distinctive, like functional couplets ending scenes in verse-dramas.
("Obscured" almost demands a grave accent — 'obscurèd'.[7]) But
cut off the couplet altogether, and you glimpse an inner texture
that is a better place:

> But if this be not happiness, who knows?
> Some day I shall think this a happy day.

I can't imagine more quintessentially Edward Thomasish lines.
And had they been allowed to *end* the poem, their simple tremor
— characterful, not just characteristic — would sink even more
resonant wells into Aeneas's words in the *Aeneid*:

> *forsan et haec olim meminisse iuvabit*
> ["Maybe some day one shall be glad to remember even these
> things"].[8]

R.S. Thomas and Dylan Thomas

Suddenly revealed is a heart-breaking signature.

II

Well then, what would represent quintessential R.S., unmistak-
able Dylan? My ultimate question is what it *means* to see R.S. as
Dylan's 'successor' as the premier English-language poet of
Wales. No amount of theorising will confuse them. R.S. has long
since developed a line in anti-South-Walian 'asides', even think-
ing fate that the Welsh he learned was not *South* Wales Welsh (*Neb*,
40). Anyone comparing the two is like the charioteer R.S. cites
from Plato's *Phaedrus* — one who has "an ill-assorted pair of horses
bridled together" (*Prose*, 64). An ideologically more agreeable
mantle fell to R.S., across the language-divide, from Saunders
Lewis. Even in 1946, he felt that "the mantle of writers like T.
Gwynn Jones and W.J. Gruffydd is falling not upon the younger
Welsh writers, but upon those of us who express ourselves in the
English tongue" (*Prose*, 31) — a pre-emptive Anglo-Welsh strike
if I ever saw one! The Thomasite 'succession' is therefore one of
chronology, not lineage. (Stylistically, Ted Hughes and Sylvia
Plath are more obvious inheritors.) And yet, if 'Welshness' of any
kind is involved, might not lineage, too, come into play? I person-
ally agree with R.S. that the glimpsed good place deserving per-
manence is Welsh Wales. But by allowing contrasts to arise first
from actual texts, we allow different voices to be heard. A good
thing, for the isle is full of noises.

But 'representativeness' is harder to agree on in Dylan than in
R.S. In terms of theme, it is R.S. who can — even while emphasis-
ing consistency — boast variety:

> ...for many years I have always been concerned with certain themes.
> Anyone who has read any of my work will know the sort of themes
> which preoccupy me — the hill country of Wales; the Welsh political
> and social existence; the natural world; the struggle between time
> and eternity; the struggle between the reason and the emotions.
> (*Prose*, 109)

Dylan, too, reflects these themes (yes, even "Welsh political and
social existence"!), but no theme disguises his one irremovable
song: man's foreshortened view of life as life-and-death. On the

other hand, *style* in Dylan varies more than has been recognised
from early to middle to late. Only at a level *beyond* style does
'Should lanterns shine' (1934) dovetail with 'There was a saviour'
(1940) or 'In the White Giant's Thigh' (1950) — even though the
very dates remind us that the career closed at the age of thirty-
nine. R.S. speaks often of changes in his material, but has no
equivalent to Yeats's 'A Coat ' or Dylan's 'Once it was the colour
of saying ', poems marking a mid-career shift in *style*. Even then,
there is the difference between 'characteristic ' Dylan and, say, the
political 'The hand that signed the paper', the realistic 'Paper and
Sticks', or the Yeatsian 'Do not go gentle into that good night' —
poems that have about them a deftly 'borrowed' power.

Without any break from the tone and timbre of the pentameter
blank-verse or stanzaic forms of his earliest poems, R.S. quickly
developed a sinuous short-lined free-verse that has relayed a
recognisable voice from the 1940s into the 1990s. It is close to the
natural voice of the man himself. ("To live in Wales is to be
conscious..." is how, in an interview, R.S. commented even on
Welsh weather.[9]) But it can also be heard in — even sculpted out
of — his prose:

> Some days
> you can't see them.
> The eye bumps into
> black cloud, low down.
> Nearer there is
> the sound of water,
> tumbling from wet heights.
> There is no light, no colour;
> only grey and green,
> and the wind blowing.
> A sheep's cry falls
> Like a stone.
>
> But suddenly
> the sun is switched on,
> and the valley is full
> of golden leaves
> like a tree undressing.
> There are clear days, too;
> the cloud's masonry
> piled up untidily

above the honeyed mountains,
the long slopes bruised with shadow. (*Prose*, 97)

Those are seven unchanged sentences from R.S.'s essay, 'The Mountains', itself very much concerned with glimpsed good places. Opening run-on lines in lower-case (unimaginable to Dylan) might suggest R.S.'s later mode, but this 1968 prose could slide either way along his poetic career. *The Echoes Return Slow* (1988) even flaunts the homogeneity, alternating cryptic prose with actual poems. This natural nearness of prose to poetry (and the potential undressing of the poetry into prose) is an index of the kind of poet he is. We recall that Edward Thomas first consciously became a poet when Robert Frost persuaded him that potential poems already lay folded in the rhythms and images of his prose.[10] Eliot said that "the moment the intermediate term *verse* is suppressed, I do not believe that any distinction between prose and poetry is meaningful".[11] Poetry is a way of seeing as well as of organising

Dylan's prose, too, is a redaction of his poetry, even changing from early surrealism to late descriptiveness in parallel ways. But, compulsively a high-definition performer, he obviously felt guiltier than R.S. about fudged borders. "When you are young," he said, "you are liable to write this bastard thing, a prose-poetry".[12] He was probably thinking of things like this:

> But on the bent grass in the seventh shade, his first terror of her sprang up again like a sun returning from the sea that sank it, and burned his eyes to the skull and raised his hair. The stain on her lips was blood, not berries; and her nails were not broken but sharpened sideways...[13]

The guilt highlights two crucial aspects of Dylan's art: the fulsomeness causing the fudging in the first place, and his delight in redeeming the seepage with heavily-crafted structures that, even across the same textures, lift the poems away from the prose.

But Eliot and Pound held that poetry "must be at least as well written as prose", that "to have the virtues of good prose is the first and minimum requirement of good poetry".[14] And in that this meant the promotion of spare forms and clear lines of 'statement', R.S. is obviously closer than baroque Dylan to Eliot's and

Pound's doctrine of "purify[ing] the dialect of the tribe"[15] — itself paradoxical since Modernism also went in for obscurity, obscurantism even. R.S. has described this verbal chasteness as, in his case, the deliberate expression of his own personality and of the landscape of Wales.[16] But it also reflects his hope that Arnold's vague talk of the 'magic' in Celtic literature might be replaced by Sir Idris Bell's perception of its "precision of utterance" (*Prose*, 52). An outside measure of the stringency is R.S.'s rejection (despite their "particularly moving effect") of the dialect words of his first parishes on the Welsh border: his examples are *nesh, feg, sniving* and *mixen* (*Prose*, 75). Geoffrey Hill or Seamus Heaney would have drawn them in — just as Dylan absorbed, say, *mitching, dingle*, or *gambo*. R.S. likes the mystery of how words come to name particular things, but holds back from applying such interests. As Donald Davie might put it, certain words "are thrusting at the poem and being fended off from it".[17]

This is neither accolade nor condemnation. But since I've raised Modernism's aim of 'purifying the dialect of the tribe' — Celtic Yeats "walking naked",[18] trans-Atlantic Eliot courting "the word neither diffident nor ostentatious"[19] — I must add that it was Dylan who was really Modernism's legatee. R.S.'s early 'Border Blues' certainly owes its mythopoeic time-shifts, mixed social tones and macaronic quotations to Eliot's *The Waste Land*, and its frenetic tone to 'Triumphal March':

> *Eryr Pengwern, penngarn llwyt heno...*
> We still come in by the Welsh gate, but it's a long way
> To Shrewsbury now from the Welsh border.
> There's the train, of course, but I like the 'buses;
> We go each Christmas to the pantomime. (*PS*, 10)

(Imagine cutting into *that*!) But, apart from isolated examples elsewhere of Imagism or dislocated syntax, it is a solitary instance. Its Modernist ventriloquialism was already passé, and stifled effects closer to R.S.'s real power, even within the same poem — the subtle evocation of Pwyll, for example, in the lines "I once heard footsteps in the leaves..." (*PS*, 12). Like *The Waste Land*'s sidelong glimpse of Christ on the road to Emmaus,[20] these more delicate coat-trailings make foreign gobbets seem thick-ankled. Anticipating Larkin's attack on Modernism's "myth-kitty",[21] R.S.

said that "there can be none of this macaronic nonsense in the writing of English poetry, *pace* Ezra Pound, and to a lesser extent T. S. Eliot. One must take the words as one finds them, and make them sing" *(Prose*, 81). But singing, presumably, certain songs. R.S.'s Welsh shifted from macaronic effect to ideological matrix.

Even in 1946 he praised contemporary Scottish writing (led by Hugh MacDiarmid) above leaderless Anglo-Welsh writing, "limping along in the rear of Eliot, Auden, and company limited" *(Prose*, 29). R.S.'s mistrust of Modernism's Babel-allusiveness places him with Dylan, the other side from David Jones. But how guilty he must think Dylan's delight in Modernism's other faith — the flight from statement into irreducible image (" 'Image, all image,' cried Marlais"[22]). Of course, all poetry is an image-making power, even for R.S. — "What I've always tried to produce is imagery. People don't give two hoots for it today".[23] But R.S.'s procedure was never really that of argument through images. It was always that of a "man speaking to men", in "language really used by men",[24] aims as Wordsworthian as Prytherch himself. Again, all this is neither praise nor blame. But we should bear in mind that if R.S. called to his side the concept of 'purifying the dialect of the tribe' — a style as clear as the messages he wanted to sing — Dylan appealed to the tradition of Keats, Tennyson and Hopkins. These poets, too, had discussable themes, but activated texture, music, and visible form at much deeper tangents to 'meaning'. If the unit is that of single words, relished in ways determining all larger structures, for Dylan their succulence is that of fruits, for R.S. that of pebbles.

III

The slim-line and the orotund are equally open to parody. So let's approach our 'representative' quotations at that angle. Slavish imitation we can set aside: younger Anglo-Welsh poets whom we don't re-read tend to be archly Dylanist or dryly R.S. Thomasish because without powerful things of their own to say. But intelligent parody is a good threshold. In 'A Letter to my Aunt', Dylan obliged us by satirising himself ("Do not forget that 'limpet' rhymes/With 'strumpet' in these troubled times..."[25]). But parody is best left to others. Dylan's contemporary, C. Day Lewis, evoked Verrocchio' s painting, *Boy with Dolphin*, with this:

> At the crack of spring on the tail of the cold,
> When foam whipped over the apple tree aisles
> And the grape skin sea swelled and the weltering capes were
> bold,
> I went to school with a glee of dolphins
> Bowling their hoops round the brine-tongued isles
> And singing their scales were tipped by a sun always
> revolving.[26]

In execution it is not a *coup de grâce*. Those "isles", for example (when Dylan meant 'islands' he *wrote* 'islands'), or the rhythmic nullity of that last line. But Day Lewis at least reminds us of Keats and Hazlitt's main criterion, sheer gusto.[27]

What parody can't reflect, however, is that orotundity is often willing to do its own blushing. 'After the funeral', suddenly seeing itself as "a monstrous image blindly/Magnified out of praise", contracts to the austerity of its last fourteen lines — giving them (like the last fifteen of 'In the White Giant's Thigh') the straitened impact of a sonnet. My 'representative' Dylan excerpt, therefore, is when 'Especially when the October wind' tightens its celebration of "the loud hill of Wales" into this:

> Shut, too, in a tower of words, I mark
> On the horizon walking like the trees
> The wordy shapes of women, and the rows
> Of the star-gestured children in the park.
> Some let me make you of the vowelled beeches,
> Some of the oaken voices, from the roots
> Of many a thorny shire tell you notes,
> Some let me make you of the water' s speeches.

"Shut, too": it is the very syntax of enclosure — but emphasising ladenness, as if from the heart of a ritual. The half-rhyme frees "rows" to mean *quarrels* as well as *lines*, even though the half-rhymes themselves are straitened into 'couplets' within the banks of full rhymes. We remember that it was the blind man healed by Christ who said "I see men as trees, walking",[28] and sense a tragic filament from the vivid "star-gestured" children (arms-and-legs outstretched) to Shakespeare's "star-crossed lovers".[29] As a merely visual conceit, "the wordy shapes of women" on the horizon are like R.S.'s "the birds' italics speckle the distance" (*Prose*, 104). But it is at a deeper level that poets know the indivisibility of thing and word. Dylan records that "When I experience anything, I experience it as a thing and a word at the same time",[30] and R.S. even specifies the problem of nominalism and universals involved: "Have you tried looking at a tree, a flower or a bird without its name echoing somewhere within you?" (*Prose*, 70). Of course, the teenage Dylan was also nudging the Symbolist notion that "the loud hill of Wales" might be evoked with *no* gap between word and thing: our stanza shows the depth of his Modernist affiliation. But above all it reminds us why the word 'poet' — unlike 'novelist' or 'dramatist' — remains unsecularised. Even so, the stanza is self-possessed, not possessed, and the ironic 'Shell-Guide-to-the-Countryside' note of a phrase like "thorny shire" shows the poetry's wry ability to deflate itself even as it moots the possibility of replacing Wales with language. Parody could hardly capture such things.

But if the orotund can blush while prevailing, the astringent can resonate while turning away. A classic satire of our time is John Davies's 'How to Write Anglo-Welsh Poetry':

> Now you can go on about the past
> being more real than the present —
> you've read your early R.S.Thomas,
> you know where Welsh Wales went.[31]

This stands off from the actual *feel* of the original, rocking against it — inviting, but declining, imitation. I'm even sure that, given the government's subsequent ugly neglect of the Welsh Valleys, John Davies would no longer choose to satirize "Valley Characters, the heart's dust/and the rest". But equally sobering is the superb R.S. poem that Davies's stanza specifically rocks against:

> To live in Wales is to be conscious
> At dusk of the spilled blood
> That went to the making of the wild sky,
> Dyeing the immaculate rivers
> In all their courses.
> It is to be aware,

Above the noisy tractor
And hum of the machine
Of strife in the strung woods,
Vibrant with sped arrows.
You cannot live in the present,
At least not in Wales.
There is the language for instance,
The soft consonants
Strange to the ear.
There are cries in the dark at night
As owls answer the moon,
And thick ambush of shadows. (*SYT*, 63)

"Ambush" is just right: the poem has a newcomer's sense of danger, a latecoming that evokes also the moveable priest. But it's a stance that also does some sniping of its own. No more than my re-alineation of R.S.'s prose above could imitation preserve the "thick ambush" of such lines. If Dylan's expansiveness suddenly implodes, we shouldn't assume that he didn't know, and regularly use, that fact. Nor should we assume that R.S. doesn't know exactly where his crystal voice gains viscous power. Free verse tends towards weightlessness, but R.S. avoids slighting the resonance of language. The way, for example, that first line-break allows us to hear that "To live in Wales is to be conscious" — period; for "to be conscious is not to be in time".[32] (Anyone doubting how consciously R.S.'s sense pauses while crossing his line-breaks should read 'Making' (*H'm*, 17), a veritable exercise in stop-go.) Or take that nicely judged tautology: "cries in the dark at night". It combines the challenge (the *cries at night*) of a small nation's history with its vulnerability (the *crying in the dark*). The lines also remind us of R.S.'s belief that "there is a peculiar charm in the echo of a delayed rhyme, as it comes back from a word occurring perhaps several lines later than the original word" (*Prose*, 72). The reader can test how it is possible (the intervening lines notwithstanding because not withstanding) to hear the echo — neither just rhyme nor just assonance — from "arrows" to "shadows". The cadence throws a weight on the two words that the controlled litheness of the intervening seven lines doesn't quite obliterate — though seven lines are a long time in poetry. Such echoes confirm the timbre of the poem as "strung woods,/Vibrant", not "the carcase of an old song" — the accusation thrown out against the limp Welsh world at the poem's end.

IV

Whether vatic ("Some let me make you...") or diagnostic ("There is no present in Wales..."), both poets "learn a style from a despair"[33] and set it defensively over against the Wales inherited. (Even the Dylan poem has the sublimated background of the teenager's dislike of the smug Swansea passing his window.) Behind texture, therefore, lies context, varying according to whether it is 'this world of Wales' or the more deeply cultural 'matter of Wales' that is involved. But Anglo-Welsh 'succession' is also problematic in simpler ways. In England, a native lineage of, say, Hardy — Housman — Edward Thomas — Wilfred Owen — Graves — Auden — Larkin is possible because a varied enough number of poets provides a matrix that can leave 'succession' to qualitative shakedown. Wales just doesn't have that choice-from-numbers, that visibility on a world stage. Of course, neither is the above list purely English — but it remains that Dylan's early celebrity over Offa's Dyke and overseas normalised the advantage of having attractive clout beyond. In that respect, R.S. is certainly Dylan's natural successor.

And yet the 'succession' has a chronological oddness about it, and not only because of Dylan's early death. This 80th birthday reminds us that R.S. was actually a year older than the Rimbaud of Cwmdonkin Drive. It was the different chronology of a precocious adolescence that forced Dylan's poetry to emerge — incunabula and all — under the aegis of Modernism in the early 1930s. Our sense of R.S. is of the cool commentator — no juvenilia — sprung to our attention fully-armed with a Classics degree and a parish in the 1950s. We salute Alan Pryce-Jones's taste in lauding *An Acre of Land* (Newtown, 1952) on radio that year.[34] Exactly *when* R.S. claimed attention is important. Even given his earlier publication of twenty-one poems since 1939 in *The Dublin Magazine*, and though *The Stones of the Field* (Carmarthen, 1946) heralded his potential, the portent of his future impressiveness was still low beyond the horizon at Dylan's death in 1953. In contrast, Dylan had not only been recognised by the wartime Philip Larkin of *The*

North Ship (1945) as the epitome (with Eliot and Auden) of a poet "speaking out loud and clear",[35] but ten years earlier had published, in his early twenties, two London volumes which the Yeats of the 1936 *Oxford Book of Modern Verse* must have had to shut his eyes to ignore — ignoring in the process the poet who later most intelligently manifested Yeats's own influence.

But *The Stones of the Field* and *An Acre of Land* did overlap with Dylan. This usefully reminds us that R.S.'s stylistic stringency was not a redress, that it wasn't an early Welsh version of the anti-Dylan Welfare-State Augustanism of the English 'Movement' poets of the 1950s. Edward Lucie-Smith's view that Dylan was "Modernism making its last, baroque gestures before the reaction against it set in"[36] shows how myopically English the baroque gestures of such views are. They can't imagine that Dylan might also have been writing out of an alternative culture. Anyway, "last gestures" hardly measures a poet whom half the world still talks about forty years after his death. However much R.S. represents poetry come down off its stilts, he himself ungrudgingly placed Dylan with Joyce and Hopkins as one of the "chief influences of English literature...over the last half-century" (*Prose*, 52). What the reaction of the English poets of the 1950s showed was an envious *English* need to get out from under such influences! That those influences were so often Celtic shows that the difference between Dylan and R.S. was radical, not reactionary, reflecting different views of poetry-in-English *within Wales*. Quite apart from a style's potential to be, inter-culturally, the end or beginning of anything, it can be, within its own culture, an alternative. R.S. is Wales's own, out-of-synch 'Movement'!

This in-house version (neither Modernist nor just Fiftyish) of 'purifying the dialect of the tribe', when coupled with the need to save a language dearer to him than the English of his poems, makes R.S. easier to place in time than Dylan. Ideologically he stems from the renewed Welsh-language confidence — that refusal to be a victim — that, from roots in the Welsh 1930s, blossomed anew in the 1960s. Dylan's poetry (unlike his prose) is less easily contextualized. This is because of the at-an-angle way in which it manifests, not only its Welshness, but its very times. Two world wars helped shape both poets. But for R.S. the 'scorched earth' of war is subject, not image: "you waited till the ground was

cool,/The enemy gone, and led your cattle/To the black fields"
(*T*, 10). Compare the idea of crossing enemy lines in Dylan's image
of incarnation: "And flesh was snipped to cross the lines/Of
gallow crosses on the liver...".[37] Even while deftly forging the
Marxist fingerprints of the English 1930s — in the metaphor of the
dole-queue, for example,

> On no work of words now for three lean months in the bloody
> Belly of the rich year...[38]

or the Audenesque Secret-State of "pursed lips at the receiver"[39]
— Dylan always impressively resisted the *de rigeuur* contempo-
raneity of that low dishonest decade. And something deep in his
resistance was also Welsh. We must pursue it, for I think R.S. was
completely off the mark when he said "There's nothing Welsh
about Dylan Thomas except that he knew his Bible".[40]

V

Our comparisons were bound to anchor, not just in Welshness, but
in *Welsh*, the language of the first place. Compensating the concave
of English fame is the deep convex of the Welshness R.S. reclaimed
by learning the language itself. There was a time when a com-
promising Anglo-Welshness in him was ascendant. And here it is
worth remembering that no 'Anglo-Welsh' solidarity sustained
the young Dylan in his first flowering to 1934 — so different from
the burgeoning Anglo-Irish situation of that period, with the
towering examples of Yeats, Joyce and Shaw, and the founding of
the Irish Academy of Letters in 1932. Out of a relative vacuum, the
Swansea poet had had to make himself *individually* audible — and
to a London the governing wisdom of which was, as V.S. Pritchett
recorded, that regionalism was dead.[41] By the mid-1940s, how-
ever, Dylan was himself central to an Anglo-Welsh confidence
that succoured also a new Welsh-*language* pride. Even so, the R.S.
of that period, though sharply nationalistic, stressed that "the
muse is not to be browbeaten into singing an accompaniment to
an ideology" (*Prose*, 34). It's a view so different from his later
confession to being "guilty of propaganda" (*Prose*, 109) — though
R.S. never betrayed what he calls (echoing Yeats's "the Muses'

sterner laws"[42]) "the poem's/Harsher conditions" (*NBF*, 26). Even more oddly, in 1946 R.S. was conceding that Wales faced the danger, not of "the disappearance of Welsh, but of its inadequacy as a medium for expressing the complex phantasmagoria of modern life" (*Prose*, 38). He would now not even dream such concessions!

But, then, R.S. is no longer a 'learner'. He is one of our sharpest Welsh stylists in prose and conversation, with an alert (not just 'alerted') love of the history sleeping in his nation's words: in a Seamus Heaney phrase, an inwardness with "the musk of their meaning".[43] This is literary history in the grain of the language. When an English person "hears the cuckoo", Heaney says, "he may well not only hear its bare and beautiful music but unconsciously his pleasure in those notes may be sustained by the mediaeval poet's delight who wrote and sang 'Summer is icumen in, lhude sing cuckoo'".[44] R.S. would counter(point) with "*Yn Aber Cuawc yt ganant gogeu* — In Abercuawg the cuckoos sing". And yet R.S. says he cannot write poetry in his reclaimed Welsh because his reach in it exceeds his grasp — a stunning measure of the depth at which real poetry works. It is a loss R.S. describes as "the creative writer's suicide" (*Prose*, 169), a too long divorce of his talents from the language to whose service he now dedicates them. It is the first things that go in deepest.

In this way, the Welsh language itself — which Dylan did not speak — is a catalyst. We have, in a sense, three models. One is the native Welsh speaker who simply chooses to write in English; the second is R.S. himself, who writes in English but with a daily world-view refracted through the Welsh learnt in adult life; the third is that in which Yeats boasted Gaelic as his "national" language even while English was his only tongue.[45] But a fourth variant is *any* poet who magnetizes instinctively — not proprietorially, like Yeats — towards an identity sensed behind the language lost. Personally, I think Dylan was of that category, one who, in Seamus Heaney's words from a related context, "feels a pain of loss, of separation from the original place".[46] His parents, both first-language Welsh speakers, denied him that birthright. His English-Master father felt, in the 1910s and '20s, that the signposts to a successful career were in English. In particular we should ponder the fact that that withholding father, a natural scholar in Welsh as well as in English, went out to teach Welsh to adults in evening classes.[47] First things go in deepest; but in a bilingual situation we may not know even which the first things are. That closeness-to-home of the language of a lost place, and the very smart of its loss, surely went deeper even than knowledge of the Bible, however familiar Welshmen feel Bethel and Bethesda to be. (Even if only an analogy, Dylan's densest poems have the attractive register of a voice heard across a language divide. Who knows what determines these things?) I can certainly imagine its opposite: that, given that *no* Welsh language reached R.S. through familial ties — not even a sense of its loss — the uncompromised English that went in first in his case went in really deep.

The depth is there in the elegance with which, compared to Dylan, he takes the English language for granted. It is ironic that he proclaimed Edwin Muir to be, not Scottish, but a poet "decidedly in the manner of English philosophical poetry" (*Prose*, 32). Linguistically, that is how R.S. himself appears. For example, I cannot imagine Dylan so unselfconsciously coming up with the word "deciduous" — "the lament of/The poets for deciduous language" (*H'm*, 22), or "pleach" — "To pleach his dreams with his rough hands" (*PS*, 23). Or "immaculate" —

> Dyeing the immaculate rivers
> In all their courses. (*SYT*, 63)

(In his reading of this last poem on record one shouldn't miss, either, R.S.'s immaculately English enunciation of "tractor".[48]) Such relaxed inwardness contrasts markedly with Dylan's reached-for vocabulary (*altarwise, parhelion, Christ-cross-row*), his boosted adjectives (*mussel pooled, heron priested*), his shuffled idioms (*the man in the wind and the west moon, wild boys innocent as strawberries, once below a time*[49]) and his own, obviously adopted, 'cut-glass' accent, betrayed only by its short 'a's'. These arch locutions, regularly stretched across daunting formal structures, blazon an essentially 'outsider' relationship to the English imagination, a high-definition performance that takes out very different patents on the dialect of the tribe.

"Twixt devil and deep sea, man hacks his caves".[50] Empson's line always reminds me of Dylan's formal energy — and its compensatory motives . But this is not limited to Dylan. R.S. has said "I feel now, in middle life [1969], that it is the actual *craft* of poetry which is important" (*Prose*, 111), adding that it is a Welsh bulwark against English 'fashion'. And in craft, of course, R.S. recognises a higher sacrifice. In George Herbert's 'Easter', that most musical of poets saw the tuning and playing of his lute as a figuring of Calvary. R.S. makes the same connection while watching, close up, Kreisler's passion on the violin:

> So near that I could see the toil
> Of his face muscles, a pulse like a moth
> Fluttering under the fine skin...
> This player who so beautifully suffered
> For each of us upon his instrument...
> Making such music as lives still.
> And no one daring to interrupt
> Because it was himself that he played
> And closer than all of them the God listened. (*T*, 19)

The idea that "the God listened" shows the mark of R.S.'s favourite theologian, Kierkegaard: "God sits in heaven and listens... 'That is the right note!' He says, 'Here it is!' ".[51] And at this point one shouldn't forget sacrifices that also take poets *away from* their craft: Dylan's sacrifice of personal survival; the sacrifice R.S. saw in Saunders Lewis's deliberately leaving "unfulfilled his early promise as a poet in order to try to avert...national extinction" (*Prose*, 35); R.S.'s own 'creative writer's suicide'; even his meticulous omission of the Kreisler poem from his *Later Poems* because its suggestion that no one dared interrupt the crucifixion was just not true of that noisy affair.[52] Who knows how morally deserving *any* sacrifices are?

But craft as the welcoming of formal obstacles is in R.S. exquisitely micro not macro: "I believe that the inner ear which goes into operation as the eye runs along a line of poetry is more delicate and subtle than the outer ear" (*Prose*, 111). In the lines about Kreisler, for example, the phrase "as lives still" —

> Making such music as lives still —

is as superior to the easier *as still lives* as Hamlet's "so long life" is to the more elegant *so long a life* —

There's the respect
That makes calamity of so long life.[53]

They are what Yeats would call "words often commonplace made unforgettable by some trick of speeding and slowing".[54] The trick also gives R.S.'s "still" (glinting between adverb and adjective, mixing memory and desire) the ambiguous stasis of the "still unravished bride" of Keats's Grecian Urn, the "stillness" of Eliot's "chinese jar".[55] It is a defter touch than R.S.'s talk elsewhere of the "stillness/about certain Ming vases" (*LS*, 44). Given our link between craft and sacrifice, such care over one word confirms Wallace Stevens's point that the "slightest sound matters. The most momentary rhythm matters. You can do as you please, yet everything matters".[56]

Yet even if Dylan's raids on English are larger, more external, there remain Welshnesses that just do not surface in that way. Nigel Jenkins can only call R.S.'s Welshness "spectral" by adding, "subject matter apart".[57] But setting apart so much subject, so much matter, just isn't possible. For example, despite his increasing mysticism, R.S. never escaped a deep need to measure his cool Anglicanism against the zeal of Nonconformity, even graduating his response from early jibe (extravagantly projecting Nonconformity as "Protestantism — the adroit castrator/Of art" [*SYT*, 92]) to middle-phase sneaking respect ("narrow but saved/in a way that men are not now" [*LS*, 19]) to his late amending homage to Ann Griffiths as the embodiment of the moment when Nonconformist Wales superseded Anglican vision (*WA*, 50). No priest was ever more significantly employed by 'The Church *in Wales*'. Or take 'Traeth Maelgwn' (*NBF*, 20): is it understandable at all without knowing its Welsh equivalent to the Canute myth? Or consider the subject matter 'set aside' that caused R.S. to correct one critic that the "namesake" of William Morgan in 'Llanrhaeadr ym Mochnant' (*NBF*, 21) was the fourth-century Pelagius, not the seventeenth-century pirate, Henry Morgan.[58] Deeper still, you sense what the moving love poem, 'The Way of It' ("If there are thorns/in my life, it is she who/will press her breast to them and sing" [*LP*, 91]) owes to Alun's 'Cathl i'r Eos': "Ac os bydd pigyn dan dy fron/Yn peri i'th galon guro,/Ni wnei, nes torro'r wawrddydd hael,/Ond canu, a gadael iddo".[59] One should never take substantive Welshness for granted. It can cross linguistic, not just geographic, borders. Wherever it is only cosy 'subject matter' it is regional, not national.

It was more complicated in Dylan, too, than celebrating specific parks, farms and estuaries. Whether in the line "When I whistled with *mitching* boys through a reservoir park", the custom and ceremony of the charabanc outing of 'A Story' and the "stuffed fox and stale fern" of 'After the funeral', the immemorial *gambo* harvests of 'Fern Hill' and 'In the White Giant's Thigh', or Carmarthenshire's marine landscapes — I wouldn't feel confident in separating freight from vehicle in any of them. More important, the worlds enshrined in such icons, cameos and vistas were *Welsh-language* worlds that the poet was conscious of glamourising in English. R.S. makes these part of a further *self*-consciousness — as in his recent tribute to "the *'gambo'* and the *'car llusg'*".[60] Both poets are sad historians of the pensive plain.

Unfortunately, today's case for a non-Welsh-speaking Welshness dangerously ignores that original language at the heart of the glimpsed good place. It is not whether today's non-Welsh-speaking Welshman is Welsh. Of course he is. The significance of R.S. is that he realised the frightening degree to which non-Welsh-speakers *within even earshot* of the core voice have thinned out since Dylan's filial proximity. The question is, will our great-great-grand-children be Welsh — after the death of the language, and the erosion of even the accent? It would be nice to think an 'otherness' will survive, shortening the passage through the post-imperial problems of a featureless 'British' identity. But the argument that, even with loss of the Gaelic languages, the demise of that 'otherness' hasn't happened in Ireland or Scotland dangerously ignores the preserving effect of distance in those cases. In Wales, we face an infinitely closer border. Even then, we're not talking mere strategy. A Biblical verse particularly dear to R.S. is "The Lord did not set his love upon you, nor choose you, because ye were more in number than any people; for ye were the fewest of all people".[61] The poet I respect in R.S. is the poet demanding long vistas.

Geographic vistas shape the very migrations of our two poets. Relevant here is the demographic forecast for the Welsh language. On the human geographer's skeletal maps, curved lines of retreat step westwards — in fact, being curved, *north*-westwards. The geographer's phrase is "the retreating frontier".[62] It is at that exact border of the Welsh language's century-long decline that 'quantification' is most difficult. I would also argue that it is at the same border that the penultimate stand of a characterful non-Welsh-speaking nationhood has always been made, as if a deep instinct sought to renew strength along lines of stress and fracture. The 'retreat' is of Anglo-Welsh, not just Welsh, identity. It is here that Dylan and R.S. most intimately meet. When Brecon's Welsh-speaking Henry Vaughan achieved London recognition in the seventeenth century, the border was literal, dividing Wales and England as well as Welsh and English. (I leave aside the sobering fact that the provenance of the earliest Welsh verse of all — Taliesin and Aneirin — was what is now southern Scotland and northern England!) When Dylan first opened his eyes on Swansea, the language border ran straight through that "ugly, lovely town".[63] It even marked his parents' house, in Swansea's Uplands, as being "the uglier side of a hill",[64] the other side of which was the Fern Hill country of Welsh-language West-Wales whose very people had at the turn of the century fed the industrial, Anglicising grind of the south-east. After 1938, heartened by London acclaim from the east, Swansea's Dylan moved — westwards. In being drawn to Laugharne, he may have been susceptible to what R.S. sees as landscape's emptier charms: "What is Wales to England after all but a kind of western county that is not worth bothering about apart from its scenery and its natural resources? Wild Wales! Yes, but it all resides in the landscape" (*Prose*, 37). Yet the literature Laugharne produced in Dylan feels like an atavistic return to first places. Anyway, the outsiderness of its approach to the English language was forged long before that retreat west. The America that finally tempted him even further west didn't know that this poetic voice that seemed, not idly 'alternative', but the very *fons et origo*, had been tempered at the linguistic geographer's "retreating frontier".

R.S.'s migrations show an even clearer inverse-trajectory. Raised as a boy on Anglesey, he felt, on reaching Aberdaron in 1967, that he had reached more than a last parish. The third-person narrative of his autobiography deepens our sense of the inexorable. He had "returned to the very source of his personal pilgrimage" (*Neb*, 85). "If you took a map of Wales, it would be easy to trace his geographic journey from his period as a child on Anglesey to that of the old man in Lleyn" (*Neb*, 86). And at this point R.S. uses — not the vague cliché of things coming full circle — but the literal oval of his career: "*Ffurfiodd ryw fath o hirgylch*" — "It formed some kind of oval" (*Neb*, 86). A recent interview with Jim Walsh, the octogenarian Irish writer now living in Wales after America, and insisting on Welsh lineage, shows how older waves fold behind the sweep of this vanishing frontier. "Looking back on things now," Walsh says, "I suspect my whole life's journey has been a moving towards Wales".[65] Even the young R.S. had no idea where his final pole lay, and certainly did not feel its Welsh-language magnet. But the completion of the 'oval' in his pastoral movement from Chirk to Hanmer to Manafon to Eglwys-fach to Aberdaron to Rhiw personalises a retreat. Obscurely cultural strings are touched even when R.S. notes that the kite, reduced by 1900 to three or four pairs in the Welsh highlands, had been a very common bird in the England of the Middle Ages (*Neb*, 63). But nothing shows more clearly how the frontier held him like a dream than his recurrent nightmare of finding his own migration reversed, and himself back in Manafon. "Mysterious the ways of the man lodged within me," he says, "but how frighteningly real!"[66]

VI

Pained strategic withdrawal fits our view of R.S.'s poetry because the poetry's own view — moral and geographic — has always had about it the hauteur of the eyrie. "Too far for you to see" is the refrain in one of his finest early poems, 'The Welsh Hill Country'. But anyone thinking the perspective callous has missed R.S.'s tone of stunned admiration:

> There's a man still farming at Ty'n-y-Fawnog. (*SYT*, 46)

If you ask of such a line, 'How does it go?', you discover a tone of amazement that in 'The Airy Tomb' is spelt out:

> No, no, you must face the fact
> Of his long life alone in that crumbling house. (*SYT*, 41)

The final line of 'The Welsh Hill Country' — "The embryo music dead in his throat" — poignantly individualises the national withdrawal, "the carcase of an old song". Elsewhere, the empathy is even more individual. R.S.'s middle-period poem about 'Marged' — "one of life's/throw-offs" (*LS*, 47) — parallels Dylan's 'The hunchback in the park'. The imbecile Marged cannot transcend her fate for "song is denied her"; Dylan's hunchback creates, in his mind, "a woman figure without fault". This objectifying of personal deficiencies transcended by art is deeply autobiographic and sympathetic. Anyway, 'The Priest' suggests that more guilty of hauteur ("the mind's height") is the reader's jibe that there are "contented" people who don't need R.S.'s sullen ministry — to which the poet answers with the *nunc dimittis* of "'Let it be so', I say. 'Amen and amen'" (*NBF*, 29). And the poetry at least finds its life amidst contingent things — farmers, a parish, the survival of a language, the effects of science, the life of birds, retreating landscapes.

More important, it does so in a style whose purification of the dialect of the tribe opens the poems bravely to disagreement, even hate. Take this other glimpse of the "bright field" —

> In Wales there are jewels
> To gather, but with the eye
> Only. A hill lights up
> Suddenly; a field trembles
> With colour and goes out
> In its turn. (*NBF*, 38)

It's a glimpse more simply brilliant than the wry glosses of his poems-about-paintings, a visual sharpness that Dylan achieves more easily in his prose. But in R.S. it modulates into a health warning:

> This wealth is for the few
> And chosen. Those who crowd
> A small window dirty it
> With their breathing. (*NBF*, 38)

Imagine trying to persuade Dylan that poetry's truth is ideologically negotiable! "The aim of a poem," Dylan said, "is the mark that the poem itself makes; it's the bullet and the bullseye; the knife, the growth, and the patient".[67]

R.S. is Dylan's significant successor exactly because of this difference in cultural commitment. For R.S., it is Wales that is not negotiable — the stance that has most crucially changed the perception of Wales since Dylan's death. For R.S. the role of the 'Anglo-Welsh' was to relate back to a core Welshness (*Prose*, 53), and fame brought disinterested acclaim alongside native partisanship in this challenge to Dylan's view that "you can't be true to party and poetry".[68] R.S.'s openness to actual disagreement evokes specific audiences. It rivals Dylan's tonally democratic embrace ("Some let me make you of autumnal spells,/The spider-tongued, and the loud hill of Wales") with a shuttering pride, the "small window" through which the "bright field" is seen. More critically, R.S.'s example brought to an end a phase of Anglo-Welsh poetry that tended to link identity to self-conscious materials and methods. In an interview with Dylan Iorwerth (significant Christian-name) he said that he deliberately changed his subject-matter when he reached Aberdaron. "By the time I reached Llŷn I felt I had come home, I had achieved my aim — I changed my subject-matter but became more of a Welshman, a straightforward Welshman, speaking Welsh every day, and therefore I was ready to act like a Welshman, so there was no need for me to write like a Welshman" (*Prose*, 16). The distinction between acting and writing — reminding us that, morally, there is no distinction — is a Keatsian insight ("I must tell you a good thing Reynolds *did*: 'twas the best thing he ever *said*"[69]), and recalls Eliot's claim that, in the end, "the poetry does not matter".[70] At such a point R.S. sees his achievement as the completion of a Welshness that shuts out the English side of the hyphen in 'Anglo-Welsh', a matter of life not of art. Perhaps this shift could only have been effected by a poet who is also a priest, drawing on the ultimate in 'alternative' subject-matter.

The cultural difference can be underlined via one of Yeats's finest lyrics, 'The Fisherman'. Like the tragic fisherman from Synge's Aran, Yeats's fisherman symbolizes a living divide.

> All day I'd looked in the face
> What I had hoped 'twould be
> To write for my own race

And the reality.[71]

"My own race/And the reality": the very line-break emphasises the chasm between ideal and real audience. Against an entrepreneurial bourgeoisie, Yeats sets an ordinary fisherman, "A man who does not exist,/A man who is but a dream". But of course, that man did exist — speaking Irish. As Seamus Heaney put it, "while Yeats was busy imagining this man, others were busy learning his language and discovering respect for his ethos", glimpsing what Daniel Corkery calls *The Hidden Ireland*.[72] R.S.'s glimpsed good Wales is a *hidden* one. He remembers once, hopelessly homesick, crossing back to his childhood Anglesey. It was a summer's evening, with young Welsh fishermen outlined "like a classic tapestry" against the hills. "An exciting word arose amongst them that sounded to the non-Welsh-speaking R.S. like 'mikrish'. He later realized the word was *mecryll* [mackerel]" (*Neb*, 119). Like Stephen's "tundish" in Joyce's *Portrait*[73], the word was a border on another language, another country.

No wonder therefore that, asked by the magazine *Wales* in 1946 'For whom do you write?', R.S. quoted Yeats's 'The Fisherman'. Over twenty years later, his own poem 'The Fisherman' was a subtle inversion of Yeats's:

> I could have told of the living water
> That springs pure.
> He would have smiled then,
> Dancing his speckled fly in the shallows,
> Not understanding. (*NBF*, 19)

This more literal stranger is the ignorant tourist, whose blankness at the poet's offer of "the living water/That springs pure" troubles many pools. The "living water" is all at once the priest's Christian witness, the sense of Welsh history that crossing the border should bring, and the cold spring of the original language. Prytherch survives in such a fisherman. Prytherch's "farm-prices mentality"[74] had kept Welsh words (not to mention *the* Word) from being the bottom line.

It's amazing just how central Yeats's 'The Fisherman' is:

> The clever man who cries
> The catch-cries of the clown,

The Page's Drift: R.S. Thomas at Eighty

The beating down of the wise
And great Art beaten down.

The language evokes more than social injury (Hopkins once spoke of Christ as "this majesty beaten down"[75]) and deepens the attack on the secular philistines. Here is R.S. quoting William Power in praise of Scotland's MacDiarmid:

> it is the quislings and lickspittles in his own country that are his chief enemies.... "His fulminations have been directed against people who in some way were preventing Scotland's full expression of the best that was in her. He wants to see Scotland 'respected like the lave,' not for her ships and engines, banks and investment companies...but for her intellect and art, her developed national culture." (*Prose*, 36)

Audience-less, such poets turn to satire. The bulk of later Dylan, poetry and prose, is warmly forgiving, but we should not forget the social disaffection of his early work, and the filaments it offers into R.S.'s more obviously satiric world. For example, anyone reading Dylan's early story 'The Enemies' will see how cognate its imagination is, not only with Caradoc Evans, but with R.S.'s 'The Priest':

> Women, pouring from the black kettle,
> Stir up the whirling tea-grounds
> Of their thoughts; offer him a dark
> Filling in their smiling sandwich.
>
> Priests have a long way to go. (*NBF*, 29)

This is the dark brew that Dylan homogenised in *Under Milk Wood*, and which R.S., too, left behind.

But what 'ideal' drives the satire? How hopeful is the poet of, some day, not *needing* satire? MacDiarmid, quoted by R.S., helps explain why Yeats needed to imagine an ideal native audience: "To bring to bear a material imagination on everyday reality, so as to emphasise the beauty which it possesses *normally and in use*" (*Prose*, 37. My emphasis). In an equally beautiful phrase, Hopkins said of ordinary domestic good grace that it "seemed of course, seemed of right".[76] R.S. yearns to "change the people and lead them to their *essential* dignity" (*Prose*, 38. My emphasis) — as a matter of course, not the patronising "of course" of politicians. But he adds that "it is a formidable task this winnowing and purifying of the people" (*Prose*, 38). He realises, like Yeats, that the poet doesn't match the audience, either: "When a country produces a man of genius he never is what it wants or believes it wants; he is always unlike its idea of itself".[77] Given that behind R.S. lies an alternative language with a poetic tradition of the highest impressiveness since the sixth century, there is in English in our time no equal to the sheer radicalness of this link between 'purifying the dialect of the tribe' and a "purifying of the people".

VII

But "before a poet can get into contact with society he must, surely, be able to get into contact with himself". The comment is striking because it is the bohemian Dylan who made it, and not any more orthodoxly 'moral' artist. He made the point originally because he couldn't "accept Auden as head-prefect" or ignore that "Spender has only tickled his own outside with a feather".[78] The young Dylan, too, had refused to join abstract ideologies across the border. Celebrating elemental themes above merely fashionable ones, he too had felt his own way back to a Welsh Wales glimpsed across the loss of language. His need to get "into contact with himself" came significantly in 1938. That was the year in which marriage, approaching fatherhood, and his first home in Laugharne — domesticities that Larkin said pushed people "to the side of their own lives"[79] — made the unangelic Dylan look homeward. And in order to register the experiences, the imagistic autonomy of his early poetry started breaking down. It was the year of the densely human 'After the funeral', which fled the trapped iconoclasm of his Swansea self for a more ventilated response to his dead aunt Ann, the human face of the Welsh-language place from which he'd been exiled. I'm not sure that the section beginning "It was my biggest funeral..." in R.S.'s 'The Minister' (*SYT*, 90) doesn't outline something emotionally similar — Brueghelian mourners set against the life of nature — just as the earlier image of a bird "dead, starved, on the warm sill" of the mouldy manse matches the stuffed fox and stale fern of Ann's best room (*SYT*, 86). R.S.'s nationalism shouldn't be divorced too completely from the place-rootedness of the Swansea poet. Without slighting the Welsh language separating them, I think they invested, not only major talents, but cognate needs in their love of Wales. Not understanding Dylan Thomas, we risk not really understanding R.S. Thomas, either.

Their different loves converge. R.S. claims that the true Wales is rural Wales (*Prose*, 53). After the warm embrace of Swansea, Dylan's ultimate good place, too, was incorrigibly rural. And because his hermetic early poems had been strangely unpeopled, he had to repopulate that landscape. The Swansea stories led ultimately to the New-Quay-and-Laugharne pastoralism of *Under Milk Wood* which, though a simplifying work, is one we should think twice about before patronising. We understand our artists best in their own time. *Under Milk Wood* isn't terminally soiled by the 'regional' delight it took in entertaining urban(e) London. In the 1950s, no less than in the 1930s, the sheer visibility of a Welsh poet in English *depended* on London, and R.S. is still published in England. More important, the 'childhood' poems, the broadcasts and *Under Milk Wood*, circling as they do on the theme of innocence, sublimate Dylan's tragic need after 1945 to find norms in "a place of love",[80] against a world demoralised by Hiroshima and Nagasaki. R.S.'s references to these, and to the Holocaust, are later, cooler and more direct ("composer of the first/radio-active verses" [*ERS*, 75]). Post-Gorbachev, we even risk forgetting the immediacy such fears had in the last eight years of Dylan's life. It was for honourable reasons that his later work sought the good place by going back down the track of his own life, to childhood itself.

But that, R.S. says, "is Wales's weakness... Is there for Wales no future?" (*Neb*, 101). And yet, as we have seen, R.S.'s career, too, was a driven return to a first place — to an Anglesey seen from Lleyn, with time nicely confused with space: "a headland from which he could look back over forty miles of sea to his boyhood some forty years distant" (*ERS*, 66). He even confesses a Dylanish guilt at having "no future but the one that is safeguarded by a return to the past" (*ERS*, 66). But, he adds, "Was his poetry wiser than his action?" (*ERS*, 66), a caution now restoring writing above living, perhaps because it had already restored religion above politics.

For the truth is that what ultimately divides our two poets are different perceptions of Time. Eliot's wisdom that "the end of all our exploring/Will be to arrive where we started/And know the place for the first time"[81] counts tremendously with R.S., who so often echoes it ("your destination/is where you began" [ERS, 33]), and for whom 'knowing the place for the first time' has the stunning literalness of experiencing it for the first time in its own language! Dylan's 'Poem in October' and 'Fern Hill', with their Victorian solidity of recall, busily reconstitute an unfaded childhood. Though they recognise the psychological gap between then and now (compare R.S.'s title 'Between *Here* and Now'), and though their aim is re-creation not recreation, Dylan's poems feel able to relay the child's holistic happiness from the past into the present for the future: "O may my heart's truth/Still be sung/On this high hill in a year's turning".[82] R.S., on the other hand, thinks us mistaken even in feeling this "need to go back to the first places for the early dew upon them; the dew is not there; the contemporary world is over-populated, over-industrialised, the world of the machine" — stressing, in an oddly disturbing image, that "the dew, the Welsh dew, is tarnished".[83] Of course, even Dylan knew that childhood's literal places were now only a childhood-in-the-mind. But, like Eliot, R.S. is concerned to rid us in the first place of that linear notion of time. Eliot had been the first major poet of post-Einstein space-time, of physical (not just 'mystical') warps in duration. As R.S. puts it, "Is it/the Orient infiltrating/our science, or science bringing/a myth up to date?" (*ERS*, 33). Once again, a different, *inner* chronology had moulded the young Dylan before Eliot's *Four Quartets* and R.S. afterwards. And Eliot's influence on R.S. deepened. 'The Bright Field'(1975) had simply reprimanded man for "hurrying//on to a receding future", for "hankering after/an imagined past" (*LS*, 60). No mystery there. Thirteen years later *The Echoes Return Slow*, describing the poet returning to the actual North Wales of his past, rebukes itself with the example of Christ on the road to Emmaus, a consciousness actually "contemporary with a future/never to be overtaken" (*ERS*, 67). There *is* mystery there, and it takes R.S.'s punning wit to normalise its use of Yeats's cones and gyres:

The Page's Drift: R.S. Thomas at Eighty

> ...in our journeys
> through time we come round not
> to the same place, but recognise it
> from a distance. It is the dream
> we remember, that makes us say:
> 'We have been here before.' (*EA*, 3)

We "come round" not just because of time's helix but as anaesthetised patients, or suddenly concurring antagonists, "come round".

That modern theoretical science has underpinned religion by making time negotiable — and not just as *déjà vu* — is ironic. R.S. hates the scientific mind, often quoting Coleridge's view that the opposite of poetry is not prose but science (*ERS*, 88), and delivering a deft put-down to science's response to ultimate questions: "We pass our hands/over their surface...feeling for the mechanism/that will swing them aside" (*LP*, 121). The swinging-aside merges into the rolled-away stone dis-covering Christ's body risen. The eighteen year-old Dylan, equally sceptical about abstract philosophic enquiry, had, in his early 'Egyptian' mode, also used the image of a presumptuously invaded tomb:

> Should lanterns shine, the holy face,
> Caught in an octagon of unaccustomed light,
> Would wither up, and any boy of love
> Look twice before he fell from grace.[84]

R.S. rightly admires the lyric which Yeats detonated at the philosophic roots of the scientific mind:

> Locke sank into a swoon;
> The Garden died;
> God took the spinning-jenny
> Out of his side.[85]

Lost with Eden at the Industrial Revolution was the 'community' that Yeats saw as heirs to Chaucer's Canterbury pilgrims: a unified culture travelling to a common shrine, later dissolved by abstraction and the Cartesian dream of a mathematical universe.[86] It is therefore no accident that Chaucer's pilgrims and Yeats's view of a unified culture are merged at one point in *The Echoes Return Slow* (*ERS*, 94). But "there are other pilgrimages/to make beside Jerusalem, Rome..." (*WA*, 52). R.S. answers his own conundrum with a shrine geographically closer than Canterbury, historically closer than Bardsey, humanly closer than "the no-man's-/land" of the microscope:

> How close
> need a shrine be to be too far
> for the traveller of to-day who is in
> a hurry? Spare an hour or two
> for Dolanog. (*WA*, 54)

Dolanog was Prytherch country, now recognized from Lleyn as having been also Ann Griffiths country when, in a pre-industrial community, the Word coincided with Welsh words. Another Abercuawg.

Of course, without science, in at least the engineering sense, one cannot now imagine an acceptable future for any country. Abercuawg — R.S.'s tangential "place of love", one of the gardens that died — seems unrealistically 'literary'. But human resistance to a merely accidental future is still healthful, especially when the alternative yearned for involves the survival of a language, and therefore of a whole world. But it does mean that "the glimpsed good place" is seen increasingly through the corner of the eye. Lleyn, sighted from Aberystwyth, always had the magic of "a country seen across the water"; yet he knew that there, too, only "a very ordinary life" was lived, and was later shocked to find it a practice-space for fighter-planes (*Neb*, 116). Ireland, the only independent Celtic land, glimpsed from Lleyn, has for him a magic unreconcilable with its materialism and loss of Gaelic (*PMI*, 30-33). Though the 'oval' of his priestly movements around Wales afforded "a comprehensive picture of Wales itself", when asked what region or spot his early poetry described, R.S. replied "they did not exist" (*Neb*, 63). It is a bracingly unscientific hyperbole. Imperfect Wales, like Yeats's ideal fisherman, does not "exist"! Only potentialities survive.

It is why he so often records fleet undisappointing sunshine — what an early poem calls "light's peculiar grace" (*SYT*, 101). In his autobiography he actually logs the hours of sunlight in his various homes (*Neb*, 105). Even the denaturing title of his autobiography — *Neb* [Nobody] — is "a nobody with a crown of light around his head", who recalls Pindar's "Man is only a dream of shadow. But

---

when some splendour falls upon him from God, glory is his, and a sweet life" (*Neb*, 87). Then suddenly, out at sea, a sunbeam illuminates "a pool of golden light far from land" and a peregrine falcon flies "strong and purposely towards the pool of light, as if entranced by it".[87] R.S. adds that poems, too, come unbidden. Even the peregrine falcon seems 'given': the first animal listed as endangered in the U.S., its very name is the best description of R.S. — from *Four Quartets* — a "spirit unappeased and peregrine".[88]

Though no longer literally on the move, R.S. retains Eliot's brief that "old men ought to be explorers".[89] He is bent on escaping what Eliot called "a provincialism, not of space, but of time; one for which history is merely the chronicle of human devices which have served their turn and been scrapped, one for which the world is the property solely of the living, a property in which the dead hold no shares."[90] R.S.'s feel is for the geological as well as the human past, and Hardy joins Eliot behind the poems. In a dark February, a beam of light suddenly illuminates one of the "centuries-old stones" in R.S.'s kitchen wall at Rhiw,[91] sparking individual thought off ageless event, as in Hardy:

> Primeval rocks form the road's steep border,
>   And much have they faced there, first and last,
> Of the transitory in Earth's long order.[92]

Repeated references to Lleyn's pre-Cambrian rocks even borrow Hardy's adjective for 'overhanging' — "a *beetling*/headland" (*ERS*, 71). 'Pre-Cambrian' claims that "My shadow/sunning itself on this stone/remembers the lava" (*LP*, 106). The lit stone, like the bright field, is a repeated *fiat*. It throws literal light on Wittgenstein's logic that "it is not how things are in the world that is mystical, but that the world exists at all".[93] But when R.S. claims, of the light slanting in from a side window as he stands at the altar, that "you can't just say 'This is the sun: S-U-N.' It's much more miraculous than that",[94] we see that glimpsed good places — however sidelong, literary, or nationalist — have for him *religious* sanction. Conversely, the theme of the *deus absconditus* is made to raise not only the limits of language but Wales's own language border, "the innocent marches/of vocabulary" (*LS*, 43). R.S.'s Welsh Wales is Eliot's "timeless moment", a glimpsed reality that may not last (anyway, "human kind/Cannot bear very much reality"[95]) but a reality that, if we are not to be mired in the present, we can't afford to stop imagining, either.

VIII

R.S. has always had, like poetry itself, this abstracting power. Distilling huge argument into pellucid statement is the very genius of his style. But he also specifically 'abstracts' concrete landscapes. When he moved to Eglwys-fach the landscape of his mind apparently remained Manafon.[96] But even in Manafon his poetry's early landscape had in fact been the moorland to the west, of Adfa and Cefncoch. As his Welsh-cultural fears increased, landscape became "not landscape for its own sake but a modern reality beginning to take shape". He translated Caledfryn's 'Diwedd y Cynhauaf' into 'Harvest End' (*EA*, 15) because he felt that the theme, persistent since Llywarch Hen, had "something abstract about it: in Caledfryn's three short stanzas what you have is, not a particular landscape, but the human condition". Moving from solid mid-Wales hill country to peninsular Lleyn, R.S. began to "abstract even more from the natural scene". And, with his poems-on-paintings (a pastiche genre he dubs wryly "this illicit occupation"), he admits that he "was now really abstracting from the landscape", these poems being art-out-of-art.

Complementing the 'abstraction', there is the uncanny rightness of our poets' last places. Laugharne is an English-speaking town enisled in Welsh-speaking Carmarthenshire, and Lleyn the eyrie of Welsh-speaking Wales, traditionally aloof from the south-west let alone any resurgent south-east. But our image of an eyrie must give way to the different 'abstraction' of the peninsula. Keeping the wide sea narrowly "either side of him" (*Neb*, 89), it is a place not of 'retirement' but of vertigo, "a branch of rock hanging between the sea and heaven, encompassed by the blossom of clouds. Now grown old, I sometimes like to think of myself as having crept far along it, waiting for the end. When I fall, my flesh and bones will go into the depths".[97] The same image in *The Echoes Return Slow* (*ERS*, 68), asking what audience he had found in Lleyn, quotes Yeats's lines on Synge's return to the Aran islands

— to "a race/Passionate and simple like his heart",[98] evoking community and Yeats's 'fisherman' again. But what 'Emerging' calls Lleyn is a "peninsula/of the spirit" (*LP*, 117), however giddy. In a favourite metaphor of "the reciprocating touch" of Michelangelo's Adam (*BHN*, 110), the mind claims that

> A promonotory is a bare
> place; no God leans down
> out of the air to take the hand
> extended to him. The generations have
> watched there
> in vain. (*LP*, 117)

In vain, yes, but "when was that ever a bar/To any watch they keep?"[99]

R.S. and Dylan represent the sundered halves of a whole: north/south, Welsh/Anglo-Welsh, circumspect/prodigal. Their careers are also inverse. Dylan moved from abstract creationist themes to populated landscapes, and R.S. from peasant landscapes to an absent God. The former involved a retreat from poetic Modernism, the latter a refinement of some of its sparest forms. But something consistent in their very styles is figured in this final contrast between narrow peninsula and broad bay. Dylan's Boat House and writing-shed are steadied not only by their "stilts" but by the formal columns of 'Prologue' and the solid stanzas of 'Over Sir John's hill' and 'Poem on his Birthday':

> There he might wander bare
> With the spirits of the horseshoe bay
> Or the stars' seashore dead,
> Marrow of eagles, the roots of whales
> And wishbones of wild geese,
> With blessed, unborn God and his Ghost,
> And every soul His priest.[100]

Compared to these formal bays and orchestrations, the peninsulas of R.S.'s free-verse have the vertigo of notes on a violin.

And yet they too break hearts. Cognate loves converge even more decisively at land's end. Both poets relish storms literally 'brought home' — to the cottage a stone's throw from the sea at Rhiw as to the "house on stilts" at Laugharne, homes celebrated in ways reminiscent of Yeats's Tower, a reminiscence that R.S. subtly acknowledges (*ERS*, 79, 104). And both would second Conrad's insight that the sea is the great leveller: "faithful to no race after the manner of the kindly earth, receiving no impress from valour and toil and self-sacrifice, recognising no finality of dominion, the sea has never adopted the cause of its masters" like the land.[101] R.S. would rightly counter with the obscenity of oil-slicks and nuclear submarines. But these are facts that separate today's world no less from Dylan's than from Conrad's. That unimpressionability of the sea underlies the religious vision of the late poems of both Thomases. The view over the estuary at Laugharne brought even Dylan's time-ridden temperament to a sense of Eliot's eternal present.

Equally timeless are deeper disturbances. R.S. speaks of the eternal "antitheses that the sea's presence brings" (*Neb*, 79). "To a thinking person," he says, "the sea has two sides, outer and inner. Or if you like, it is both mirror and window. The mirror reflects all the beauty and glory of the creation.... But the window reveals the permanent war of creatures mercilessly, endlessly, devouring each other...through the seaweed, as through a forest, seals, cormorants and mackerel hunt like rapacious wolves" (*Neb*, 87-8). It's an emphasis that prompted critics to say that *H'm* was in thrall to Ted Hughes's *Crow*. But this seeing-beyond is Wordsworthian ("my fancy has penetrated into the depths of that sea — with accompanying thoughts of shipwreck, of the destruction of the mariner's hopes, the bones of drowned men heaped together, monsters of the deep, and all the hideous and confused sights"[102]), and Keatsian ("I saw / Too far into the sea; where every maw / The greater on the less feeds evermore"[103]) and Dylanish:

> Dolphins dive in their turnturtle dust,
>   The rippled seals streak down
> To kill and their own tide daubing blood
>   Slides good in the sleek mouth.[104]

Amongst what Dylan here calls "the beaks and palavers of birds" ("Porth Neigwl is full these days of the great noise of sandwich terns flocking for their flight south"[105]), the birdwatching R.S. says Lleyn is "a place for poetry" not "because of its views" but "because of its peace" (*Neb*, 105). Obviously, even aircraft noise hasn't forced peace to mean literal silence, and R.S. says that he turned consciously from man to noisy birds because "birds haven't changed, whereas Wales has".[106] His delight in seeing "the creatures still going about their immemorial business" (*Neb*, 117) is Dylan's delight in "Flounders, gulls, on their cold, dying trails,/Doing what they are told".[107] Of course, R.S.'s birds are scientifically watched, not emblematically seen: he even yearns for storms, to drive strange birds closer to land! (*Neb*, 90). But it isn't a science that carries into poetry: just as Dylan quipped that "all birds are robins, except crows, or rooks",[108] R.S. says that poetry is about birds, not Stone Curlews and Dartford Warblers (*Prose*, 84). But bird-noisy Lleyn also evokes a more existential blankness. The use in 'Sea Watching' of Stevie Smith's painful phrase "not waving but drowning"[109] — "Nothing/but that continuous waving/that is without meaning" (*LS*, 64) — ripples the poem's surface before its more profoundly precarious close. "Spending an hour or two looking out to sea, hoping to spot a foreign bird, he realized the similarity there was between this and praying" (*Neb*, 117-8):

> There were days,
> so beautiful the emptiness
> it might have filled,
>   its absence
> was as its presence; not to be told
> any more, so single my mind
> after its long fast,
>   my watching from praying. (*LS*, 64)

There are moments when R.S's effects seem more 'heady' than Dylan's. The elegant vertigo, the free fall, of the syntax here leaves us to 'catch' the meaning. The poem so risks its own form that we have to reconstitute the idiom 'watching cannot be told-apart from praying'. And, leaning to realign the syntax, we hear momentarily its opposite — "not to be told/any more, so single my mind" — like a stubborn Yeatsian 'aside', which it isn't.

This liquid pace and tone, merging contraries, is R.S.'s most crucial gift. It increasingly matched a need (as Cleanth Brooks said of Yeats's decision to 'walk naked') "to deal with a cultural situation now radically re-envisaged".[110] One can't imagine Dylan's structured forms matching the antipoetic and political reflexes of the decades since 1953. And that platform of disappointment is what made R.S.'s voice sensitive also to a numinous waiting. What freed forms do is capture a more individual movement of mind. Of the two, perhaps surprisingly, Dylan is the more subtly allusive. In his capacious villanelle, for example, even the dead who "forked no lightning" evoke Romeo's "How oft when men are at the point of death/Have they been merry! which their keepers call/A lightning before death".[111] R.S.'s "Eliot said that" (*ERS*, 53), his appeal to Keats's "the holiness of the heart's affections" (*ERS*, 92), or his poems about crucial influences such as Kierkegaard, Wallace Stevens, or Saunders Lewis are more openly allusive. Both are lyric poets, but R.S. has insisted that by 'lyric' he himself means 'changeable'.[112] Even with its shifts, Dylan's style was always a more impersonal 'utterance for the race'. But we should rejoice that neither poet does without humour. The sheer wit of Dylan's conceits still awaits its due credit. And one of R.S.'s main imaginative fingerprints is surely the splicing of the serious and the demotic meanings within clichés: "Priests have *a long way to go*" (*NBF*, 29), "Being *taken for a ride* by a rich/Relation" (*H'm*, 37), "the *clapped* ranks of/the peerage" (*WW*, 9), "*to move/in divine circles*" (*WA*, 53), "Time *would have its work cut out*" (*ERS*, 2), "Jacob wrestled/*to no end*" (*C*, 14). R.S. has said "I think there's a certain amount of misunderstanding of my work, a lot of my work is ironic"; "What I've tried to do...is...to operate on more than one level, to try to bring ambivalence and so on into the phrases".[113]

But even if clarity appeals first via worked surfaces, R.S.'s structural openness remains his major legacy to others with things of their own to say, whether in Wales or elsewhere. No one should pass that by — or off — as simplicity. R.S. is an impressive love poet, and there is no better image for the depths beyond troubled surfaces than the magnificent last line of a late poem to his wife: "Over love's depths only the surface is wrinkled" (*ERS*, 121). At the same time, comparisons must outgrow the silly charge that Dylan's bulkier surface craft is somehow 'dishonest'.[114] As Robert Lowell put it, specifically in Dylan's defence, "there's a lot of bull about poetry being spontaneous".[115] Having, as he once told me, "nothing at all against Dylan",[116] R.S. will smile if I salute them both by quoting Larkin:

I don't say, one bodies the other
　　One's spiritual truth;
But I do say it's hard to lose either,
　　When you have both.[117]

Notes

1. T.S. Eliot, 'The Love Song of J. Alfred Prufrock' (ll. 104-5).
2. James Smith, 'Wordsworth: A Preliminary Survey', *Scrutiny* 7 (1938), 53.
3. William Wordsworth, *The Prelude* (1850 version), Bk VI, 1. 626; *The Excursion*, Bk IV, 1. 1147; *The Prelude*, Bk VI, 1. 608.
4. R.S. Thomas, Introduction, *Selected Poems of Edward Thomas* (London: Faber and Faber, 1964), 11.
5. Seamus Heaney, poem xlii of 'Squarings', *Seeing Things* (London: Faber and Faber, 1991), 102.
6. I am grateful to my wife, Hazel Davies, for this information, based on her recent discovery of correspondence between Edward Thomas and O.M. Edwards.
7. Indeed, Faber's *Selected Poems* wrongly prints it as "obscurèd".
8. Vergil, *Aeneid*, Bk I, l. 203 (my translation).
9. R.S. Thomas, interviewed by J.B. Lethbridge, *The Anglo-Welsh Review* 74 (1983), 39.
10. See Lawrance Thompson. *Robert Frost: The Years of Triumph 1915-1938* (New York: Holt, Rinehart and Winston, 1970), 87; R. George Thomas, *Edward Thomas: A Portrait* (Oxford: Oxford University Press, 1985), 223-32.
11. Eliot, Introduction to a translation of Valéry's *Art of Poetry* (1958).
12. John Malcolm Brinnin, ed., *A Casebook on Dylan Thomas* (New York: Thomas Y. Crowell, 1960), 196.
13. Dylan Thomas, 'A Prospect of the Sea', *A Prospect of the Sea* (London: Dent, 1955), 6.
14. Eliot, 'Poetry in the Eighteenth Century', Boris Ford, ed., *The Pelican Guide to English Literature* (London: Penguin Books, 1957), vol. 4, 272-3.
15. Eliot, 'Little Gidding' (l. 127), *Four Ouartets* (London: Faber and Faber, 1944), 39. All quotations from *Four Quartets* are from this volume. The phrase is Mallarmé's — "Donner un sens plus pur aux mots de la tribu" — from his 'Le Tombeau d'Edgar Poe'.
16. R.S. Thomas, interviewed by Bedwyr Lewis Jones, *Barn* 76 (February 1969), n.p.
17. Donald Davie, *Purity of Diction in English Verse* (London: Routledge and Kegan Paul, 1952), 5.

18. W.B. Yeats, 'A Coat', *Collected Poems*, second edition (London: Macmillan, 1950), 142. All poetry by Yeats is quoted from this volume.
19. Eliot, 'Little Gidding' (l. 219), *Four Quartets*.
20. Eliot, 'What the Thunder Said' (ll. 359 - 65), *The Waste Land*.
21. Philip Larkin, 'Four Conversations', *The London Magazine* IV (November 1964), 71-2.
22. Dylan Thomas, 'The Orchards', *A Prospect of the Sea*, 85.
23. R.S. Thomas, interviewed by Byron Rogers, *The Sunday Telegraph Magazine* (7 November 1975), 29.
24. Wordsworth, Preface to the second edition of *Lyrical Ballads* (1800).
25. 'A Letter to my Aunt, Discussing the Correct Approach to Modern Poetry', Paul Ferris, ed., *The Collected Letters* (London: Dent, 1985), 69.
26. C. Day Lewis, 'Boy with Dolphin: Verrocchio (D.T.)', *Collected Poems* (London: Jonathan Cape with The Hogarth Press, 1954), 344.
27. E.g. Keats's letter to Woodhouse, Hyder E. Rollins. ed., *The Letters of John Keats 1814-21*, two volumes (Cambridge: Cambridge University Press, 1958), volume one, 387.
28. Mark, 8:24. C.f. "And the trees walked like men", 'The Enemies', *A Prospect of the Sea*, 37.
29. *Romeo and Juliet*, prologue, l. 6.
30. Recalled by Alastair Reid, E.W. Tedlock, ed., *Dylan Thomas: The Legend and the Poet* (London: Heinemann, 1960), 54.
31. John Davies, 'How to Write Anglo-Welsh Poetry', *At the Edge of Town* (Llandysul: Gomer Press, 1981), 37.
32. Eliot, 'Burnt Norton' (l. 85), *Four Quartets*.
33. William Empson, 'This Last Pain', *Collected Poems* (London: Chatto and Windus, 1955), 33: "Imagine, then.../What could not possibly be there,/And learn a style from a despair."
34. John Betjeman, Introduction, *Song at the Year's Turning* (London: Rupert Hart-Davis, 1955), 11.
35. Larkin, Introduction, *The North Ship* (London: Faber and Faber, 1966), 8.
36. Edward Lucie-Smith, ed., *British Poetry Since 1945*, second edition (London: Penguin, 1986), 271.
37. Dylan Thomas, 'Before I knocked', Walford Davies and Ralph Maud, eds., *Dylan Thomas: Collected Poems 1934-1953* (London: Dent, 1988), 12. All poetry quotations are from this edition.
38. Dylan Thomas, 'On no work of words'.
39. Dylan Thomas, 'I have longed to move away'.
40. Cited in John Ackerman, *A Dylan Thomas Companion* (London: Macmillan, 1991), 154.
41. V.S. Pritchett, 'Scott', *The Living Novel* (London: Chatto and Windus, 1946), 43.

42. Yeats, 'The Grey Rock', *Collected Poems*, 117.

43. Seamus Heaney, 'The Interesting Case of John Alphonsus Mulrennan', *Planet* 41 (January 1978), 35.

44. Heaney, 'The Interesting Case', 34.

45. Yeats, 'A General Introduction for My Work', *Essays and Introductions* (London: Macmillan, 1961), 520.

46. Heaney, 'The Interesting Case', 38.

47. Paul Ferris, *Dylan Thomas* (London: Hodder and Stoughton, 1977), 34.

48. *R.S. Thomas Reading His Own Poems* (Cardiff: Welsh Arts Council Oriel Records, 1976).

49. Davies and Maud, eds., *Collected Poems*, 58, 28, 9, 86, 56, 94, 134.

50. Empson, 'Arachne', *Collected Poems*, 23.

51. Quoted by John Drury in the series 'Faith and Reason', *The Independent Weekend* (1 June 1991), 33. The comment by Kierkegaard is from the final page of his Journal.

52. Private conversation

53. *Hamlet*, III, 1, 68-9.

54. Yeats, Introduction, *The Oxford Book of Modern Verse* (Oxford: Oxford University Press, 1936), xvii.

55. Eliot, 'Burnt Norton' (l. 142), *Four Quartets*.

56. Wallace Stevens, *Opus Posthumous* (London: Faber and Faber, 1957), 226.

57. Nigel Jenkins, 'Commentary', *Western Mail* (7 March 1991).

58. R.S. Thomas, Letter, *The Anglo-Welsh Review* 18 (Summer 1969), 187.

59. John Blackwell (Alun), *Ceinion Alun* (Rhuthun: Isaac Clarke, 1851), 199.

60. R.S. Thomas, *Cymru or Wales?* (Llandysul: Gomer Press, 1992),19.

61. Deuteronomy, 7:7. See *Neb*, 107.

62. John Aitchison and Harold Carter, 'Rural Wales and the Welsh Language', *Rural History* 2 (1991), 62.

63. Dylan Thomas, 'Reminiscences of Childhood', *Quite Early One Morning* (London: Dent, 1954), 1.

64. Dylan Thomas, 'Once it was the colour of saying'.

65. Joe Kelly, 'Finding a Fresh Voice at Journey's End', *Newlines* 7 (1991), 19.

66. R.S. Thomas, *Blwyddyn yn Llŷn* (Caernarfon: Gwasg Gwynedd, 1990), 78. (My translation, as in each Welsh text quoted.)

67. Ferris, ed., *Collected Letters*, 297.

68. *Ibid.*, 185.

69. Rollins, ed., *The Letters of John Keats*, volume two, 207.

70. Eliot, 'East Coker' (l. 71), *Four Quartets*.

71. Yeats, 'The Fisherman', *Collected Poems*, 166.

72. Heaney, 'The Interesting Case', 37.

73. James Joyce, *A Portrait of the Artist as a Young Man* (Triad/Panther, 1977), 227.
74. R.S. Thomas, Lecture and Reading on the theme of 'Landscape' (Extra-Mural Department, UCW Aberystwyth and Gregynog), Gregynog, 17 July 1991. Hereafter cited as 'Gregynog'.
75. Christopher Devlin, ed., *The Sermons and Devotional Writings of Gerard Manley Hopkins* (Oxford: Oxford University Press, 1959), 36.
76. Gerard Manley Hopkins, 'In the Valley of the Elwy'.
77. Yeats, 'The Death of Synge', *Autobiographies* (London: Macmillan, 1955), 520.
78. Ferris, ed., *Collected Letters*, 281.
79. Larkin, 'Afternoons', *The Whitsun Weddings* (London: Faber and Faber, 1964), 44.
80. Dylan Thomas, *Under Milk Wood*, (London: Dent, 1954), 76.
81. Eliot, 'Little Gidding' (ll. 240-2), *Four Quartets*.
82. Dylan Thomas, 'Poem in October'.
83. Gregynog.
84. Dylan Thomas, 'Should lanterns shine'.
85. Personal conversation. The Yeats lines are from 'Fragments', *Collected Poems*, 240.
86. Yeats, 'Four Years: 1887-1891', *Autobiographies*, 193.
87. R.S. Thomas, *Blwyddyn yn Llŷn*, 88.
88. Eliot, 'Little Gidding' (l. 121), *Four Quartets*.
89. Eliot, 'East Coker' (l. 202), *Four Quartets*.
90. Eliot, 'What is a Classic?', *On Poetry and Poets* (London: Faber and Faber, 1957), 69.
91. R.S. Thomas, *Blwyddyn yn Llŷn*, 17.
92. Thomas Hardy, 'At Castle Boterel', *Collected Poems* fourth edition, (London: Macmillan, 1930), 331.
93. Ludwig Wittgenstein, proposition 6.44 ("Nicht wie die Welt ist, ist das Mystische, sondern daß sie ist") in *Logischphilosophische Abhandlung*.
94. R.S. Thomas, interviewed on London Weekend Television's 'The South Bank Show', 17 February 1991.
95. Eliot, 'Burnt Norton' (ll.42-3), *Four Quartets*.
96. Gregynog. The next six unattributed references are also from R.S.'s Gregynog lecture. (See note 74 above.)
97. R.S. Thomas, *Blwyddyn yn Llŷn* 35-6.
98. Yeats, 'In Memory of Major Robert Gregory', *Collected Poems*, 149.
99. Robert Frost, 'Neither Out Far Nor In Deep', *The Complete Poems of Robert Frost* (London: Jonathan Cape, 1951), 330.
100. Dylan Thomas, 'Poem on his Birthday'.
101. Joseph Conrad, *The Mirror of the Sea*, twenty-second edition (London: Methuen, 1947), 165.

102. Wordsworth, 'Essay Upon Epitaphs', printed as a note to *The Excursion*, Bk V (1814).
103. Rollins, ed., *The Letters of John Keats*, volume one, 262.
104. Dylan Thomas, 'Poem on his Birthday'.
105. R.S. Thomas, *Blwyddyn yn Llŷn*, 67.
106. Gregynog.
107. Dylan Thomas, 'Poem on his Birthday'.
108. Dylan Thomas, 'The Crumbs of One Man's Year', *Quite Early One Morning* (London: Dent, 1954), 44.
109. Stevie Smith, 'Not Waving But Drowning'.
110. Cleanth Brooks (interviewed by Robert Penn Warren) in Lewis P. Simpson, ed., *The Possibilities of Order* (Baton Rouge: Louisiana State University Press, 1976), 62.
111. *Romeo and Juliet*, V, 3, 88-90.
112. Interviewed by J.B. Lethbridge, *The Anglo-Welsh Review*, 39.
113. *Ibid.*, 40, 46.
114. Cf. C.B. Cox, 'Welsh Bards in Hard Times: Dylan Thomas and R.S.Thomas', Boris Ford, ed., *The New Pelican Guide To English Literature* (London: Penguin Books, 1983), 209-23.
115. Robert Lowell, interviewed in *Dylan Thomas: The World I Breathe*, an 'N.F.T. Festival' film, produced and directed by Perry Miller, narrated by John Malcolm Brinnin, New York, 1964.
116. Personal correspondence, 11 November 1987.
117. Larkin, 'Toads', *The Less Deceived*, sixth edition (Hessle: The Marvell Press, 1966), 33.

Ned Thomas

R.S. Thomas and Wales

To take this title in its broadest sense would mean dealing with the poet's whole work. R.S. Thomas has spent virtually his entire life in Wales. Most days he has walked the Welsh countryside observing the hills, the sea, the rocks, the distant prospects, the trees in their seasons, the fields and unfenced uplands, the people and the birds. When he writes of geological time, the pre-Cambrian rocks are those on which he sits. If he describes himself as having crawled out "on to a bough/of country that is sus-pended/between sky and sea" (*EA*, 38), it is the Llŷn peninsula. If he sees a small field light up, it is, of course, a field in Wales.

But if Wales provides many of the elements out of which the poetry is made, the poetry also constructs a world that is unmistakably R.S. Thomas's . Insofar as that world presents itself as the world of Wales or the world seen from Wales, it can, and has been, argued with as selective and biased — what writer's world is not?

Now where the boundaries of language, territory and audience are coterminous, there is a natural corrective to this selectivity, in that the writer's reputation has, sooner or later, to live or die by the confirmation which the work obtains or fails to obtain from those who share these communities in space and time. It exists, in Daniel Corkery's phrase, "by native suffrage".

But this is not true for the Anglo-Welsh writer, whose situation is much more complicated. First, his or her language and concepts come already shaped to a high degree outside Wales — there are already in English, well-established "moulds" (Corkery again) for conceptualising Wales, the influence of which it is hard even for very self-conscious writers to escape entirely. Secondly, the competing definitions of Wales which Anglo-Welsh authors advance live or die by foreign as much as by native suffrage. Finally, even the Anglo-Welsh part of the audience, though it may be in touch with the same Welsh social reality as the author, will take its concepts and critical language to some degree from outside — indeed often to a greater degree and less questioningly than the authors themselves do.

Nor can the critic avoid these shifting sands. Are judgements on R.S. Thomas's construction of Wales in his poetry to be made within the framework of mainstream English literary criticism, through an extension to Anglo-Welsh of the concepts common in Welsh-language criticism of Welsh literature, from some notional (because still-to-be-defined) Anglo-Welsh position, or from (as I would myself argue) a comparative standpoint which would, on the one hand, set the poetry against representations of Wales in the Welsh language. and on the other against the products of new literatures in English during the post-colonial period?

Critics of all persuasions might agree that the profile of Wales which emerges in R.S. Thomas's work is overwhelmingly rural, but the perception of that rurality would be very different in each case. In the tradition of English literature there is a Romantic status, after Wordsworth, to be derived from hills and solitude, where the poet pens a few sheets in a gap of cloud. This perception merges very easily with a view of the Celtic west which chooses not to see the industrial and modern aspects of the Celtic countries. The Anglo-Welsh critic from industrial (or post-industrial) south Wales is more likely to stress the limitation, indeed the suppression involved in constructing Wales in a rural image, but may unite with the English critic in perceiving R.S. Thomas as geographically 'remote'. This the Welsh-language critic is less likely to do, since many of Welsh literature's dominant figures in the twentieth century have come from rural backgrounds (or what are perceived from outside as such) and have created a consciousness which is no less modern for not being urban. Such a critic may however feel a different kind of remoteness in the emphasis within R.S. Thomas's work on place as landscape rather than as community. But a comparative viewpoint might see that very emphasis as symptomatic of a fractured culture and of the attempt to establish a relation with the past through landscape, as can be observed in Australian literature. The comparatist might also note a development in the work of R.S. Thomas which can be parallelled in other places and in relation to other nationalisms: a received Romanticism of the far horizon, the erotic periphery, enters the literary vocabulary of the young poet from outside, is challenged, problematised and then redefined by a more profound understanding of the philosophic roots of Romanticism so as to create a new centre of consciousness here and for the poet's own people.

It is necessary to raise these complex critical questions at the very start. Ideally I would go on to address them in the context of R.S. Thomas's whole work — anything less risks making a selection to fit a particular case. The rest of this present essay has to content itself with a more narrow focus on those poems where Wales or the condition of being Welsh is self-consciously addressed or explored, where these terms help to define the self, to proclaim a complex loyalty, or stand in enforced contrast with England and English.

I have set these poems within a biographical context because I think there is a special importance to the inner development of Anglo-Welsh writers — it is not merely a question of personal maturing, but of voyaging to a discovery of who they are in relation to their country.

* * * * *

The trajectory of R.S. Thomas's life and work in relation to concepts of Wales and the Welsh nation is not difficult to plot. He has plotted it himself in various autobiographical prose pieces and there is no reason to doubt him — since his poems of various periods fit that account. Born into a Welsh family that was undergoing its own process of anglicisation within the same wider social process: brought up in Cardiff and Holyhead, and educated entirely in English, he was by birth and upbringing outside the Welsh language but sufficiently close to become aware as a young adult of his outsider's condition.

As has happened in the case of other Anglo-Welsh writers his first approach to the 'other' Wales from the one he inhabited in daily life was through landscape and history — a 'Romantic' landscape and a 'Romantic' history: The well-known lines from 'Welsh Landscape' (*SYT*, 63),

> To live in Wales is to be conscious
> At dusk of the spilled blood
> That went to the making of the wild sky,
> Dyeing the immaculate rivers

echo the passage in *Y Llwybrau Gynt* where he describes his feelings on the train journey from theological college in Cardiff home to Holyhead:

> As you know, the line from Cardiff to Shrewsbury runs through the Marches, with the plains of England on one side and the Welsh hills on the other. I was often stirred by the sight of these hills rising in the West. It sometimes started to get dark before we reached Ludlow. In the west the sky would be aflame, reminding one of ancient battles. Against that light, the hills rose dark and threatening as though full of armed men waiting for a chance to attack. There was in the west a land of romance and danger, a secret land. But when I arrived home, I would forget about all that for a while. There was an English life to live. and work to do for the next term at college. (*Prose*, 137-38)

If the young R.S. Thomas sees "the West" through the eyes of late English Romanticism, Arnold and maybe Housman, he is also able to identify himself as an insider via the Irish analogy. In the Irish literary movement of the beginning of the century he found an example of Romanticism turned around and used as a weapon by the peripheral nation. He also interested himself in the Scottish literary renaissance, and visited both the West of Ireland and the West of Scotland. Why should the same kind of literary movement not be possible in Wales, the writers steeping themselves in the native tradition but mobilising the nation through English?

The young Saunders Lewis, a quarter of a century earlier, had attempted his first and only play in English in the manner of a Welsh Synge but had then decided to commit himself to a literary career in Welsh. The choice was open to him since Welsh was the language of his home, even though that home was in Wallasey. R.S. Thomas, too, came up against the question of language, both in respect of everyday life and literary ambition. He also had to contend with the exemplary commitment of Saunders Lewis to Welsh.

When he moved from his first curacy in Flintshire to be Rector of Manafon in Montgomeryshire R.S. Thomas found himself just on the English side of the linguistic border, and would walk westwards to learn and practise his Welsh. But to change his poetic language was not so easy. He did attempt a Welsh version of his celebrated poem 'A Peasant'. It is technically competent, the dictionary meanings are preserved, but the angst and the tension get lost, and with them the poetry. After that he was to speak Welsh and write prose in Welsh with increasing fluency, but to stick to English for his central work of poetry.

The idea of nationhood which R.S. Thomas had embraced now made it difficult to persevere with the early dream that he might be a national poet for the Welsh people through the English language rather as he imagined Yeats had been for the Irish. If territory and history were bound up with a people through its language, in an organic fashion, as Herder and the Romantics asserted, and as Saunders Lewis also maintained, and if that language were still a living force in society and literature (which could be posited of the Welsh language much more plausibly than it could of Irish), then it was clear where a writer's first duty lay; but within the same philosophical framework, poetry was not a matter of doing your duty, but of drawing on deep springs of feeling outside the poet's conscious control. Hence an impasse, and a perception that to write of Wales in English was to write out of a contradiction. In his essay 'The Creative Writer's Suicide' he considers the temptation for writers in a minority culture in crisis to devote their energies to saving the nation at the expense of their true talent, and then turns to the Anglo-Welsh, whose situation he finds far worse:

> An Anglo-Welsh writer is neither one thing nor the other. He keeps going in a no-man's land between two cultures. For various reasons he is obliged to write in English. Whatever may be said to the contrary, therefore, he is contributing to English culture, and deserves the strictures of his fellow-Welshmen on that account. If he endeavours to make his work more Welsh, he either gains the hostility of his English readers or loses their interest...
>
> If he is a true Welshman, one who is sensitive to the feeling and the traditions of his own country and nation, he will have some desire to learn Welsh in order to take possession of his true birth-right. Very good ! But that is not the end of the matter. The desire then comes to write in Welsh in order to prove to himself and to the public that he is a true Welshman. Vanity of vanities....
>
> Where are the poets who have composed truly great poems in a foreign language? (*Prose*, 172-3)

In the above passage the very language reinforces the contradiction. At different points Welsh is perceived as the writer's "true birth-right" and "a foreign language".

At its strongest this sense of contradiction at the root of the poetic endeavour becomes self-disgust:

> The
> industrialists came, burrowing
>   in the corpse of a nation
> for its congealed blood. I was
>   born into the squalor of
> their feeding and sucked their speech
>   in with my mother's
> infected milk, so that whatever
>   I throw up now is still theirs. (*WW*, 12)

It seems likely that R.S. Thomas found a personal resolution to this dilemma by living increasingly through the Welsh language (which became more possible after his move to Aberdaron in Llŷn) and joining in the language struggle. In recent years he has become a defender of the rights of Welsh as a majority language in those few areas (such as Llŷn) where the long continuity of the speech community has not been finally breached. His position has made him unpopular even with some nationalist politicians, for today in the 'Welsh-speaking areas' they, too, have to play to an electorate that is linguistically mixed. But the social angst which R.S. Thomas the public figure expresses is quite different from the personal angst about his identity which the younger poet knew, and, unlike that earlier angst, scarcely finds expression at all in the poetry. He told Dylan Iorwerth in 1983 that by the time he reached Aberdaron in Llŷn he did not need to identify himself as a Welshman in his writing, because he lived and spoke and acted as a Welshman in his life (*Prose*, 16).

* * * * *

In the earlier period one can note a gradual drift from poems with a strong historical and mediaeval frame of reference to those which relate to more contemporary events and to language. This not only reflects his own voyage of self-discovery and the crossing over into Welsh, but possibly also the climate of different times to which R.S. Thomas has always been very responsive. Welsh nationalism as he first met it in the work and person of Saunders Lewis had a strong historical orientation. The language was a main concern, but the language campaigns proper came later, with the activities of Cymdeithas yr Iaith Gymraeg (the Welsh Language Society) dramatising the crisis. Throughout, R.S. Thomas has responded to particular events and processes in the social and political life of Wales, such as the drowning of valleys ('Reservoirs', *NBF*, 26), the afforestation of a previously inhabited countryside ('Afforestation', *WA*, 20), or the investiture of the Prince of Wales in 1969 (see 'Loyalties', *NBF*, 31). While the idea that Welsh people might survive by keeping close to nature was dear to the poet from early on, in 1978 he can express this feeling in the language of the green times:

> The dinosaurs have gone their way
> into the dark. The time-span
> of their human counterparts
> is shortened; everything
> on this shrinking planet favours the survival
> of the small people, whose horizons
> are large only because they are content to look at them
> from their own hills.   ('The Small Country', *F*, 19)

This responsiveness to the evolving crisis of Welsh society makes R.S. Thomas an intense and passionate poet; his responsiveness to the evolving language of the times gives that intensity a contemporary edge. His philosophic bent often manages to lend distance and an extra dimension to the contemporary event. But none of these things makes the poet a political thinker, nor would he claim it. For this reason there seems no good reason here to illustrate at length the recurrent Welsh topics. They are often the staples of nationalist thought and feeling in their time — the gap between the servile contemporary reality and the proud past, the loss of dignity that goes with the loss of language, laments for the lost places, the contrast between the spare uplands of Wales and the beckoning rich lowlands of England where the Welsh grow fat and forget who they are. But when one is just beginning to think that these are predictable topoi, R.S. Thomas will suprise one. In 'Plas Difancoll' (*LP*, 164) he meditates on the decay of a mansion which he perceives as alien and colonial:

> The owls' home and the starlings',
> with moss bandaging its deep wounds
> to no purpose, for the wind festers in
> them and the light diagnoses
> impartially the hopelessness
> of its condition. Colonialism
> is a lost cause. Yet the Welsh
> are here, picknicking among the ruins
> on their Corona and potato
> crisps, speaking their language without pride,
> but with no backward look over the shoulder.

In the rhetoric of nationalism the Welsh would speak their language with pride; and they would look to their past with pride as they do in a much earlier poem 'Welsh Landscape' (*SYT*, 63). In an R.S. Thomas poem one might have expected the Corona and potato crisps to be wielded by the philistine trippers from Birmingham not by the Welsh. It is no doubt true to a particular experience, but it is also true to a strand in nationalist feeling that coexists in powerful and productive tension with feelings for the past. Nationalism looks to the past in order to gain strength for change: like Walter Benjamin's angel of history it rushes backwards with wings outspread into the future. If it is *merely* backward-looking, it is not nationalism, but an antiquarian fashion. In this poem it is the forward dynamism that has won. The "but" which introduces the last line is at first suprising. If it were to read "and" it would introduce a parallel, and reinforce a negative tone; instead, what is introduced is a contrast (which becomes a positive assertion), paralleling the larger contrast introduced a few lines earlier by "Yet", between the decaying colonial structure and the triumphant philistine instinct for survival of the Welsh.

Some of the same forward surge can be felt at the end of 'Welsh History' (*SYT*, 61) when the historical backward glance is discarded for the powerful if partly obscure assertion:

> We were a people, and are so yet.
> When we have finished quarrelling for crumbs
> Under the table, or gnawing the bones
> Of a dead culture, we will arise,
> Armed, but not in the old way.

R.S. Thomas and Wales

* * * * *

Beyond the laments and wounds and internal tensions of nation-alism, one looks to the national poet for something to love. That is perhaps the greatest, and in the profoundest sense, most political gift that poets can give their country. Celebration is not easy in our time and anyone who thinks it easy will wither in the irony of their readers. Perhaps it came more easily in Wales than in England at an earlier stage of R.S. Thomas's life (the comparison with Larkin in this respect is interesting), but the internal contradictions and cynicisms of politics, and their general discrediting, have taken their toll here too. R.S. Thomas's affirmations, whether they are of God, of human love, or of love of country are made at the very margins, when negation has achieved its worst:

> I know that bush,
> Moses; there are many of them
> in Wales in the autumn, braziers
> where the imagination
> warms itself. I have put off
> pride and, knowing the ground
> holy, lingered to wonder
> how it is that I do not burn
> and yet am consumed.
>
> And in this country
> of failure, the rain
> falling out of a black
> cloud in gold pieces there
> are none to gather,
> I have thought often
> of the fountain of my people
> that played beautifully here
> once in the sun's light
> like a tree undressing. ('The Bush' *LP*, 194)

Wales is certainly celebrated here, though through a sense of loss which can also be a spur to action. But maybe the highest celebra-tion occurs where the sense of being at home is so pervasive as to make the word Wales unnecessary:

> In front of the fire
> With you, the folk song

The Page's Drift: R.S. Thomas at Eighty

Of the wind in the chimney... ('The Hearth', *H'm*, 18)

Who is to say that this is not a Welsh poem? Or 'The Small Field' (*LS*, 60) where Moses and the lit bush recur without the sense of loss, and where the Welsh scene has become a metaphor for true understanding beyond the kinetic forces which drive human activity, including, as we have seen, nationalism:

> Life is not hurrying
>
> on to a receding future, nor hankering after
> an imagined past. It is the turning
> aside like Moses to the miracle
> of the lit bush, to a brightness
> that seemed as transitory as your youth
> once, but is the eternity that awaits you.

or 'Good' (*LS*, 65) in which Wales is not named nor its dilemmas invoked, but where the kestrel flies over a familiar Welsh scene in which valley and hill not only furnish the setting but yield a metaphor for life's journey as they do in the lines of the Welsh hymn: "*O fryniau Caersalem ceir gweled /Holl daith yr anialwch i gyd*".

This essay has inevitably focused on many poems which express anguish — springing from the sense of division and incompleteness which arises in invaded cultures, from the very wound from which nationalism itself springs. But it is important to stress two things. The poems where R.S. Thomas has been stung into self-consciousness about Wales are not more 'Welsh' than those which use the imagery of his country to explore time and inner space. But nor are the more 'political' poems less 'poems' as imperialist criticism sometimes finds it convenient to suggest. They in fact speak to levels of feeling in Welsh people far deeper than those of politics as these are normally understood in Britain, and find other audiences throughout the world in those places where loss of land, of language, and the desire to make good those losses have also been experienced.

The Poet

We sweat the afternoon
in the muslin-light of the marquee
under the shadows of birds.
Outside, pigeons complain in the heat
to the harp's sharp fire.

Then his voice,
the first unthreading of a sea-wind,
his needle set true north
by some cold star that crackles
like a grit in the mind.

His hands are shaking, his gaze fixed
on a far shore of the spirit
beyond the flowers and the footlights.
His words cast shadows
restless as bird griefs.

Like that time in a restaurant
when he and the Gael were talking
about song and language, he sat haloed
against a window of tropical fish
he could not see.

All the time they spoke,
I watched an angel-fish
flaunting its silks about his head,
a cold flame shaken out
of the oceans and the galaxies.

Gillian Clarke

Select bibliography

Essays conveniently collected in the volumes edited by Anstey and by Dyson (see below) are not separately listed in this bibliography. I am very grateful to Dr John Harris, Aberystwyth, for permission to use the R.S. Thomas section of his forthcoming *Welsh writing in English: a bibliographical guide to twenty-four modern Anglo-Welsh authors* (Cardiff: University of Wales Press) when compiling this selection.

1. Publications by R.S. Thomas

The stones of the field (Carmarthen: Druid Press, 1946).
An acre of land (Newtown: Montgomeryshire Printing Co., 1952).
Song at the year's turning: poems, 1942-1954 (London: Hart-Davis, 1955).
Poetry for supper (London: Hart-Davis, 1958).
Tares (London: Hart-Davis, 1961).
The bread of truth (London: Hart-Davis, 1963).
Pietà (London: Hart-Davis, 1966).
Not that he brought flowers (London: Hart-Davis, 1968).
H'm: poems (London: Macmillan, 1972).
Selected poems: 1946-1968 (London: Hart-Davis; MacGibbon, 1973. St Albans: Granada, 1979. Newcastle upon Tyne: Bloodaxe Books, 1986. US ed., New York: St Martin's, 1974).
What is a Welshman? (Llandybie: Christopher Davies, 1974).
Laboratories of the spirit (London: Macmillan, 1975. US ed., Boston: Godine, 1976).
The way of it; poems/drawings by Barry Hirst (Sunderland: Ceolfrith Press, 1977).
Frequencies (London: Macmillan, 1978).
Between here and now (London: Macmillan, 1981).
Later poems: 1972-1983 (London: Macmillan, 1983. Reissued 1984, pbk.)
Selected Prose , edited by Sandra Anstey (Bridgend: Poetry Wales Press, 1983. Reissued 1986 pbk.).
Ingrowing thoughts (Bridgend: Poetry Wales Press, 1985).
Neb, golygwyd gan Gwenno Hywyn (Caernarfon: Gwasg Gwynedd, 1985). An English précis of this autobiography appears in

Bibliography

Contemporary authors: autobiography series, Vol.4, ed., Adele Sarkissian (Detroit: Gale, 1986), 301-313.
Welsh airs (Bridgend: Poetry Wales Press, 1987).
Pe medrwn yr iaith ac ysgrifau eraill, golygwyd gan Tony Brown a Bedwyr Lewis Jones (Abertawe: Christopher Davies, 1988).
The echoes return slow (London: Macmillan, 1988).
Counterpoint (Newcastle upon Tyne: Bloodaxe Books, 1990).
Blwyddyn yn Llŷn (Caernarfon: Gwasg Gwynedd, 1990).
Cymru or Wales? (Llandysul: Gomer Press, 1992).
Mass for hard times (Newcastle upon Tyne: Bloodaxe Books, 1992).

2. Publications about R.S. Thomas

Ackerman, John, 'R.S. Thomas: poet for our time', *Anglo-Welsh Review* 85 (1987), 103-111.
Allchin, A.M., 'The poetry of R.S. Thomas: an introduction', *Theology* (Nov., 1970), 488-495.
Anstey, Sandra, ed., *Critical Writings on R.S. Thomas* (Bridgend: Poetry Wales Press, 1982). New revised and expanded edition, 1992.
Babel 1 (1983): R.S. Thomas section, 3-61.
Barnie, John, *The king of ashes* (Llandysul: Gomer Press, 1989), 3-13, 14-19, 20-27.
....'The candle in the window', *Planet* 86 (1991), 68-77.
Bedient, Calvin, 'On R.S.Thomas', *Critical Quarterly* 14 (1972), 253-268.
....*Eight contemporary poets* (London: Oxford University Press, 1974), 51-68.
Brown, Tony, 'Language, poetry and silence: some themes in the poetry of R.S. Thomas', in William Tydeman, ed., *The Welsh connection* (Llandysul: Gomer Press, 1986), 159-185.
Carpanini, Rudolf G., 'Romanticism in the poetry of R.S. Thomas', *Annali dell' Instituto di Lingue e Letterature Germaniche* (Universita di Parma) 6 (1980-81), 113-148.
Castay, Marie-Thérèse, 'R.S. Thomas', *Apex* 3 (1978), 8-27.
....'Nature and some Anglo-Welsh poets', *Poetry Wales* 15.2 (1979), 100-110.
....'Développement de la poésie anglo-galloise (1930-1980)', *Caliban* 18 (1981), 21-32.
Conran, Anthony, 'R.S. Thomas and the Anglo-Welsh crisis',

Poetry Wales 7.4 (1972), 67-74.

....'R.S. Thomas as a mystical poet', *Poetry Wales* 14.4 (1979), 11-25.

....*The Cost of Strangeness: essays on the English poets of Wales* (Llandysul: Gomer Press, 1982), 220-262.

Cox, C.B., 'Welsh bards in hard times: Dylan Thomas and R.S. Thomas', in Boris Ford, ed., *The new Pelican guide to English literature*, Vol.8 (Harmondsworth: Penguin, 1983), 209-223.

Davie, Donald, 'R.S. Thomas's poetry of the Church in Wales', *Religion and Literature* 19.2 (1987), 35-48.

Davies, James A., 'Participating readers: three poems by R.S. Thomas', *Poetry Wales* 18.4 (1983), 72-84.

Davies, Walford, 'R.S.Thomas: the poem's harsher conditions', *The New Welsh Review* 3.3 (11) (1991), 15-25.

Davis, William V., 'An abstraction blooded: Wallace Stevens and R.S. Thomas on blackbirds and men', *Wallace Stevens Journal* 8.2 (1984), 79-82.

....'R.S.Thomas: poet-priest of the apocalyptic mode', *South-Central Review* 4.4 (1987), 92-106.

....ed., *Miraculous simplicity: essays on R.S. Thomas* (Fayetteville: University of Arkansas press, 1993).

Dyson, A.E., 'The poetry of R.S. Thomas', *Critical Quarterly* 20.2 (1978), 5-31.

.....*Yeats, Eliot and R.S. Thomas: riding the echo* (London: Macmillan, 1981), 285-326.

....ed., *Three contemporary poets: Thom Gunn, Ted Hughes and R.S.Thomas* (London: Macmillan, Casebook series, 1990).

Gitzen, Julian, 'R.S. Thomas and the vanishing God of form and number', *Contemporary Poetry* 5.2 (1983), 1-16.

Hardy, Barbara, 'Region and nation: R.S. Thomas and Dylan Thomas', in R.P. Draper, ed., *The literature of region and nation* (London: Macmillan, 1989), 93-107.

Herman, Vimala, 'Negativity and language in the religious poetry of R.S. Thomas', *ELH* 45.4 (1978), 710-731.

Hooker, Jeremy, *The presence of the past: essays on modern British and American poetry* (Bridgend: Poetry Wales Press, 1987), 128-140.

Humfrey, Belinda, 'The gap in the hedge: R.S. Thomas's emblem poetry', *Anglo-Welsh Review* 26.58 (1977), 49-57.

Keith, W.J., 'R.S.Thomas', in Vincent B. Sherry, ed., *Poets of Great Britain and Ireland*, 1945-1960 (Detroit: Gale, 1984), 346-356.

Bibliography

Knapp, James Franklin, 'The poetry of R.S. Thomas', *Twentieth Century Literature* 17.1 (1971), 1-9.

Mathias, Roland, *A ride through the wood: essays on Anglo-Welsh literature* (Bridgend: Poetry Wales Press, 1985), 186-205.

Merchant, W. Moelwyn, 'R.S.Thomas', *Critical Quarterly* 2 (1960), 341-351.

....*R.S. Thomas* (Cardiff: University of Wales Press, 1989). Reissue of volume first published in the Writers of Wales series, 1979.

Newman, Elizabeth, 'Voices and perspectives in the poetry of R.S.Thomas', in Theo D'haen, ed., *Linguistics and the study of literature* (Amsterdam: Rodopi, 1986), 56-71.

Phillips, D.Z., *Through a darkening glass: philosophy, literature and cultural change* (Oxford: Blackwell, 1982), 165-190.

....*R.S. Thomas: poet of the hidden God: meaning and mediation in the poetry of R.S. Thomas* (Basingstoke: Macmillan, 1986).

....*From fantasy to faith: the philosophy of religion and twentieth century literature* (London: Macmillan, 1991), 201-211.

Poetry Wales: R.S. Thomas special number 7.4 (1972).

Thomas, M. Wynn, ed., *R.S. Thomas: y cawr awenydd* (Llandysul: Gwasg Gomer, 1990).

....*Internal Difference: literature in twentieth-century Wales* (Cardiff: University of Wales Press, 1992), 107-129, 130-155.

Thomas, Ned, 'R.S. Thomas: the question about technology', *Planet* 92, 54-60.

Thomas, R. George, 'The poetry of R.S.Thomas', *Review of English Literature* 3.4 (1962), 85-95.

....(and Leonard Clark), *Andrew Young and R.S. Thomas* (Longmans for the British Council and National Book League, 1964), 27-41.

Triggs, Jeffery Alan, 'A kinship of the fields: farming in the poetry of R.S. Thomas and Wendell Berry', *North Dakota Quarterly* 57.2 (1989), 92-102.

Vicary, J.D., 'Via negativa: absence and presence in the recent poetry of R.S. Thomas', *Critical Quarterly* 27.3 (1985), 41-51.

Volk, Sabine, *Grenzpfähle der Wirklichkeit: approaches to the poetry of R.S. Thomas* (Frankfurt am Main; London: Peter Lang, 1985).

Ward, J.P., *The poetry of R.S.Thomas* (Bridgend: Poetry Wales Press, 1987).

....'R.S.Thomas's poems of Wales', *Poetry Wales* 23, 2-3 (1988), 20-25.

Notes on contributors

SANDRA ANSTEY is the Officer for English at the National Language Unit of Wales. She was awarded her Ph.D. in 1981 for a thesis on R.S. Thomas's literary achievement which included a list of uncollected poems in manuscript or in printed form, or which had been broadcast. She has edited a selection of R.S. Thomas's English prose works and a collection of printed reviews and essays on his writings. A revised and extended edition of this collection was published in 1992. She has also edited a selection of Wordsworth's poetry for Oxford University Press.

TONY BROWN is Senior Lecturer in English at the University College of North Wales, Bangor. He edited *Edward Carpenter and Late Victorian Radicalism* and was co-editor (with Bedwyr Lewis Jones) of *Pe Medrwn yr Iaith*, a collection of R.S. Thomas's writings in Welsh. He is currently working on a critical biography of Carpenter and preparing an edition of the collected short stories of Glyn Jones.

MARIE-THÉRÈSE CASTAY is Senior Lecturer in the English Department of the Université de Toulouse-La Mirail. She has been a close friend of R.S. Thomas's since 1967 when she completed a M.A. on his early poetry. She has published several articles on his work in British and in European journals.

GILLIAN CLARKE has published several volumes of poetry, including *Letter from a Far Country*, *Selected Poems* and *Letting in the Rumour*. She is a former editor of the *Anglo-Welsh Review* and now teaches creative writing in primary and secondary schools throughout the United Kingdom. She is the present Chair of the English Language section of *Yr Academi Gymreig* (the Welsh Academy of Writers) and her latest collection of poetry, *The King of Britain's Daughter*, will be published by Carcanet in Spring, 1993.

WALFORD DAVIES is Director of the Department of Extra-Mural Studies at the University College of Wales, Aberystwyth, where he also holds a Personal Chair in English Literature. His work on

Dylan Thomas includes two studies of the poet and an edition of the early prose writings. He is the editor (with Ralph Maud) of Dylan Thomas's *Collected Poems*. His other publications include editions of the poetry of Wordsworth, Gerard Manley Hopkins, and Thomas Hardy.

WILLIAM V. DAVIS is Professor of English and writer-in-residence at Baylor University. He has been a Fulbright scholar at the Universities of Vienna and Copenhagen, and a visiting scholar at University College, Swansea. In addition to *One Way to Reconstruct the Scene* (winner of the Yale Series of Younger Poets' Award for 1979) he has published *The Dark Hours* (winner of the Calliope Press Chapbook Prize, 1984) and *Winter Light* (1990). His critical works include two books on the poetry of Robert Bly and he is the editor of *Miraculous Simplicity: essays on R.S. Thomas* (University of Arkansas Press, 1993).

ANNE STEVENSON, born in England in 1933, was educated in the United States. After graduating from the University of Michigan in 1954, she came to Britain where she established herself as a poet, critic and biographer. Her *Selected Poems* was published by Oxford University Press (1987). In 1989 *Bitter Fame*, her radical biography of Sylvia Plath, appeared to mixed acclaim and fury in the British press. The latest of her nine books of poems is *The Other House*, 1990. The University of Michigan awarded her the Athena Award for distinction in literature in 1990.

NED THOMAS is Director of the University of Wales Press and director of the Mercator project on minority languages (Aberystwyth) for the E.C. For twenty years he taught at the University College of Wales, Aberystwyth, having previously worked as a journalist for the *Times* and edited the Russian periodical *Angliya* for the British Government. His books include *The Welsh Extremist; A Culture in Crisis* and studies of George Orwell, Derek Walcott and Waldo Williams. He was the founder and for many years the editor of the Welsh internationalist journal, *Planet*.

M. WYNN THOMAS, Senior Lecturer in English at University College, Swansea, recently completed a period as Visiting Professor at Harvard. His books include editions of works by Emyr Humphreys and Morgan Llwyd, as well as critical studies of both writers. He is also the author of *The Lunar Light of Whitman's Poetry* and *Internal Difference: literature in twentieth century Wales*. In 1990 he edited a collection of essays in Welsh on R.S.Thomas's poetry.

HELEN VENDLER is A. Kingsley Porter University Professor at Harvard and Poetry Critic for *The New Yorker*. She has written books on Yeats, Stevens, Herbert, and Keats; her critical essays are collected in *Part of Nature, Part of Us* and *The Music of What Happens*. She has edited the *Harvard/Faber Book of Contemporary American Poetry* and *Voices and Visions: American Poets*. She is working on a commentary on Shakespeare's Sonnets.

ROWAN WILLIAMS recently became Bishop of Monmouth, having previously been Lady Margaret Professor of Divinity and Canon of Christ Church, Oxford. His books include *The Wound of Knowledge, The Truce of God* and *Arius: heresy and tradition*.

Index of Works by R.S. Thomas Cited in the Text

ABERCUAWG (poem) 108, 116n, 127, 128
Abercuawg (essay), 55n, 127, 167, 172
"A blue snake in the valley ran", 23
The Absence, 88, 111, 128
Absolution, 45, 50, 52
An Acre of Land, 28, 29, 31, 40, 44, 181, 182
A Choice of George Herbert's Verse (ed), 116n
Adjustments, 106, 108, 122
A Farmer, 26, 27, 34n
Affinity, 29, 36-38, 44
Afforestation, 217
After Jericho, 94
The Airy Tomb, 40, 190
All Right, 145
Anniversary, 120
The Answer, 88, 111
Ap Huw's Testament, 120, 156-57, 158
Approaches, 129
Aside, 49
Astronauts, 170n
At It, 83, 107
Auguries, 32, 34n
Autobiography, 157-58

BALANCE, 106, 112, 117n, 165
The Bank, 94
The Bat, 24, 25, 33n
Being, 96
Bequest, 129
Between Here and Now, 11, 57-76, 101, 126, 128, 130, 145, 163, 170n, 202
Birches, 25
Bleak Liturgies, 115n
Blwyddyn yn Llŷn, 170n, 208n, 209n, 210n
Boatman, 159, 160
Border Blues, 176-77
The Boy's Tale, 121, 155-56, 158-59
The Bread of Truth, 11, 42, 50, 51, 120, 121, 144, 150, 154, 155, 158, 163
The Bridge, 23
The Bright Field, 94, 128, 197
Brothers, 149
The Bush, 122, 219

CALLING, 89, 166
Captain Cook's Last Voyage, 170n
Careers, 120, 131
Castaway, 159, 170n
Cezanne: The Bridge at Maincy, 75-76
Circle, 159, 161

Coda, 164
The Combat, 84, 86, 96
Commision, 32, 35n
Confessions of an Anglo-Welshman, 26, 34n
Correspondence, 163-64
Counterpoint, 11, 15, 129, 145, 146, 205
Country Church, 119, 134
The Creative Writer's Suicide, 55n, 117n, 215
Cyclamen, 24, 25, 26
Cymru or Wales?, 208n

THE DARK WELL, 53
Darlington, 34n
Dau Gapel, 47
Degas: Portrait of a Young Woman, 59-61, 170n
Degas: Two Women Ironing, 72-75
Depopulation of the Hills, 151
Derelict, 169n
Dialectic, 94, 106
Dialogue, 83
Directions, 170
Drowning, 153

THE ECHOES RETURN SLOW, 11, 13, 89, 94, 99, 100, 113, 116n, 117n, 118n, 122, 129, 130, 131-33, 135-37, 138, 141-43, 144, 145, 146, 169n, 175, 196-97, 198, 200, 201-02, 203, 205
Emerging (*F*), 82, 87, 88, 110, 117n
Emerging (*LS*), 82, 84, 87, 88, 202
The Empty Church, 109
Enigma, 44
Epiphany, 112
Epitaph, 52
Evans, 150
Experimenting With An Amen, 14, 19n, 83-84, 89, 90, 94, 101, 126, 129, 143, 145, 166, 167, 198, 201, 211

FABLE, 94
The Fair, 170n
Farm Wives, 35n
The Farmer Speaks (see also The Hill Farmer Speaks), 29
Farming Peter, 164-65
The Figure, 150
The Film of God, 106, 128
The Fisherman, 192-93
Fishing, 106, 161
Fragment, 24, 25, 33n
Frequencies, 11, 82, 83, 84, 86, 87, 91, 94, 96, 97,

Index

99, 100, 101, 102, 105, 106, 107, 108, 109, 110, 111, 112, 113, 114n, 117n, 122, 126, 127, 128, 152, 161, 163, 164, 165, 170n, 183, 217
Fugue for Ann Griffiths, 168

THE GAP, 84, 86, 101-04, 105, 114n
The Gap in the Hedge, 49, 115n
Gaugin: Breton Landscape: the Mill, 75
Gideon Pugh, 26, 27, 34n
God's Story, 83
Gone?, 109, 152-53, 170n
Good, 220
A Grave Unvisited, 117n
Green Categories, 52, 56n, 151
Groping, 107, 163
Growing Up, 32, 35n
Guernica, 76
Y Gwladwr, 29, 34n

HAFOD LOM, 11
The Hand, 83, 84
Harbour, 159
Harvest End, 201
Headline, 161, 170n
The Hearth, 220
Henry Jones, 106
The Hill Country, Montgomeryshire (see also The Welsh Hill Country) 29
Hill Farmer, 29, 34n
The Hill Farmer Speaks (see also The Farmer Speaks) 29
Hiraeth, 148
H'm, 14, 100, 126, 127, 128, 143, 145, 170n, 180, 185, 205, 220
"How many men have loved", 23

"I KNOW NO CLOUDS", 25, 26
Iago Prytherch, 45, 50, 55n
In a Country Church, 45
In Great Waters, 163
Ingrowing Thoughts, 9, 10, 19n, 57, 58, 76-80, 130
Invasion on the Farm, 44, 149
Islandman, 162

JUDGEMENT DAY, 144

KIERKEGAARD, 117n

LABORATORIES OF THE SPIRIT, 82, 83, 84, 86, 87, 96, 97, 98, 107, 114n, 122, 125, 126, 128, 164, 168, 172, 187, 191, 197, 204, 220
A Labourer, 44, 150
The Labourer, 149

Landscape, 209n
Later Poems, 109, 121, 126, 144, 145, 155, 164, 186, 187, 198, 200, 202, 217, 219
A Lecturer, 16
A Life, 129
"Like slender waterweeds to my mind", 23
A Line from St David's, 11
Lines from Taliesin, 29, 34n
Llananno, 128
Llanddewi Brefi, 34n
Llanrhaeadr ym Mochnant, 187
Y Llwybrau Gynt, 40, 41, 122, 123, 124, 126, 131, 138, 141, 214
The Lonely Furrow, see also The One Furrow, 29, 31
Looking at Sheep, 11
Looking Glass, 145
"Look, look at the sky", 25, 33n
Lost Christmas, 159
Loyalties, 217

MAE GANDDO BLEIDLAIS, 34n
Maes-yr-Onnen, 31
Making, 180-81
The Making of a Poem, 38, 80
Marged, 191
Mass for a Hard Time, 115n
Meditations, 94
Memories, 41, 49, 150
Midnight on the Farm, 35n
The Minister, 30-31, 32, 34n, 47-48, 195
Monet: Lady with a Parasol, 62-69
The Mountains, 173-75

NEB, 55n, 99, 114n, 121, 122, 123-25, 126, 130, 131-34, 135, 139-40, 142, 144, 146, 147, 149, 155, 162, 168n, 169n, 173, 190, 193, 196, 199-200, 201, 203-04
Night and Morning, 38
Ninetieth Birthday, 119
No Answer, 32
No Through Road, 42-43, 119
Not That He Brought Flowers, 11, 39, 97, 120, 121, 128, 144, 154, 184, 187, 191, 193, 194, 205, 217

ON THE FARM, 50
"Once through the friendless dark so close I came", 23
The One Furrow (see also The Lonely Furrow), 29, 31
One Way, 101
Original Sin, 32, 34n

Index

PARDON, 84
A Peasant, 28, 29, 40, 44, 49, 54n, 119, 214-15
Peasant Girl Weeping, 34n
Peasant Greeting, 151
Pe Medrwn yr Iaith, 22, 199
The Penguin Book of Religious Verse (ed), 79
Perhaps, 83, 109
Petition, 127
Pietà, 10, 11, 49, 100, 149
Pilgrimages, 109, 113, 164
Pissarro: Landscape at Chaponval, 69-72
The Place, 53-54
Plas Difancoll, 217-18
Poetry for Supper, 42, 45, 50, 54, 120, 150, 151, 156, 172, 176, 185
The Porch, 105, 122
The Possession, 106, 109
Prayer, 44, 122
Pre-Cambrian, 86, 91, 94, 162-63, 200
The Presence, 145
Present, 105, 145
A Priest to his People, 28, 47, 119
The Priest, 97, 191, 194
Proportions, 32, 34n

THE RED MODEL: RÉNÉ MAGRITTE, 77-79
Relations, 160
Renoir: Muslim Festival at Algiers, 72
Reply, 94
Reservoirs, 217
Retirement, 118n, 129
Revision, 90, 93, 101
Roger Bacon, 83, 86, 94
Rose Cottage, 11
Rough, 83, 125, 128

SAILOR'S HOSPITAL, 121, 154-55, 169n
Salt, 121, 155, 156-57, 160, 168
Sarn Rhiw, 94, 129
Schoonermen, 153-54, 155
The Sea, 159, 161-62
Seaside, 159
Sea Watching, 107, 204
Selah, 168
Selected Poems 1948-1968, 28, 39, 49, 50, 53, 158
Selected Prose, 22, 38, 40, 41, 44, 47, 53, 55n, 58, 80, 116n, 118n, 167, 173, 176, 177, 179, 180, 182, 183, 184, 185, 186, 189, 192, 194, 195, 204, 214, 215, 216
Self-Portrait, 98
Senior, 128
Servant, 50-51

Shadows, 107, 108
The Small Country, 217
The Small Field, 220
Somersby Brook, 35n
Song (*AL*), 29, 34n
Song (*SYT*), 122
Song at the Year's Turning, 22, 25, 28, 30, 31, 32, 33, 36, 37, 38, 39, 40, 41, 42, 44, 45, 47, 49, 115n, 119, 120, 122, 134, 144, 149, 150, 151, 180, 185, 187, 190, 195, 196, 199, 213, 218
Song for Gwydian, 120
Sorry, 120
The Stones of the Field, 22, 25, 26, 28, 31, 40, 45, 48, 55n, 148, 181, 182
Strands, 129, 167
Strangers, 144
Sub Post Office, 161
The Survivors, 121, 154, 169n
Synopsis, 165

TARES, 42, 50, 53, 100, 120, 144, 151, 186
Temptation of a Poet, 50
Text, 159
That, 128
Their Canvases Are, 94
A Thicket in Lleyn, 90, 92, 94, 97
This One, 129
Those Others, 151-52
Three Countries, 34n
Threshold, 163
Too Late, 50
The Tool, 85
Traeth Maelgwn, 187
The Tree: Owain Glyn Dwr Speaks, 45
A True Poet, 19n
Two Children Menaced by a Nightingale: Max Ernst, 76-77
The Two Sisters, 29, 34n

THE UNTAMED, 158, 160

VIA NEGATIVA, 128
The Village, 151

WAITING, 108, 163
"The waters strive to wash away", 23
The Way of It, 121, 187
Welsh, 120
Welsh Airs, 153, 168, 187, 198, 199, 205, 217
A Welsh Ballad Singer, 35n
The Welsh Hill Country (see also The Hill Country, Montgomeryshire), 29, 45, 190-91
Welsh History, see also Welsh Nation, 29, 31,

218
Welsh Landscape, 213-14, 218
Welsh Nation, see also Welsh History, 29
Welsh Shepherd, 29, 34n
West Coast, 94
What Is A Welshman?, 205, 216
Words and the Poet, 115-16n

YOUNG AND OLD, 159-62, 170n
Young and Old, 161, 166